THE 25 BEST
World War II Sites
Pacific Theater

Launched in 1999, Greenline Publications introduces a list of unique books: *Extraordinary Guides for Extraordinary Travelers. The 25 Best World War II Sites: Pacific Theater* is the first in the **Greenline Historic Travel Series.** Greenline's willingness to explore new approaches to guidebooks, combined with meticulous research, provides readers with unique and significant travel experiences.

Never settling for the ordinary, Greenline's first travel series, **The Fun Also Rises,** covered the world's absolute most fun events and destinations. The first two books in the series, *The Fun Also Rises Travel Guide North America* and *The Fun Also Rises International Travel Guide* took readers to the world's 100 most fun places—from the Opera Ball in Vienna to the Calgary Stampede to the world's greatest food fight, the Tomatina in Buñol, Spain. The series continues this year with the Fun Seeker's destination guides, beginning with Las Vegas and Los Angeles.

To reach us or for updated information on all Greenline books, visit the Greenline Publications website at www.greenlinepub.com.

The 25 Best World War II Sites: Pacific Theater is an independent guide. We welcome your views on our selections.

The information contained in this book was checked as rigorously as possible before going to press. The publisher accepts no responsibility for any changes that may have occurred since or for any other variance of fact from that recorded here in good faith.

ISBN: 0-9666352-6-4
Library of Congress Control Number: 2002095160
Distributed in the United States by National Book Network (NBN)
Printed in the United States
First Edition
All rights reserved
Copyright © December 2002 Greenline Publications

GREENLINE PUBLICATIONS
Extraordinary Guides for Extraordinary Travelers
P.O. Box 590780
San Francisco, CA 94159-0780

The Ultimate Traveler's Guide
to Battlefields, Monuments
and Museums

THE 25 BEST
World War II Sites
Pacific Theater

CHUCK THOMPSON

GREENLINE PUBLICATIONS • SAN FRANCISCO, CALIFORNIA

Russia

Korea

Japa

China

Nanjing

21

Shanghai

5 Hiroshima

11 Tokyo

14

Nagasaki/Kyushu

9

Okinawa

Taiwan

Iwo Jima

Hong Kong

Myanmar

Rangoon

17 Kanchanaburi

Bangkok

Thailand

Bataan

22

Philippines

19

2 Manila

Corregidor

Tinian

16

4

Saipan

20

Guam

Leyte

15

South
China Sea

Malaysia

6

Palau/Peleliu

Singapore

3

Borneo

Indonesia

Papua New Guinea

Port Mores

Darwin

Australia

Kodiak

8
Unalaska/Dutch Harbor

Adak

Attu
Kiska

Aleutian Islands

Aurile Islands

International Date Line

Pacific Ocean

United States
mainland
(25)

Midway Island

Hawaiian Islands

1
Pearl Harbor/Oahu

Wake Island

Eniwetak

Marshall
Islands

Kwajalein

10 Majuro

18
Chuuk (Truk)

Emiej Island
23

13
Tarawa

Gilbert
Islands

Solomon
Islands

7

12 Guadalcanal

N

ACKNOWLEDGEMENTS

Anyone who has been involved in an undertaking as ambitious as this one understands that the name that appears on the cover represents merely the intersection of the work, talent and generosity of innumerable participants. Though it's impossible to catalog each favor done—among other benefits of travel is the discovery that anonymous Samaritans around the world still need no motivation beyond compassion to rush to the aid of confused visitors—apologies are nevertheless extended to anyone inadvertently left off this list who made this book possible.

Because a two-minute conversation can sometimes be as valuable as a two-hour airplane ride, I've listed names below without note of relative importance. No matter how much expertise, time or other considerations were involved, all assistance received during the course of this project was necessary, valuable and, above all, greatly appreciated. I would be remiss, however, for not paying special attention to Mr. Ernie Teston of the Philippine Department of Tourism, who essentially gave up his life in order to live mine during my lengthy stay in the Philippines. Philippines Secretary of Tourism Mr. Richard Gordon and Director of PIDOT San Francisco Mr. Rene de los Santos also provided invaluable assistance across their beautiful country. Ms. Megumi Ishihara of the Japan National Tourist Organization was exceptionally patient and helpful in dealing with far too many requests from me concerning her spectacular country.

Thanks and gratitude are extended to those who made invaluable contributions in the following locations. Bataan/Olongapo: Gina Augustin, David Contrerar, Ceasar Cuayzon and Jose Diego. Chuuk: Larry Burton, Mason Fritz, Mitory Matsuo, Bill Stennet and Stefan Thomas. Guadalcanal: Dennis Anii, Wilson Maelaua, Jeff Saemanea and John Vandenheever. Guam: Cathy Gogue, Tom Goresch, June Sugiwara and Loretta at GVB. Hawaii: Jim Austin, Jim Cone, Olav Holst, Nikki and Tom O'Rourke and Glen Tomlinson. Japan: Yoko Takano and the incomparable Tuan Robert Glasser and Tamiko Shimizu. Kanchanaburi/Thailand: Rod Beattie, William John Slape and the irrepressible "Shanghai" Bob Hill. Kodiak: Pam Foreman and Curt Law. Leyte: Efron Fuentes, Bing Lumbre, Norma Morantte, Dr. Manuel Veloso. Manila: Marie Jean Cordero Dela Cruz, Tony Estrada, Rene Garcia, Benji Guy, Chi Chi Lopez and the spectacular Lopez sisters, Maita Oebandas, Jose Victor Torres, Augusto de Viana and Eugene Yap. Marshall Islands: Jennifer Brush, Bernie Cotter, Matt Holly, Brian Kirk, Tom Maus, Suzanne Murphy, Jack Niedenthal, Terry Sasser, U.S. Ambassador Michael Senko, Mark Stege and the Friday night poker club. Nanjing: Ignatius T. Ding and Xia Yumin. Okinawa: Dave Davenport. Peleliu/Palau: Teddi Anderson, Leah Asanuma, Tony Campbell, Kevin Davidson, Tangie Hesus, Bradley Kloulchad, Ron Leidich, Sam Scott. Saipan: Kathryn Acorda, Vicki Benavente, Frank Cabrera, Victor Cabrera, Jonas Ogren, Wayne Pangelinan, Scott Russell and Charlotte Vick. Singapore: Brent Burkhardt, Hugh Caitlan, Mike Chua, Peiling Huang, Shien Yau Lim, Mohamed Yusoff Mahmood, Nelyn Nah, Tresnawati Prihadi, Jimmy Yong and the fabulous Peter Chen and friends. Solomon Islands: Bob Reynolds and the entire crew and passengers of the *Spirit of Solomons,* especially the map- and book-toting Doug Drumheller and World War II veterans Paul Alvers, Ed Lynch and O.K. Williams. Tarawa: Don Allen. Tinian: the indefatigable Ellen Ikehara and Carmen Sanchez. Unalaska/Dutch Harbor: Lauren Adams, Stan Cohen, Jeff Dickrell, Bobbie Lekanoff, Wendy Marriott, Laresa Moses, Mya Renken and Jack Walsh.

Special thanks are extended to everyone at Greenline Publications, in particular Gerard Gleason, Terrance Mark, Roger Migdow, Harry Um, Debra Valencia and especially Kristin Poss. Greenline publisher Alan Davis remained at all times the dedicated and driving force behind this project, which he believed from the start was not just interesting but important. For that he deserves thanks and gratitude from veterans and all those who walk in their footsteps.

My parents, family and friends have all indulged me in this and other projects in one way or another and deserve endless thanks.

Without Joyce Leong, none of the names above would appear on this list for without her nothing would be possible, much less worth doing.

CREDITS

Kristin Poss, Editor

Additional research and writing contributed by Jordan Rane (Kyushu, North America, Saipan, Tokyo), Donald K. Allen (Tarawa) and Paul Zemanek (Papua New Guinea).

Book Design by DeVa Communications, Los Angeles
Debra Valencia, Creative Director
Production team: Will Soper, Robert Bruzus, Tritia Khournso and Sahar Rafat

Photos by Chuck Thompson except where indicated

TABLE OF CONTENTS

INTRODUCTION

Events of the 1930s and '40s excepted, this book got its start in 1987 among the brush-covered hills of Guam. My brother, Mike, and I had become intrigued by vague stories of a World War II tank graveyard somewhere near a place called Yona. The local U.S.O. office reportedly led hikes to the tanks on Saturdays. Alas, we couldn't wait and set out on a poorly considered boony stomp through razor-sharp kunai grass and steep hills that, three hours later, resulted in numerous cuts and scrapes, a fair amount of arguing, much colorful language and no tanks found. We retreated with bloody calves, and I spent the rest of my time on Guam closer to the beach.

Traveling through Southeast Asia a few years later, girlfriend Joyce and I stumbled upon the excellent World War II exhibits on Singapore's Sentosa Island—the wax figure of Lieutenant-General Arthur Percival surrendering Singapore to the wax figure of General Tomoyuki Yamashita providing a lasting image of the trip. Weeks later we came upon a large statue of Filipino guerrillas heaving grenades in the middle of the road to Olongapo—a monument to the participants of the Battle of Zigzag Pass, one of the many forgotten but important actions in the massive Allied campaign to liberate the Philippines in 1944-45.

Having arrived in the region with an abiding interest, I began spending free time seeking out various points of wartime interest around the Pacific. The results were hit and miss. The Hiroshima Peace Memorial Museum was well documented and worth the trip. But what about the "wrecked planes, guns, relics and monuments all over the Pacific" I kept hearing about? Few of these appeared readily evident to one not given to scouring microfiche files in dusty archives offices or spending days gaining the confidence of local looters. I decided to go out and buy a book that catalogued war sites in the Pacific ... and discovered that no such book existed. If any World War II research seemed overlooked, this was clearly it.

It should be noted that much (though not close to all) of the information presented in this book has existed in some form in a number of sources—brochures, asides in travel guides, Web sites and small books, usually published privately or within limited locales. Such books have long been the domain of war buffs, local historians and inveterate artifact hunters. But what few copies of these materials exist tend to concentrate on small areas. Furthermore, these sources are hard to come by, often involving a trip to whatever region they cover and some amount of chance. Even a visit to the Marshall Islands Historic Preservation Office in Majuro, for instance, doesn't guarantee one will find Henrik Christiansen's excellent though somewhat faded monograph series on *The Archaeology of World War II in the Marshall Islands*. No single guide book attempts to cover a comprehensive list of Pacific War sites, weed out the existing mountain of misinformation or present details in a way that might lead the casual traveler to places both historically significant and intrinsically fascinating.

This is not a book for war buffs. Though it's hoped those with a more intense interest will find the book useful, its main concern isn't with whether it was Marine Company A or B that took Hill 57 (or was it Sector X?); or whether the SB2A dive-bomber that supported the mission was known as the Buccaneer or the Helldiver; or if the 75mm

A/T guns the company carried had a range or 5,500 or 9,00∪ yards; or even what A/T stood for. (Anti-tank, as it turns out, as well as the Buccaneer, built by Brewster, and 9,000-plus yards.) With respect to the personnel who built and used that equipment and served in those battles, their families and anyone else interested in such detail, the technical end of the war has already been covered more thoroughly and expertly than I could ever hope to fake. Though major figures, weapons, technology and battles provide the framework, this book is more interested in the beaches, battlefields, cities, artifacts, museums and monuments left behind. In other words, the tangible materials that lift the war off of textbook pages, television and movie screens and provide a tactile connection to the great story of the twentieth century, a story, as of this writing, still firmly in charge of shaping the century that followed it.

Travel does something to the ordinary person's interest in history. Someone who might never bother with a book on the ancient Mayan or Roman civilizations is suddenly gripped by the unshakeable need to see Tikal when visiting Guatemala or the Coliseum in Rome. Many trips abroad are centered around such excursions. This makes perfect sense. Along with food and drink, a look at local history is often the most accessible and efficient way of connecting with a foreign culture. In the case of the Pacific War (the term used synonymously here with World War II Pacific Theater, or any Allied fighting anywhere against the military of Imperial Japan) such sites carry an added bonus, providing an entry point to American, Japanese and Allied nations' history, as well. Nearly all of East Asia and the Pacific were reconstructed by the "Typhoon of Steel"—a phrase popularly used to describe the Battle of Okinawa, but applicable on a wider scale—that swept across the region in the 1930s and '40s. This book seeks to guide Asia-Pacific travelers to those places of greatest importance and interest.

Word count being the implacable foe of every writer and unbreakable ally of every editor, various factors were brought into play when deciding which locations to leave in and which to leave out when compiling this limited list of "25 Best." The final ranking, admittedly subjective, was constructed around a set of only slightly flexible guidelines. Sites were judged on the basis of three equally weighted qualities. First, its historic significance—the Aleutians were a horrible battlefield, but what occurred there pales in importance next to Singapore. Second, the amount and quality of relics or attractions remaining at a given site—more Americans remember the name Bataan, but there's much more to see on Corregidor. Third, excluding any association with the war, each site was considered purely on its merits as a travel destination, its services, natural beauty and general desirability—Palau was a big winner here.

At or near the top of all three categories, Pearl Harbor/Oahu finished first in overall score. Regrettably, there has to be a spot at the bottom of any list. Further down, sites may get tougher to travel to, or have slightly less to look at, but every destination covered here is worth a visit. In the end, it's a question of taste. For those who prefer to see wrecked planes or coral-encrusted ships exactly where they went down in the 1940s, places such as the Marshall and Solomon Islands, Palau and Chuuk (Truk) are superb. For world-class museums and more accessible attractions, several destinations across Japan and Singapore are tough to beat.

Although I'd previously visited many of the locations included in this book, I was aware that fiftieth anniversaries of various battles celebrated through the 1990s, as well as a new crop of successful Hollywood films, had inspired the creation of monu-

Points of Interest Ratings

Individual points of interest are awarded scores of one to five stars based on the following rough description:

★★★★★ Major site, must visit

★★★★ Extraordinary site or development

★★★ Worth a side trip

★★ Interesting, not vital

★ Only if you have time or special interest

All attractions are free unless noted otherwise.

ments and museums, or refurbishment of many major battle sites. Just as surely, I knew that neglect, development, looting and weather had altered or taken away others. What I liked in 1990 might have changed, for better or worse, in the intervening years. To that end, through the summer and fall of 2002, I embarked on a massive trip visiting all the sites here (with a couple of exceptions noted) and reevaluated each in the manner described above. Most heartening was the discovery of many new facilities—the top-flight Aleutian World War II National Historic Area Visitor Center, which opened in the summer of 2002, being just one example.

Among other happy finds was that, although the U.S.O. office in Guam had in the meantime closed down, the mythical Yona tank farm that inspired this project does, in fact, exist (the description is on page 184). As it had in 1987, my hike there fifteen years later ended on a symbolic note. Encroaching on the once uninhabited, hilly land around the tanks is a large, modern golf resort catering to Japanese tourists. After a sweaty hour over a rough, muddy trail to the tanks, I looked across the hills with some despair, then cut across a field, hopped a fence and wandered into the resort. A maintenance worker took me to the top of one of the condo towers and pointed to the tanks, about 700 yards from the resort's property line. He looked at my dirty shoes, shook his head and said I'd walked all that way down the trail for nothing. I could have driven to the resort. Worse, I'd have to go back up the hill for the car.

He was right, in a way, but, I was nevertheless happy to have taken the hard road to this site. The tanks were fine, but in the end I did in Guam what I'd done there the first time—spent time at the beach. Those less inclined to hike muddy hills and hop fences will be glad to know that relics are there, too. A short walk from my hotel on Guam's main tourist drag along Tumon Bay is Gun Beach, where a large Japanese coastal defense gun sits amid the sand and low cliffs just as it did during the 1944 U.S. invasion of the island.

Relaxing on Gun Beach after suffering for the Yona tanks crystallized the point of the entire project. The fact is, there really are "wrecked planes, guns, relics and monuments all over the Pacific." Most of them require no more effort than riding in a car, hiking a hill or walking down a beach. The trick is knowing where to look. If this book has succeeded, the best way to start is by turning the page.

A NOTE ON DISTANCES, DIRECTIONS AND GUIDES

Like any travel guide, this one strives to present its information with a certain level of consistency. Unfortunately, the terrain it covers—the battlefields of the Pacific War—can hardly be regarded as uniform. In many places, traditional street addresses and directions are easy to provide and simple to follow—Honolulu and Singapore come to mind. Other sites present greater challenges—the Marshall Islands, Tinian, Peleliu—necessitating the sort of "walk south 100 yards from the big rock" landmark-based set of instructions normally found on a child's treasure map. In each case, and at the regrettable expense of consistency, I've provided the type of direction that seems to best suit the area concerned.

Similarly, long distances have been listed in miles or kilometers, following both the convention of the country to which they apply and the assumption that travelers will be using local road signs and possibly odometers to get from point to point. If signs and other indicators in a given location are listed in kilometers, it seems counter-productive to list mileage (and vice-versa) no matter what the nature of one's native familiarity with such measurements. In this regard the rule is ancient—do as the Romans. All walking distances, however, are presented in feet, yards and miles, units most familiar to the largely American audience anticipated for this book.

Many of the distances, those included particularly for walking or general orientation, are estimates and should not be considered precise unless stated as such (1.2 miles, 138 feet, ninety-six steps, etc.). More importantly, particularly in jungle and urban areas, travelers should bear in mind that given the rapid growth of both human development and tropical foliage, trails, roads and other paths may over time (even within weeks) become overgrown or disappear entirely. Even with the directions included here, finding some of the more obscure sites in this book often amounts to looking and looking, retracing steps and looking again before actually finding that wrecked tank or gun emplacement. In times of trouble, asking a local is always the best way.

None of this should be regarded as intimidating. With the aid of a good local map (or cab driver), the vast majority of sites herein are easy to find. To the degree that this book has been written to aid independent travel, every effort has been made to direct the reader to sites without the assistance of a guide. This largely reflects the way I prefer to travel. Few things annoy me more than being hostage to someone else's schedule. Guides tend to be slow when I want them to be fast, fast when I want slow. They like to take rest stops, take it easy and break for bad, boxed lunches. They're forever telling me to be careful. Many are misinformed. And they have to be paid.

That said, though most sites in this book are easily found without assistance, some are simply inaccessible without it. For the submerged wrecks of Truk Lagoon, a dive guide is an obvious necessity. But Palau's Rock Islands, among others, require at the very least a boat and knowledgeable captain. While Saipan's points of interest are easily covered in a rental car, the Solomon Islands' are not. Manila has familiar-sounding street addresses, but most foreign visitors tend to drive there but once. Finally, tightened security at U.S. military facilities (Hawaii and Guam being most important to this book) at the very least argues in favor of established tour operators who often have pre-arranged access to bases for legit tour groups.

For all my complaints about tour guides in general, it would be a disservice to many fine men and women throughout the Pacific not to note that World War II guides are by and large a different breed. Both locals and expats (Americans and Australians, usually), they consistently display a devotion and knowledge of their subject that borders on the fanatical—hell on their permanent relationships, I presume, but great fortune for those who make their acquaintance whether on the way to a museum in the city or a downed Corsair in the jungle.

In addition, many of these guides and local experts are among the only people actively engaged in preventing the continual looting of wartime artifacts, and lobbying various governments to take a more proactive role in preserving their historic heritage. Being prepared to concede that my experiences in the Pacific may have softened my position, and accepting that my overall prejudices might not be shared by all, I've listed guides and tour services in chapters where they seem most helpful.

1

Pearl Harbor/ Oahu

THE WAR YEARS

Considering the overwhelming amount of analysis devoted to the Japanese attack on Pearl Harbor, the principle facts are quite simple. On the morning of December 7, 1941, approaching undetected from the north, a massive Japanese Navy fleet centered around six aircraft carriers launched two waves of fighter and bomber aircraft against American military installations across the Hawaiian island of Oahu, concentrating on the destruction of the U.S. Pacific Fleet anchored in Pearl Harbor. Masterminded by Admiral Isoroku Yamamoto (and a number of rarely credited staff officers), the surprise attack caught the entire island off-guard, resulted in a resounding Japanese victory and immediately propelled the tenuously isolationist United States into World War II in both the Pacific and Europe. The first strike wave of 183 red-balled aircraft swarmed over the island and began dropping bombs and torpedoes at 7:55 a.m. To ensure no challenges from American fighters, airplanes on runways at Hickam, Wheeler and Bellows airfields were among the first targets hit. Also decimated were patrol planes and fighters at Ford Island, Kaneohe Naval Air Station and Ewa Airfield. Creating terror and confusion, Japanese pilots flew so low that Wheeler commander Colonel William Flood later said, "I could see the Japanese pilots lean out of their planes and smile as they zoomed by. ... Hell, I could even see the gold in their teeth!"

Simultaneously, the Japanese attacked the some 100 U.S. Navy ships at Pearl Harbor, focusing on Battleship Row, seven neatly arranged battleships that comprised the soul of the Pacific Fleet. (The flagship U.S.S. *Pennsylvania* was dry docked on December 7 at the nearby Navy Yard.) Hardest hit was the U.S.S. *Arizona*, which took a direct strike to its forward magazine and exploded in a gargantuan fireball, spreading a billowing cloud of black smoke across the harbor. Officially, 1,177 *Arizona* sailors were killed, representing almost half of all deaths in the massive conflagration that seized Oahu. A second wave of 171 strike planes arrived at 8:54 a.m. and inflicted more damage.

In all, eighteen ships of the Pacific Fleet—all eight battleships, three light cruisers, three destroyers and four auxiliary vessels—were sunk, capsized or badly damaged. Of 394 aircraft at Hickam, Wheeler and Bellows airfields, 188 were destroyed and another 159 were damaged. Including sixty-eight civilians, 2,403 died in the attack, 1,178 were wounded. Japanese losses were limited to twenty-nine planes (lost to anti-aircraft fire and the few American fighters that managed to get off the ground), one submarine, five midget submarines and fifty airmen. (As with virtually all statistics in this book, variations are found in casualty reports from various official sources).

Damage to American forces might have been worse. Fortuitously for the American military, Pearl's three aircraft carriers—the *Saratoga, Lexington* and *Enterprise*—were out of port on the fateful morning. The harbor's critical fuel reserves and elaborate ship-repair facilities were left largely unmolested.

A few hours after the attack, martial law was declared at Honolulu's Iolani Palace and was not lifted until October 24, 1944. Oahu was transformed into a massive forward base—during the war, fifty bases and about 700 training ranges were built on the island. Most of the battleships hit in the attack would be raised, repaired and put back into service. Pearl Harbor never lost its position of primacy as the main American fleet base in the Pacific.

Nevertheless, in less than two hours, the attack on Pearl Harbor changed the course of history and sealed Japan's fate. "One can search military history in vain for an operation more fatal to the aggressor," wrote naval historian Samuel Eliot Morrison. On December 8, President Franklin Delano Roosevelt delivered his "day of infamy" speech to a joint session of Congress. Within an hour, Congress declared war. The sole dissenting vote came from Montana Representative Jeannette Rankin, the remarkable suffragist and pacifist who in 1917 had also voted against U.S. entry into World War I.

Following an investigation completed shortly after the disaster, Pearl Harbor's top Army and Navy commanders—Lieutenant-General Walter Short and Admiral Husband Kimmel—were found guilty of dereliction of duty and forced to resign. (The controversial scapegoats were posthumously exonerated and their original ranks restored by Congress in 1999, following a campaign by family members and others.) Admiral Chester Nimitz was appointed commander-in-chief of the Pacific Fleet—"Tell Nimitz to get the hell out to Pearl and stay there till the war is won," Roosevelt ordered famously—and 130,000,000 Americans were galvanized as never before for a single purpose: Avenge Pearl Harbor, defeat Japan.

The date which will live in infamy now also seems fated to live in controversy. Too detailed to cover here, the American and Japanese collision course in the Pacific that developed through the 1920s and '30s is treated in many of the sources listed below. Such matters as the Japanese invasion of China and the American oil embargo imposed against Japan in July 1941 deserve examination, but among the more enduring questions surrounding the attack are those concerning who knew what and when. A considerable body of work continues to grow suggesting that while Roosevelt, Winston Churchill and others were aware of Japanese plans in advance, they allowed the Pearl Harbor attack to take place in order to draw the United States into the war in Europe. Long before December 7, 1941, America had broken Japanese communication codes and was routinely deciphering top-level communications. This and other facts make conspiracy theories compelling at the very least. Whether or not officials in Washington, D.C. were in fact surprised by the attack, it's safe to say that the military and civilian residents of Oahu were completely unprepared for the carnage that would mark them to the end of their lives, and live on as one of the most world-altering events in history.

SOURCES & OTHER READING

At Dawn We Slept: The Untold Story of Pearl Harbor, Prange, Gordon W., Penguin, 1982
Day of Infamy, Lord, Walter, Bantam, 1987
Infamy: Pearl Harbor and Its Aftermath, Toland, John, Doubleday, 1982
Pearl Harbor: Final Judgement, Clausen and Lee, Crown, 1992
Day of Deceit: The Truth About FDR and Pearl Harbor, Stinnett, Robert, Simon & Schuster, 2001
Days of Infamy: MacArthur, Roosevelt, Churchill—The Shocking Truth Revealed, Costello, John, Nimbus Communications, 1994

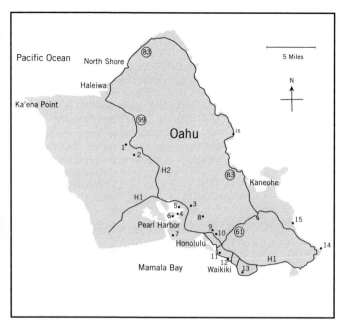

1. Schofield Barracks/Tropic Lightning Museum
2. Wheeler Army Airfield
3. Ft. Shafter
4. U.S.S. *Arizona* Memorial
5. U.S.S. *Bowfin* Submarine Museum and Park
6. Battleship *Missouri* Memorial
7. Hickam Air Force Base
8. Natsunoya Teahouse
9. Japanese Consulate
10. Punchbowl (National Memorial Cemetery of the Pacific)
11. Iolani Palace
12. Ft. DeRussy Museum (U.S. Army Museum of Hawaii)
13. Diamond Head State Monument
14. Makapuu Wayside Trail
15. Bellows Field Beach Park
16. Kualoa Ranch

Pearl Harbor/Oahu Today

Population (Oahu): 876,156 • Area code: 808 • Currency: U.S. dollar

Already considered among the world's most beautiful islands, the massive influx of mainland American influence during the war propelled Oahu into the modern age and elevated it to one of the globe's great travel destinations. Today, most of Oahu's five million annual visitors congregate in Waikiki, the two-mile stretch of golden-sand, beachfront property bookended by Diamond Head and Honolulu Harbor, and jammed with expensive resorts, high-rise hotels, bars and excellent restaurants.

Beyond the famed bikini-covered beaches and congested capital city of Honolulu, Oahu quickly becomes rural and slower paced. The emerald Koolau Mountains plunging into the sea on the island's windward (east) side provide the kind of lush, dramatic scenery associated with classic Hawaiian images. The North Shore—a world-class haven for winter surfers—is relaxed and culturally diverse. Naval Station Pearl Harbor remains the home of the commander-in-chief of the Pacific Fleet and thirty home-ported ships.

Other destinations have a greater number of relics, but for the combination of historical significance, major sites, ease of travel, natural beauty and wealth of first-rate accommodations, restaurants and activities, Oahu has no equal. A short day is recommended to tour the main Pearl Harbor sites (shaded box). An additional one or two busy days are needed to cover the remaining points of interest.

POINTS OF INTEREST

1. Schofield Barracks/Tropic Lightning Museum ★★★

Foote Gate (aka Main Gate) off of H-2 on Kunia Road
Museum at Carter Hall, Building 361, Waianae Avenue at Macomb Drive
T: 808-655-0438 (Museum)
T: 808-655-0216 (Community Commander's Office)
Museum open Tuesday-Saturday, 10 a.m.-4 p.m.
Closed Sunday, Monday, federal holidays. Mission and security conditions allowing, daytime visitors with proper ID checking in at Foote Gate on Kunia Road are usually allowed to enter the base to see the museum and tour the facility.

Home of the 25th Infantry Division, Schofield is where *From Here to Eternity* and *The Thin Red Line* author James Jones was stationed when Pearl Harbor was attacked (he was later wounded in Guadalcanal). With relics, photos and small exhibits, the museum chronicles the exploits of the 25th Infantry in Guadalcanal, Leyte, Korea, Vietnam and the Gulf War. Available at the museum, a free historic guide to the base marks the location of twenty points of interest including the Post Cemetery and soldier's barracks. On the property is Kolekole Pass. Contrary to widespread published accounts, Japanese planes did not fly through the mountain pass on December 7. Schofield was hit during the attack, but wasn't a primary target.

2. Wheeler Army Airfield ★★★

On Kamehameha Highway, adjacent to Schofield Barracks
T: 808-655-0216 (Schofield Barracks Community Commander's Office)
Mission and security conditions allowing, daytime visitors with proper ID checking in at Kawamura Gate on Kamehameha Highway are usually allowed to enter and tour the facility.

From this small base, pilots Ken Taylor and George Welch viewed the initial phases of the December 7 attack then drove north to airplanes at Haleiwa Field. Each pilot was officially credited with four kills of Japanese planes. Several less-celebrated pilots took off from Wheeler and also recorded kills. The replica P-40 fighter near Kawamura Gate on Kamehameha Highway is painted with Taylor's numbers and markings. On base are several old hangars, barracks and office buildings that were bombed. Except for the modern aircraft, the airfield, with its line of hangars, looks just as it did in 1941.

3. Ft. Shafter ★★★

Main Gate off of H-1 (Ft. Shafter/Aiea exit) on Sunston Drive
T: 808-438-6996 (Community Coordinator's Office)
Mission and security conditions allowing, daytime visitors with proper ID checking in at the Main Gate on Sunston Drive are usually allowed to enter and tour the facility.

Richardson Hall (aka the Pineapple Pentagon) was and is the U.S. Army Pacific Headquarters. Inside the entrance is a stunning mural titled "Marching Men" depicting victorious U.S. soldiers marching home through an unspecified jungle. Among other operations, plans for the invasion of Okinawa and Japan were drawn up inside this building. Lieutenant-General Walter Short lived across the street in the eighth house in from the one-way entrance to Palm Circle Drive. Near the house is the site (not the original structure) of the information center where early radar detection of incoming Japanese planes was incorrectly determined to be American aircraft arriving from the West Coast. The Roberts Commission that investigated the Pearl Harbor disaster and found Short and Kimmel guilty of dereliction of duty convened at Ft. Shafter.

7. Hickam Air Force Base ★★★

Main Gate off of H-1 (Hickam exit) northwest of Honolulu International Airport
T: 808-449-2490 (Public Affairs Office)
When scheduled two weeks in advance, guided tours have been offered in the past. As of this writing, only retired and active military personnel can visit.

Hickam Air Force Base tours include Flagpole Circle, which features bronze plaques and a memorial listing the names of those who died at the base during the December 7 attack. Across the street, shell holes can still be seen in the Pacific Air Forces Headquarters building. Inside is a display on the war along with the same flag that flew over the base during the attack, and later over the White House after the Japanese surrendered. A restored B-25J Mitchell Bomber built in 1945 and used as a trainer is on display next to the Wing Headquarters building. Still bearing the Army Air Corps star above their doors, the four restored double hangars at Hangar Row were heavily damaged during the attack. This is another spot where aircraft had been lined up wingtip to wingtip and dovetailed, making them vulnerable to aerial attack.

8. Natsunoya Teahouse ★

1935 Makanani Dr., Honolulu
T: 808-595-4488
Rental for private functions only

Once called "the most important spy in the world," Takeo Yoshikawa, Japan's leading authority on the U.S. Navy, arrived in Honolulu in March 1941. In a dramatic 1961 TV interview, he revealed many of his secrets, including the location of this teahouse in the hills overlooking Pearl Harbor from which he tracked the movements of the U.S. Pacific Fleet. The humble, two-story wooden house is mostly impressive from inside the second-floor tatami room with large windows looking out over Pearl Harbor.

9. Japanese Consulate ★

1742 Nuuanu St.

The diplomatic office was a pipeline to Japan for information regarding U.S. military preparedness. The old building no longer exists, but the site at 1742 Nuuanu St. is the same as prewar.

10. Punchbowl (National Memorial Cemetery of the Pacific) ★★★★

2177 Puowaina Dr.
T: 808-532-3720

Pearl Harbor

The following three sites share a parking lot and are within easy walking distance of each other. Shuttle buses make the five-minute run between the U.S.S. *Bowfin* and U.S.S. *Missouri*.

4. U.S.S. *Arizona* Memorial ★★★★

1 Arizona Memorial Place
T: 808-422-0561
Daily, 7:30 a.m.-5 p.m.
(last program begins at 3 p.m.)
Closed Thanksgiving, Christmas
and New Year's Day
Free

Opened in 1962, the memorial is administered by the National Park Service and receives about 1.5 million visitors per year. Taken in groups of 150, the mandatory itinerary follows a set program and includes a twenty-minute introductory film, five-minute boat ride to the memorial for a fifteen-minute stay (seats on the right provide the best picture views on the boat ride out) and a visit to the museum. Not counting the wait, the whole experience takes about seventy-five minutes. Early morning is the best time to avoid lines. Because of the sun and light harbor traffic, it's also the best time to see the rusted, barnacle-encrusted,

608-foot-long *Arizona*, which rests with eighty percent of her crew entombed just below the waterline beneath the memorial. The dip in the center of the recognizable, white memorial represents the initial defeat at Pearl Harbor; the upward swing on both ends signifies ultimate American victory. The memorial is moving, but it's the significance of the site—the *Arizona* has unofficially come to commemorate all military personnel killed in the Pearl Harbor attack—that makes it a major attraction.

5. U.S.S. *Bowfin* Submarine Museum and Park ★★★★★

11 Arizona Memorial Dr.
T: 808-423-1341
Daily, 8 a.m.-5 p.m. (Last U.S.S. *Bowfin* tour begins at 4:30 p.m.)
Museum only: $4 Adult, $2 Child
Museum and U.S.S. *Bowfin*:
$8 Adult, $3 Child
Museum, U.S.S. *Bowfin* and U.S.S. *Missouri* package: $18 Adult, $9 Child
For guided tours, add $6 to all prices

The park includes several steam-powered torpedoes (the U.S. Navy's primary torpedo during World War II), plaques telling the story of all fifty-two American submarines lost during the war and a captured Japanese *kaiten* manned suicide torpedo. The museum details the history of the "silent service" with an extensive Pacific War section that includes the dive-stand from the U.S.S. *Swordfish*. The narrow, 312-foot long *Bowfin* is spectacular to walk through. Nicknamed the "Pearl Harbor Avenger," the *Bowfin* was launched December 7, 1942, completed nine Pacific War patrols and, as indicated by the flags on its conning tower, destroyed forty-three Japanese ships. Highlights of

the immaculately preserved sub include the torpedo room (with tiny sleeping berths shoved in between massive torpedoes), control room and engine room.

6. Battleship *Missouri* Memorial ★★★★★

11 Arizona Memorial Dr.
(Tickets and access through U.S.S. *Bowfin* ticket office)
T: 808-973-2494 or 877-6444-8966
Daily, 9 a.m.-5 p.m.
(Ticket sales end at 3:55 p.m.)
$14 Adult, $7 Child
U.S.S. *Missouri*, U.S.S. *Bowfin* and Submarine Museum package:
$18 Adult, $9 Child

For guided tours, add $6 to all prices

The last and biggest American battleship ever built, the 900-foot-long behemoth provided gunfire support in the battles for Iwo Jima and Okinawa. On the spectacular teak deck, General Douglas MacArthur accepted Japan's surrender in Tokyo Bay on September 2, 1945. The Surrender Deck is commemorated today with a large copy of the Instrument of Surrender and an audio track of MacArthur's surrender-ceremony speech. The guided or self-guided tour includes the flying bridge, elegant ward room and (failed) kamikaze attack site on the starboard side of the fantail. The high point is the awesome set of forward gun mounts with sixteen-inch guns in each turret. The massive guns, the most powerful ever mounted on a U.S. warship, fired projectiles up to twenty-three miles. The *Missouri's* overwhelming size is commensurate with her place in history. She's anchored just beyond the U.S.S. *Arizona* Memorial, succinctly marking the beginning and end of the war for the United States.

Daily, 8 a.m.-5:30 p.m.,
September 30-March 1
Daily, 8 a.m.-6:30 p.m.,
March 2-September 29
7 a.m.-7 p.m., Memorial Day

Covering 116 acres in Puowaina Crater (aka Punchbowl), Hawaii's most-visited attraction was opened to burials of Pacific War veterans in 1949. Including the remains of 848 Korean War veterans, the immaculate cemetery has 33,230 gravesites, including that of famed war correspondent Ernie Pyle, who was killed during the Battle of Okinawa. His gravesite is D109 and a small tribute to his life and work is on display in the visitors center. Overlooking the grounds is a massive memorial dominated by a thirty-foot-tall female figure known as "Columbia," standing on a prow representing a U.S. Navy aircraft carrier. Two large outdoor map galleries depict principal Pacific War campaigns. The Courts of the Missing record the names of 18,094 World War II soldiers missing in action, as well as names of MIA soldiers from Korea and Vietnam. The forty-eight spectacular Chinese banyan trees, representing each U.S. state during wartime, were a gift from China commemorating U.S. assistance in China's fight against Japan. At the end of the short Memorial Walk, views of Honolulu and Diamond Head are superb. Along with the Manila American Cemetery and Memorial, this is one of two hallowed national resting places for the remains of Pacific War veterans.

11. Iolani Palace ★★

364 S. King St., Honolulu
T: 808-522-0832 (reservations)
T: 808-538-1471 (recorded information)
Tours every fifteen minutes (reservations recommended), Tuesday-Saturday,
9 a.m.-2:15 p.m.
$10 Adult
$3 Child (5-12)
Children under 5 not admitted

At America's only royal palace, barbed wire was erected and martial law declared on December 7, 1941. The building was Hawaii's government seat until the State Capital was opened in 1969. Tours of the restored palace primarily recall the glory days of Hawaii's monarchy.

12. Ft. DeRussy Museum (U.S. Army Museum of Hawaii) ★★★

Corner of Kalia and Saratoga Roads, Waikiki (next to Hale Koa hotel)
T: 808-438-2821

Tuesday-Sunday, 10 a.m.-4:15 p.m.
Closed Monday

Chronicling military history in Hawaii, the museum includes large and excellent Pearl Harbor and Pacific War exhibits. Items include weaponry (American and Japanese tanks are out front), uniforms, photos and pieces of Japanese aircraft shot down on December 7. Just behind Waikiki Beach, the museum is located in the historic Battery Randolph building (a key coastal defense installation completed in 1911) at Ft. DeRussy.

13. Diamond Head State Monument ★★

Off Diamond Head Road, between 18th and 22nd Avenues
T: 808-587-0300
Daily, 6 a.m.-6 p.m.
$1

A 0.7-mile trail leads to the 761-foot peak of Hawaii's most recognizable landmark. Along the way are several bunkers and gun emplacements. Built into the side of the mountain, Diamond Head's once-extensive complex of batteries and command positions anticipated an assault by warships. The airborne attack of December 7 showed it to be largely obsolete, though positions were manned for coastal watch throughout the war. The concrete remnants are interesting, but the payoff for the moderately difficult hike is the panoramic view of Waikiki, Oahu and the Pacific Ocean. The hike up takes thirty to forty-five minutes.

14. Makapuu Wayside Trail ★★

Highway 72, on ocean side of road about 1.5 miles north of Sandy Beach Park

The paved one-mile trail leads to a scenic point overlooking a lighthouse and the windward coast of Oahu. The hike is mostly uphill. It takes thirty to forty-five minutes to reach the ten or so coastal defense fortifications (mostly concrete pillboxes) at the top. As on the Diamond Head trail, the wartime leftovers are interesting, but this one is more about the great views.

15. Bellows Field Beach Park ★★

41-043 Kalanianaole Hwy.
Bellows Air Force Station
T: 808-449-2490 (Hickam AFB Public Affairs Office)

With airplanes parked wingtip to wingtip, without fuel or ammunition, Bellows Field was badly damaged on December 7. Little evidence remains of the old flying field. Though Bellows Air Force Station is not normally open to the public (the area is used primarily as a recreational facility for military personnel), this park on the eastern shore of Oahu beside Bellows AFS has historical markers and a nice beach.

16. Kualoa Ranch ★★

49-560 Kamehameha Hwy.
T: 808-237-8515 or 800-231-7321
Tours from $49 (ATV, horseback) to $148 (deluxe tour)

The 4,000-acre working cattle ranch offers tours of its gorgeous mountain valley. The U.S. military controlled the property during wartime and turned it into an airfield. A fairly extensive bunker system remains. The ranch was used for the scene of the young boys hiking as Zeroes flew overhead in the film *Pearl Harbor*. *Windtalkers, JurassicPark* and scenes from other movies have been filmed here as well. A World War II bunker has been turned into a small "Hollywood comes to Kualoa" museum.

World War II Tours

Home of the Brave
Military Base Tour

T: 808-396-8112
Adult: $69, plus tax
Child (2-11): $59, plus tax

After September 11, 2001, security and access to Hawaii's military bases tightened considerably. An easy way to avoid access hassles and visit many of the sites in this chapter is to join a tour with an established company. Home of the Brave employs top-notch guides who provide a wealth of anecdotes and commentary concerning the Japanese attack and wartime Oahu. Its excellent Military Base Tour includes the U.S.S. *Arizona* Memorial, Schofield Barracks, Wheeler Army Airfield, Fort Shafter, a Punchbowl drive-by and the company's small but worthwhile private museum.

Islander Seaplane Service
Islander Air Tour

T: 808-836-6273
$139, plus tax
The one-hour Islander airplane tour

covers the basic Oahu sites—Waikiki, Diamond Head, etc.—but also includes fly-overs of Schofield Barracks and Wheeler Army Airfield, and flies alongside Pearl Harbor. The flight culminates by following the exact approach route and altitude (2,500 feet) used by the main body of Japanese attackers on December 7, making it a unique experience in the Pacific.

Captain Bruce
Wreck diving ◤

T: 808-373-3590 or 800-535-2487
Oahu has several good World War II dives. The *Mahi*, a 186-foot U.S. Navy minelayer sunk at ninety feet off Oahu's west shore was voted one of the United States' best wreck dives by readers of *Rodale's Scuba Diving* magazine. A decently preserved Corsair fighter, which crashed into the ocean in 1945 or 1946 while on a training flight, lies at 105-110 feet off the east shore of the island. Captain Bruce specializes in World War II dives.

OTHER AREA ATTRACTIONS

North Shore

H-2 to Highway 99 to Haleiwa

From golf to nightclubs to hiking to parasailing to fishing to luaus and hula shows, Oahu has so many diversions it's difficult to highlight one or two. One of the often-levied criticisms of the island, however, is that all of these activities make Oahu "too touristy." One place that refutes this complaint nicely is the North Shore. A forty-five-minute to one-hour drive from Honolulu puts visitors in a relaxed, less-developed part of the island that bears resemblance to the mythical "Hawaii" that Honolulu and Waikiki left behind decades ago. Starting with the surfing capital of Haleiwa, the Kamehameha Highway follows the shore past comparatively uncrowded (the area is busier during the winter surf season) surf and sunning beaches at Waimea Bay, Pipeline and Sunset Beach. For those disenchanted with the buzz of Waikiki, North Shore is a slower alternative worth a day trip or longer stay.

GETTING TO/AROUND PEARL HARBOR/OAHU

Nonstop flights to Honolulu International Airport are plentiful from many U.S. mainland cities, Guam, Japan and other international airports.

Though taxis are easy to find in Waikiki and the local transit system (TheBus) is often praised, a car is the only reason-able way to get around. All major and many minor car rental companies operate in Oahu, including Avis (800-331-1212), Budget Car Rental (800-527-7000) and Dollar Rent A Car (800-800-3665). Many airlines offer good airfare/rental car packages—ask when making flight plans.

ACCOMMODATIONS

Outrigger Waikiki on the Beach

2335 Kalakaua Ave., Honolulu
T: 808-923-0711
F: 808-921-9749
530 rooms
From $175

In the heart of Waikiki, the Outrigger is one of the island's landmark hotels. Along with excellent restaurants, lounges and shops, cultural events are regularly held in the lobby. Family and internet specials are available, but for all this it's the dramatic beachfront setting and impeccable service that makes it a favorite.

OHANA East

159 Kaiulani Ave., Waikiki
T: 808-922-5353 F: 808-926-4334
445 rooms
From: $135

Waikiki offers an endless selection of hotels, but if being a couple blocks off the beach isn't a concern, this solid hotel is a (comparative) bargain. Centrally located within a three-minute walk of the beach, four-star restaurants and gift shops. Across the street, OHANA West (2330 Kuhio Ave.; 922-5022) has even cheaper rooms, from $129.

Turtle Bay Resort

57-091 Kamehameha Hwy., Kahuku-Oahu
T: 808-293-8811 or 800-203-3650
F: 808-293-9147
445 rooms
$100-$325

Covering 880 acres of quiet North Shore property, Turtle Bay has great cottages and rooms on a long stretch of pristine beach, two pools, two championship golf courses and ten tennis courts. An hour from Honolulu, the full-service resort is the island's best alternative to the bustle of Waikiki.

Corregidor

PHILIPPINES

THE WAR YEARS

While seemingly half of Asia fell beneath Japan's blitz through the Far East in the opening months of World War II, only American and Filipino defenders on Corregidor Island (and mainland Bataan) provided resistance against Japanese territorial ambition. Following one of the most grueling sieges in the annals of warfare, historian William Manchester pronounced Corregidor—a narrow, three-and-a-half-mile-long fortress—the mythic equal of the Alamo and Dunkirk. When the fortress fell to the Japanese it marked what many considered the lowest point in American morale during the war.

Occupied by the U.S. military since the Spanish-American War in 1898, Corregidor—along with four smaller islands—defended the entrance to Manila Bay, the finest natural harbor in the Orient and front door to the Philippine Islands. Fortified with forty-five coastal guns, twenty-four anti-aircraft batteries, forty-eight heavy machine guns and about 6,000 troops, The Rock was the final key to Japan's fifty-day plan to seize Luzon, the Philippines' largest island.

After enduring three weeks of Japanese attacks on the Philippines that commenced simultaneously with the December 7 attack on Pearl Harbor, Philippine President Manuel Quezon and commander of U.S. and Filipino forces General Douglas MacArthur fled Manila to the safety of Corregidor's underground shelters on Christmas Eve of 1941. Foremost among these was the bombproof Malinta Tunnel, an 836-foot-long, twenty-four-foot wide fortification built through the base of Malinta Hill. The main tunnel's labyrinth of twenty-five, 400-foot-long laterals would provide living space, hospital rooms, offices and supply depots throughout the harrowing ordeal to come.

On December 29, Japanese bombers made their first raid on Corregidor, opening a schedule of continual bombardment that over the next five months drove inhabitants underground, denuded the island of dense forest and destroyed its defensive structures. Water and food rations were cut to starvation levels. Malnutrition, beriberi, dysentery and malaria exacted terrible tolls. Injuries mounted. MacArthur promised reinforcements, but the war in Europe was Washington's priority. The defenders of Corregidor were isolated, cut off from any hope of aid.

Aboard the submarine *Swordfish*, Quezon slipped off The Rock on February 20, 1942, to reestablish his government in the Philippines' southern islands. Following orders from President Franklin Roosevelt, MacArthur transferred command of Philippine military forces to Major-General Jonathan Wainwright and, with an escort of four torpedo boats, left the island on March 12. On March 17 he landed at Batchelor Airfield near Darwin, Australia, where, surrounded by reporters, he delivered the promise for which he would be remembered the rest of his life: "I shall return."

With the April 9, 1942 surrender of Allied forces on Bataan, Japanese artillery bombardment of Corregidor intensified. On May 4, shells fell at a rate of one every five seconds, 16,000 tons in twenty-four hours. "Those on the island began to have a feeling of standing on jelly, so intense and so continuous were the explosions," wrote Alfonso Aluit in his book *Corregidor*.

On the night of May 5, Japanese soldiers arrived on the island. Aided by heavy seas and chaotic landings, Fil-Am troops put up a desperate defense. But Wainwright knew his forces were too weak and ill equipped to repel the invaders. On May 6, he sent a telegram to Roosevelt: "With broken heart and head bowed in sadness but not in shame I report that today I must arrange for terms of surrender of the fortified islands of Manila Bay." For another month, the defenders of Corregidor—13,193 Americans and Filipinos, including 2,302 civilians—were held hostage until all organized resistance in the Philippines ended in June 1942.

Spearheaded by the 503rd Parachute Infantry Regiment and the amphibious 34th Infantry, the battle to retake Corregidor commenced on February 16, 1945. Several days of bloody fighting against 6,000 entrenched defenders featured numerous banzai charges and a Japanese attempt to blow up Malinta Hill. It cost liberation forces 225 deaths to regain Corregidor; at least 4,500 Japanese were killed. By February 25, with the island secure, MacArthur returned to lead a solemn ceremony marking the return of Fil-Am forces.

The Official U.S. Army History called the loss of the Philippines to the Japanese "the single largest defeat of American Armed Forces in history." With typical bombast, MacArthur called the recapture of Corregidor "one of the most brilliant operations in military history." Wainwright spent the rest of the war in Japanese POW camps. Expecting to be court-martialed upon his release, he instead was awarded a Medal of Honor for his tenacity on Corregidor. Aboard the U.S.S. *Missouri* at the formal Japanese surrender ceremony in Tokyo Bay on September 2, 1945, MacArthur presented to Wainwright the first pen used in signing the surrender document.

MacArthur later claimed the resolute defense of Corregidor and Bataan disrupted Japan's war timetable and bought the Allies time to regroup for its massive counterstrike through the Southwestern Pacific. Historians debate the strategic value of the battle, but undeniable was its value as a morale booster for U.S. troops and civilians who, in the first months of 1942, found little in the war news to console them.

SOURCES & OTHER READING

Corregidor, Aluit, Alfonso J., Galleon Publications, 1991

Corregidor: The American Alamo in World War II, Morris, Eric, Cooper Square Press, 2000

Corregidor: The Rock Force Assault, 1945, Flanagan, E.M., Presidio Press, 1988

Back to Corregidor: America Retakes the Rock, Devlin, Gerald M., St. Martin's Press, 1992

Corregidor: The Saga of a Fortress, Belote and Belote, Harper & Row, 1967

MacArthur and Wainwright: Sacrifice of the Philippines, Beck, John Jacob, University of New Mexico Press, 1974

American Caesar: Douglas MacArthur 1880-1964, Manchester, William, Dell, 1978

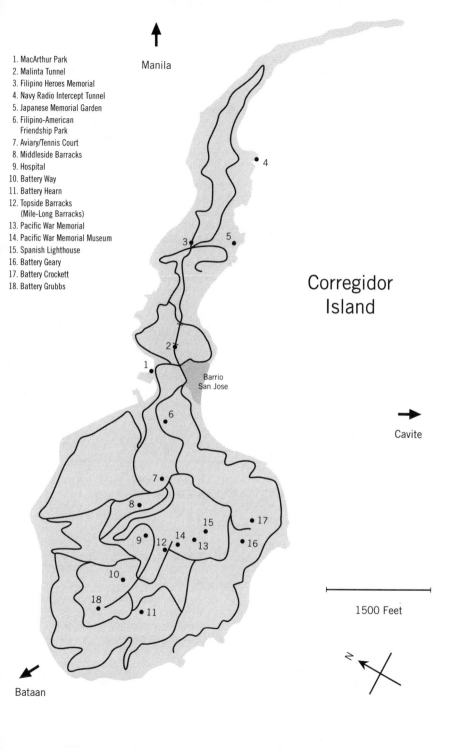

1. MacArthur Park
2. Malinta Tunnel
3. Filipino Heroes Memorial
4. Navy Radio Intercept Tunnel
5. Japanese Memorial Garden
6. Filipino-American
   Friendship Park
7. Aviary/Tennis Court
8. Middleside Barracks
9. Hospital
10. Battery Way
11. Battery Hearn
12. Topside Barracks
    (Mile-Long Barracks)
13. Pacific War Memorial
14. Pacific War Memorial Museum
15. Spanish Lighthouse
16. Battery Geary
17. Battery Crockett
18. Battery Grubbs

Manila

Corregidor
Island

Cavite

Barrio
San Jose

Bataan

1500 Feet

N

CORREGIDOR TODAY

Population: Only island employees • Philippines Country Code: 63 • $1 = 50 pesos

Modern development has paved over so much of the Pacific that it's often difficult to get a visceral sense of the wartime environment. Corregidor is the sublime exception, a sprawling destination with a 1940s look and feel that's been carefully maintained. Declared a national shrine in 1969, the entire island is managed by the Corregidor Foundation as a tourist destination and preserved war memorial. As such, it's unique in the Pacific—World War II preservation is not Corregidor's focus, it is its sole purpose.

The tadpole-shaped island is renowned for its large collection of enormous gun batteries, but the amount and quality of other relics and sites is fantastic. Tours of Malinta Tunnel are a highlight of the entire Pacific. The concentration of attractions on the Topside area is worth a full afternoon. Unspoiled vistas of Manila Bay and the South China Sea are breath-taking. The cheap commercialization that degrades so many destinations has been wisely avoided.

There are pitfalls. With no private cars, transportation is primarily limited to open-air tour buses that run on desultory schedules. Stops at points of interest are brief—one of the longest inevitably reserved for the gift shop. The amount of Japanese visitors and investment (one presumes) in the Philippines leads to occasional heavy-handed efforts to rehabilitate the image of the Japanese military.

Yet Corregidor rises above these deficiencies. Day trips from Manila quickly cover the major sites. An overnight stay allows one to walk the island at an individual pace—far better. The hub of activity and information is the centrally located Corregidor Hotel.

POINTS OF INTEREST

There are only a few main roads and no real addresses on Corregidor. The island is divided into four primary sections—Bottomside, Tailside, Middleside, Topside—designating relative position and elevation. Boats arrive and tours commence from the Bottomside docks. With the exception of Malinta Tunnel, all attractions are free.

1. MacArthur Park ★★

Bottomside

A bronze sculpture of MacArthur (looking like he's hailing a cab) is erected at the ruins of Lorcha Dock where he boarded a torpedo boat to escape Corregidor. Various guns and weapons are scattered in an area nearby.

2. Malinta Tunnel

★★★★★ (Guided tour)

★★★★ (Light and Sound Show only)
Bottomside
Light and Sound Show, 150 pesos in addition to bus tour
Evening tour (inquire at Corregidor Hotel), 50 pesos

The 836-foot-long and twenty-four-foot-wide main tunnel (with laterals branching out) is the centerpiece of the island. Originally an arsenal and hospital, it became the bombproof headquarters for MacArthur, Philippine Commonwealth President Manuel Quezon and embattled Filipino-American (Fil-Am) forces. The Light and Sound Show—included at extra cost on every bus tour—features simulated explosions, life-size models re-creating scenes inside the besieged tunnel, audio tracks of actors making decisions as the Japanese close in (MacArthur sounds reedy; the tubercular Quezon coughs through most of his lines) and a flag-waving finale to the strains of the Philippine national anthem. The show's not bad—it's a good way to spend thirty minutes inside the famed tunnel—but more rewarding are the evening guided tours organized through Corregidor Hotel. These usually begin at around 5:30 p.m. and are often led by longtime guide Syver Valenzuela, who knows as much about the island as anybody. Without the bombast of the Sound and Light Show, visitors get an informative, one-hour tour through the maze of laterals, including the 1,000-bed hospital. By contrast, Light and Sound Show visits are restricted to the main tunnel. Either way, visitors are allowed inside the tunnel only under supervision of a guide.

3. Filipino Heroes Memorial ★★

Tailside

Fourteen large tablets commemorate Filipino heroes from the 1521 Battle of Mactan to World War II to the 1986 EDSA People Power Revolution. An impressive chronology of Philippine history.

4. Navy Radio Intercept Tunnel ★★

Tailside

In addition to Malinta, there are several smaller tunnels on the island. This one near Kindley Airfield is accessible only by a rope drop of about fifty feet. The Corregidor Hotel has details about guided trips.

5. Japanese Memorial Garden ★★

Tailside

This 2.2-hectare park has a ten-foot stone Buddha, Shinto shrine, various Japanese military memorabilia, four anti-aircraft guns and a koi pond. The regimental flag of the unit that first invaded the island is displayed.

6. Filipino-American Friendship Park ★★

Middleside

Landscaped grounds and a ten-foot statue of Filipino and American soldiers leaning on one another.

7. Aviary/Tennis Court ★

Middleside

On a military preserve, the purpose of this depressing and somewhat random collection of exotic birds and animals in small wire cages is not immediately clear. Behind the Aviary, however, is the tennis court built to disguise the island's water reservoir. Through holes in the concrete, deep cavities are visible.

8. Middleside Barracks ★★

Middleside

Decent ruins of reinforced barracks built before the war from Japanese concrete and American steel.

9. Hospital ★★

Middleside

The bombed-out ruins of the original hospital—not to be confused with the 1,000-bed hospital in Malinta Tunnel—remain in recognizable shape.

10. Battery Way ★★★

Middleside

Completed in 1913, Battery Way was armed with four, twelve-inch mortars (all still here in remarkable condition) capable of firing 14,610 yards in any direction. In early May 1942, three of the mortars were disabled by direct hits from Japanese guns. The complex also includes underground magazines, support bunkers and command-post building.

11. Battery Hearn ★★★

Middleside

This awesome twelve-inch seacoast gun had a range of 29,000 yards. Built to fire on large warships, it was mostly ineffective during the fight for Corregidor. Disabled by the Americans before their surrender, it was repaired by American

Topside

Many Topside sites are concentrated in an easy-to-walk area and merit at least two to three hours for visitors with anything more than a passing interest. Tour buses usually stop for forty-five minutes to an hour in the Topside area.

12. Topside Barracks (Mile-Long Barracks) ★★★

Actually a quarter-mile long, this hurricane-proof concrete building is reputedly the world's longest barrack. The three-story ruins are still interesting to explore.

13. Pacific War Memorial ★★★★

Completed in 1968, the $3 million domed memorial stands on the highest part of Corregidor. The dome has a hole in the top configured so that on each May 6 at precisely noon the sun shines through, directly illuminating the entire, circular marble altar below. Earthquakes and other seismic shifts have, alas, moved the altar slightly off center. May 6 nevertheless remains an annual day of commemoration services. Behind the elegant memorial is a steel sculpture symbolizing the eternal Flame of Freedom. The sculpture is ugly, but on the empty bluff behind it is one of the best views on the island—Malinta Tunnel, Corregidor's tadpole tail and the expanse of Manila Bay are all visible.

14. Pacific War Memorial Museum ★★★

Adjacent to the Pacific War Memorial, this small museum has an impressive collection of American and Japanese arms, uniforms and relics. An enlarged cover of the May 8, 1944 issue of *Time* magazine depicts a forlorn General Wainwright behind a barbed-wire prison fence.

15. Spanish Lighthouse ★

Mostly this is an excuse for a gift shop, but the rebuilt tower—the original was built in 1836—does provide panoramic views of the area.

16. Battery Geary ★★★

Together with Battery Way, the eight, twelve-inch Geary mortars were considered the most effective anti-personnel weapons on Corregidor. Japanese spotters in helium balloons eventually located their position, and the battery was completely destroyed with a direct hit on the central magazine.

17. Battery Crockett ★★★

One of six "disappearing guns," on Corregidor, the battery was armed with two, two-inch seacoast guns mounted on carriages that retracted behind a concrete parapet.

POW engineers under death threats from the Japanese.

18. Battery Grubbs ★★★

Topside

Another battery of enormous "disappearing guns." Three massive ten-inch barrels remain inside a relatively well-preserved command post. This high position is the best place on the island to view the sunset over the sea.

OTHER AREA ATTRACTIONS

Hiking Trails

Three primary hiking trails (and at least three smaller ones) crisscross the island. Details on guided hikes and trail information can be obtained from Corregidor Hotel. Longtime guide Syver Valenzuela is the best person to talk to.

Easy Trail: Starts from the Main Road ascending Malinta Hill. The trail leads to the summit of the hill. The original hospital is the highlight. Takes forty-five minutes to an hour.

Moderate Trail: Starts from the flagpole at the old Officers Quarters on Topside (just in front of the Pacific War Memorial). Walk includes Battery Wheeler, Wheeler Tunnel (accessed by ladder through an air shaft), Battery Cheney, Cheney Ravine, various gun emplacements and caves. Takes a little more than an hour.

Endurance Trail: Starts at the Aviary. Trail includes Battery Morrison, Battery James, James Ravine, two Japanese caves, Battery Rockpoint, Battery Hanna, Battery Sunset and Battery Smith. Takes three to four hours.

GETTING TO/AROUND CORREGIDOR

From Manila, the easiest way to the island is via high-speed ferry operated by Sun Cruises, which controls virtually all Corregidor access through a concession with the Corregidor Foundation. Ferries depart Manila daily at 8 and 10:30 a.m. from Terminal A of the CCP Complex on Roxas Boulevard. Ferries depart Corregidor for Manila daily at 2:30 and 5 p.m. The trip takes one hour each way. The day-tour rate is 650 pesos, including round-trip ferry and guided bus tour. Overnight packages start at 1,690 pesos, including round-trip ferry, guided bus tour, lunch and accommodations. Sun Cruises Reservations: 2-831-8140 or 2-834-6858.

Independent travelers can hire private boats from the docks at Mariveles in Bataan Province, just across from Corregidor. Rates must be negotiated (usually higher than the Sun Cruises ferry), but approaching the island this way can be troublesome as bus tours and other services are generally reserved for those on the Sun Cruises package trips.

Most visitors get locked into the guided tour buses, which are adequate for those with a moderate interest in Corregidor. The are no rental cars on the island, but a limited number of private jeepneys are available. The cost per jeepney (which comfortably fits six to eight people) is 800 pesos for two hours. Information is available at the Corregidor Foundation Office at Corregidor's North Dock (cell: 0912-304-0892) or through the Corregidor Visitor's Information Center in Manila (2-550-1347).

ACCOMMODATIONS

There are only three options, all arranged through Sun Cruises (2-831-8140 or 2-834-6857) or the Corregidor Visitor's Information Center (Terminal A, CCP Complex, Roxas Boulevard, Manila; 2-550-1347.)

Corregidor Hotel

31 Rooms
1,690 pesos, as part of package tour

Restaurant, pool, decent rooms and central location. This is by far the best place to stay.

Corregidor Resort

17 beach cottages
1,690 pesos, as part of package tour

Solitude on a nice but rocky beach is the only advantage. Food is available at the restaurant up the small hill, but the out-of-the-way location is undesirable in terms of walking or catching buses.

Camping

Per arrangement with Sun Cruises, campers can pitch tents for thirty pesos per night on the beach just in front of the Corregidor Resort huts.

3

Singapore

THE WAR YEARS

With the exception of Pearl Harbor and Hiroshima, no event in the Pacific War altered the world as dramatically as the Fall of Singapore. Winston Churchill called the defeat "the most ignominious capitulation in the history of British arms." In his memoirs, Churchill referred to Japan's effortless sinking of British protector battleships, the HMS *Repulse* and *Prince of Wales*, as his greatest shock of the war.

"The convictions of two centuries were knocked topsy-turvy by this event," wrote British historian James Morris. "Asians were never to look upon Englishmen in quite the same way again."

Hailed as "impregnable," fortress Singapore stood as the island citadel that assured the security of the entire British empire east of Suez. By 1940, neighboring Malaya produced forty percent of the world's rubber and nearly sixty percent of its tin, most of which was exported to America. Singapore's strategic value to war planners in Japan was simple to adduce. Taking Singapore and Malaya would not only fuel the Japanese war drive, it would crush Britain and severely limit the United States' ability to campaign in the East.

In the early morning hours of December 8, 1941, while Pearl Harbor still lay undisturbed, Japanese fighters and bombers attacked Singapore and the Malayan coast. Coming ashore at Kota Bharu and other points hundreds of miles north of the city, troops equipped with bicycles and rubber-soled slippers advanced with brutal efficiency through the presumably impenetrable Malay jungle. Remarking on futile efforts to repulse the here-there-and-everywhere Japanese assault, one despairing British officer remarked, "It's like trying to build a wall out of quicksand."

By February 1, Japanese troops stood on the banks of the Johore Strait, the thin stretch of water that separates Singapore from the mainland. With Britain's paltry air defenses unable to repel incessant bombing raids and water supplies nearly gone, a state of siege gripped the city. Thousands were killed in daily bombing raids. Office buildings and churches became makeshift hospitals. So many lay dead in the streets that proper burial was impossible.

The final Japanese push landed on the western coast of the island. At the ruined gates of the city, 30,000 invaders faced a multinational British armed force of about 70,000. The legend that all of Singapore's guns were pointed out to sea and couldn't be turned to face an inland invader is apocryphal—but it's true that the vast Malayan jungle had been expected to defend Singapore from overland assault, and that most of the city's permanent defenses had been positioned on the seaward side of the island. It hardly mattered. Supplies and morale were exhausted. On February 15, a contingent of British officers, lead by the lean and quiet Lieutenant-General Arthur Percival, made the humiliating trek to a Ford Motors assembly plant a few miles outside the city. Surrounded by Japanese newspapermen and photographers, the stocky, ruthless General Tomoyuki Yamashita (the "Tiger of Malaya") gloated at the British arrival. Silently, Percival signed the surrender document, Japanese troops entered the city and more than 120,000 soldiers and civilians were sent to prison camps for the remainder of the war.

To the British, the collapse of Singapore was perhaps even more shocking than the assault on Pearl Harbor was to the Americans. Strategically, the victory was Japan's greatest of the war. Tokyo's *Asahi Shimbun* newspaper was more bullish than usual: "With the fall of Singapore the general situation of the war has been determined. The ultimate victory will be ours!"

The psychological victory was even more important. By sacking one of the traditional pivots of imperial power, Japan's ambitions for its Greater East Asia Co-Prosperity Sphere—the Asian world it envisioned free of European and American control— rocketed from fantasy to legitimacy. The myth of British invincibility was shattered. To drive the point home, Australian POWs were forced to sweep the streets of Singapore, a symbol that the old racial order had been overturned.

Renaming the city Shonan (Light of the South), the Japanese military occupied Singapore for the next three-and-a-half years. European and Australian prisoners were interned at the brutal Changi Prison. Others were sent to work on the infamous Death Railway. In retribution for support given to China's ongoing war with Japan, local Chinese faced the worst of the occupation atrocities. Beatings, forced labor and imprisonment were reserved for the fortunate. The number of Chinese residents massacred after the capture of Singapore is estimated as high as 100,000.

As Japanese military fortunes declined throughout Asia, all of Singapore braced for a bloody fight to retake the island. But America's island-hopping campaign bypassed Singapore, and the city was surrendered without a fight. On September 5, 1945 British warships and Commonwealth troops were greeted with a three-mile parade of cheering locals. A week later, Admiral Lord Louis Mountbatten, supreme Allied commander in Southeast Asia, accepted the surrender of the Japanese military command.

Percival spent the war in a Japanese prison camp in Manchuria, but was released in time to be flown to Tokyo and presented by Douglas MacArthur at Japan's formal surrender ceremony aboard the U.S.S. *Missouri* on September 2, 1945. After the war, Yamashita was tried for atrocities in Singapore and Manila and hanged in 1946. Even so, as Churchill had forecast after the sinking of the *Repulse* and *Prince of Wales*, the fall of Singapore "signaled the end of Great Britain's Far Eastern empire."

SOURCES & OTHER READING

Singapore: The Pregnable Fortress, Elphick, Peter, Hodder and Stoughton, 1995

Singapore 1942: Britain's Greatest Defeat, Warren, Alan, Talisman, 2002

Singapore's Dunkirk, Brooke, Geoffrey, Cooper, 1989

Scapegoat: General Percival of Singapore, Kinvig, Clifford, Brassey's, 1996

Syonan—My Story: The Japanese Occupation of Singapore, Shinozaki, Mamoru, Asia Pacific Press, 1975

Singapore 1941-1942: The Japanese Version of the Malayan Campaign of World War II, Tsuji, Masanobu, Oxford University Press, 1988

King Rat, Clavel, James, Little, Brown and Company, 1962

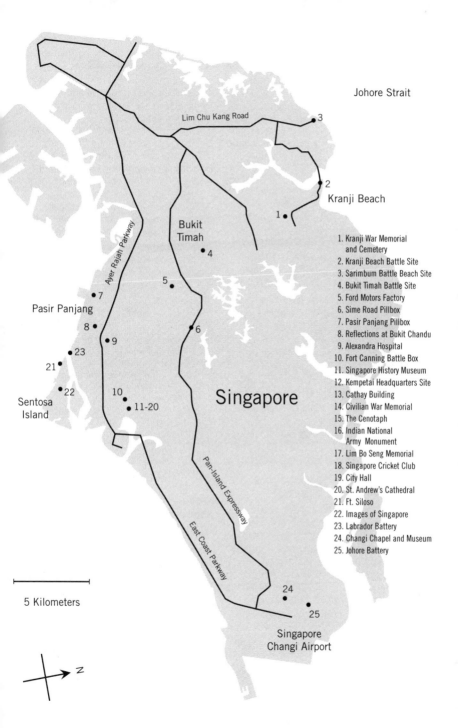

Johore Strait

Lim Chu Kang Road

3

2

Kranji Beach

1

Bukit
Timah

4

Ayer Rajah Parkway

5

7

Pasir Panjang

8

9

23

21

22

Sentosa
Island

10

11-20

Singapore

Pan-Island Expressway

East Coast Parkway

24

25

Singapore
Changi Airport

1. Kranji War Memorial
   and Cemetery
2. Kranji Beach Battle Site
3. Sarimbum Battle Beach Site
4. Bukit Timah Battle Site
5. Ford Motors Factory
6. Sime Road Pillbox
7. Pasir Panjang Pillbox
8. Reflections at Bukit Chandu
9. Alexandra Hospital
10. Fort Canning Battle Box
11. Singapore History Museum
12. Kempetai Headquarters Site
13. Cathay Building
14. Civilian War Memorial
15. The Cenotaph
16. Indian National
    Army Monument
17. Lim Bo Seng Memorial
18. Singapore Cricket Club
19. City Hall
20. St. Andrew's Cathedral
21. Ft. Siloso
22. Images of Singapore
23. Labrador Battery
24. Changi Chapel and Museum
25. Johore Battery

5 Kilometers

Z

SINGAPORE TODAY

Population: 4 million • Singapore country code: 65 • $1 = $1.8 Singapore dollars (all prices below in Singapore dollars)

Occupying all of Singapore Island (239 square miles) and fifty-four smaller islands, this urbanized city-state emerged in the 1980s and '90s as a regional economic juggernaut, particularly in technical and financial industries. A quick look around tells the story. Though exemplary examples of colonial architecture exist, business suits, luxury cars and high-rise office towers dominate the landscape.

For all the stereotypes of a nose-to-the-grindstone population under rigid government control (many of them well founded), Singaporeans tend to be energetic, outgoing and highly social. Restaurants, bars and nightclubs are crowded nightly. English is the official language. The country's three primary ethnic groups—Chinese (78.8 percent), Malay (13.9 percent), Indian (7.9 percent)—also speak various dialects of their own languages.

Intense development has destroyed most of the old city that once made the mere name Singapore synonymous with romance. Old Asia hands still grow melancholy when contemplating the sterile, featureless creature that's risen in its place, and justifiably so. Still, excluding the notoriously terrible cabbies, you can rely on just about everything here, from the immaculate subway to what one British expat called "the only honest police department in the world." Charming it may no longer be, but as a way point in often difficult Southeast Asia, Singapore can be a traveler's best friend.

A visit to all the sites listed below requires two to three days.

POINTS OF INTEREST

1. Kranji War Memorial and Cemetery
★★★★★

9 Woodlands Rd.
Daily, 5 a.m.-7 p.m.

The most immediately impressive of all of Singapore's attractions, this vast memorial honors Commonwealth soldiers who died throughout Southeast Asia. Marked graves of 4,000 men stand in symmetrical rows. An additional 24,000 names are inscribed on the memorial, which represents all three branches of the service. The massive horizontal cross section resembling an airplane wing (air force) is bisected by an eighty-foot-tall pylon recalling a submarine conning tower (navy). Twelve supporting columns represent the twelve garrisons of the land army. The area served as a POW camp and burial ground during the Japanese occupation of Singapore. A memorial service is held at the cemetery each November 15.

2. Kranji Beach Battle Site ★★

Kranji Way, a few miles north of Kranji War Memorial and Cemetery

The beach where the main thrust of Japanese soldiers landed on February 10, 1942 is now a quiet park covered with accasia, angsanna and tamarind trees. A large bronze plaque resembling an open book marks the location. The plaques, seen throughout Singapore, are meant to represent the Story of Singapore as a text opened to a particular page in the country's history.

3. Sarimbum Battle Beach Site ★

Northern end of Lim Chu Kang Road

The site of the other major Japanese invading point serves as a public dock. The Japanese crossed the Johore Strait in small boats, overwhelmed about 750 Australian defenders and proceeded up the Lim Chu Kang Road to take Tengah Air Base. Down the road several kilometers, the air base is now used by the Republic of Singapore Air Force.

4. Bukit Timah Battle Site ★

Bukit Timah Road, about eight miles west of the city center

"Bukit" means hill and seizing Bukit Timah was an important step in the Japanese advance on the city. Once under control, Yamashita set up temporary headquarters here. Singapore fell a week later. One of the ubiquitous book plaques marks the otherwise unremarkable site.

5. Ford Motors Factory ★

351 Upper Bukit Timah Rd.

The site of the British surrender was the first car assembly plant in Southeast Asia. Once popular on the Japanese World War II travel trail, it's now derelict and fenced off. Singapore's National Heritage Board is considering plans to turn it into a museum. In the meantime, the plant is off limits, but can be seen from the road.

6. Sime Road Pillbox ★★

Sime Road, near entrance of Singapore Island Country Club

Built for the defense of MacRitchie Reservoir, this squat, concrete structure is listed by the National Heritage Board as one of Singapore's "100 Historic Places." The nearby Adam Park Estate and golf course was the scene of intense fighting.

7. Pasir Panjang Pillbox ★★

Junction of Paris Panjang and Science Park Roads

Built for the defense of the southern coast, this pillbox was used by the 1st Malaya Brigade.

8. Reflections at Bukit Chandu ★★★★

31-K Pepys Rd., off Pasir Panjang Road
T: 6736-6622 (Singapore Tourism Board)
Tuesday-Sunday, 9 a.m.-5 p.m.

Opened in 2002, this museum dedicated to the heroism of the Malay Regiment in the defense of Singapore is one of the slickest, most high-tech World War II museums anywhere. The story of the Battle of Pasir Panjang, which took place in this area, is told in a "biurnal sound" audiovisual presentation featuring three-dimensional holographs. On small, invisible screens, Japanese Zeroes zoom overhead, dropping bombs and strafing Malay soldiers who pop up from entrenched positions to describe the battle to visitors. Elaborate models, Japanese bikes from the Malay campaign and other exhibits are all of high caliber. The center was designed for the education and promotion of Malays in Singapore. It's worth a visit also for its tranquil, forest setting (a rarity in Singapore) and the beautiful two-story former British officers quarters in which the center is housed.

9. Alexandra Hospital ★★

378 Alexandra Rd.

During their invasion, Japanese troops stormed the hospital in retaliation against Indian soldiers whom they believed were firing at them from inside. Many staff and patients were killed in the long-remembered slaughter. The original hospital building exists to the left of the main entrance. The hospital is in use today as part of National University of Singapore's Medical School.

10. Fort Canning Battle Box ★★★★★

51 Canning Rise
T: 333-0510

Tuesday-Sunday, 10 a.m.-6 p.m. (last admission at 5 p.m.). Closed Monday
$8 Adult, $5 Child (12 and under)

A Singapore highlight, the Battle Box is

the large subterranean bunker complex that served as Britain's Malay Command Headquarters. It was completed in 1939 with twenty-two rooms, many of which can be entered on a tour that impressively re-creates the final days of the Battle of Singapore. Life-size animatronic soldiers move and "talk" in the Communications Room (original British phone equipment); Fortress Commander's Office (the animatronic yet still corpselike Percival receiving disastrous situation reports); and Battle Box (giant table map where Japanese advances are tracked). The tour climaxes in the Surrender Conference Chamber where an even gloomier Percival discusses options with eleven of his top officers. Through it all, Percival is portrayed as a determined fighter who nevertheless bows to his field officers' wishes to surrender. The moving, talking figures and simulated explosions may be tacky to some, but the dank, gloomy bunker does give a frightening sense of how isolated and desperate Singapore was as the enemy closed in.

Heritage Trail

By themselves, few of the sites on the Heritage Trail are extraordinary. Together they constitute a compact collection of sites along an approximately two-mile walk. Sites are rated individually but taken as a whole merit ★★★★.

11. Singapore History Museum ★★

93 Stamford Rd.
Tuesday-Sunday, 9 a.m.-6 p.m., Friday, 9 a.m.-9 p.m., closed Monday
$3

Apart from three small dioramas of the war years on the ground floor, the only item of note is a tattered Union Jack. Taken at the February 15, 1942 Fall of Singapore, it was recovered from the corpse of a Japanese soldier in Burma in October 1944. The flag was taken by the Japanese soldier and kept as a souvenir throughout the war.

12. Kempetai Headquarters Site ★

Stamford Road, next to Singapore History Museum, a one-minute walk to the right as you face the museum

A bronze book plaque stands at the site of the old YMCA building used by the feared Kempetai, the Japanese military police force often compared with the Nazi Gestapo. The YMCA building there now was built after the war.

13. Cathay Building ★

2 Handy Rd.

Kitty-corner from the Singapore History Museum, Singapore's "first skyscraper" was used as an air-raid shelter during the attack on Singapore. On February 15, 1942 General Percival flew the Japanese flag from the roof as a sign that he'd accepted Yamashita's conditions of surrender. The Japanese Military Information Bureau and Military Propaganda Department used the building during the occupation. It later became headquarters of Admiral Lord Louis Mountbatten.

14. Civilian War Memorial ★★

Intersection of Beach and Raffles Roads

Soaring to 220 feet, the four narrow columns that form this landmark erected in 1967 are colloquially known as the "chopsticks." Each chopstick represents a different Singapore ethnic group: Chinese, Malay, Indian, Eurasians and other minorities. The memorial is dedicated to civilians who lost their lives during the Japanese occupation. Remains of unknown victims are interred beneath the memorial.

15. The Cenotaph ★

Across from the Civilian War Memorial, a minute or so south, in War Memorial Park, the Cenotaph was erected in 1920 to honor Singaporeans who died in World War I. The monolith was later inscribed to include World War II soldiers.

16. Indian National Army Monument ★

A short walk south from The Cenotaph through War Memorial Park

A bronze book plaque commemorates the Indian National Army, formed in 1942 to co-opt Indians in Singapore into India's fight for independence. The original monument, built during the final months of the Japanese occupation, was destroyed by returning British forces.

17. Lim Bo Seng Memorial ★★

A short walk south from the Indian National Army Monument through War Memorial Park

This Asian-style monument to Chinese resistance leader Lim Bo Seng is one of the more interesting to look at in Memorial Park. It tells how the major-general "manfully endured repeated tortures" by the Japanese "to which he succumbed on 29th June, 1944, at the age of 35."

18. Singapore Cricket Club ★★

Connaught Drive, end of War Memorial Park
T: 6338-9271

Founded in 1852 and expanded in 1877 and 1884, the gorgeous colonial building was used as a makeshift hospital in early 1942 then transformed into an exclusive club for Japanese officers during the occupation. Admission is for members only.

19. City Hall ★★★

3 St. Andrew's Rd., across from War Memorial Park
Monday-Friday, open during business hours

Built between 1926 and 1929, this was the site of the surrender of 738,400 soldiers, sailors and airmen of the Japanese Expeditionary Force. The surrender was made to Admiral Lord Louis Mountbatten on September 12, 1945, first on the steps outside then officially signed inside what is now known as City Hall Chamber. The third-floor chamber is open to the public, though since this fact is rarely publicized it generally remains dark and vacant. With minor modifications (carpet, air-conditioning), the room remains in its 1945 state, complete with eight massive, marble columns. The chamber can be rented for private functions for $800 a night. The Singapore Academy of Law, which administers the chamber, can be reached at 332-4388.

20. St. Andrew's Cathedral ★★

11 St. Andrew's Rd.

The Anglican church was used as a secret communication center by volunteer defense forces. Plaques and insignias inside and out commemorate various units who fought the Japanese.

21. Ft. Siloso ★★★★

33 Allanbrooke Rd., Sentosa
275-0388
Daily, 9 a.m.-7 p.m.
(last admission, 6:30 p.m.)
$3 Adult, $2 Child

On the southern coast of Singapore, Sentosa Island (connected by bridge to the main island) was once the military post responsible for the seaward defense of the city. Today it's a gaudy theme and amusement park, but a piece of the original Ft. Siloso remains. At the entrance of the fort are four 120mm Japanese naval guns (Japan occupied the fort during the war). Fiberglass soldiers, smoke and recorded explosions simulate the fire of a British, six-inch breech-loading coastal defense gun. The often-repeated legend about Singapore's guns "facing the wrong way" references the batteries here. The guns were in fact rotated and fired at the Japanese, but their coastal position left them in the rear of the action and rendered them mostly ineffective. The tour includes the fort's tunnel complex, interesting re-creations of its 1880s state and a large collection of guns, cannons and artillery from different eras.

22. Images of Singapore ★★★★

33 Allanbrooke Rd., Sentosa
T: 275-0388
Daily, 9 a.m.-9 p.m.
$8 Adult, $5 Child

Also on Sentosa Island, this museum uses life-size figures and high-tech exhibits to tell the story of Singapore from the landing of Stamford Raffles to the present. The extensive section devoted to World War II probably does the best job in the country of presenting the Fall of Singapore in a complete and cohesive fashion. Film, pictures, relics and signage are all engrossing. Wax figures re-create Percival's humiliating 1942 surrender to Yamashita and the 1945 Japanese surrender to Mountbatten.

23. Labrador Battery ★★

Labrador Villa Road in Labrador Park

On the main island, just across from Sentosa Island, this is one of the few surviving gun emplacements from Singapore's defense. The fort's stone walls, pillboxes and plaques are interesting.

24. Changi Chapel and Museum ★★★

1000 Upper Changi Rd. North
T: 6214-2451
Daily, 9:30 a.m.-4:30 p.m.

Small but moving, the Changi Chapel is a replica of one of several prison-camp chapels allowed by the Japanese (the only original chapel now stands reassembled at Australia's Royal Military College in Duntroon, Canberra). The Singapore replica and adjacent museum were opened in 2001 and dedicated to the more than 50,000 civilians and soldiers imprisoned at infamous Changi for more than three years. James Clavell based his classic novel *King Rat* on his imprisonment here. Exhibits include photos, drawings and personal items belonging to prisoners. Replicas of the Biblical murals painted by British POW Stanley Warren—who used female POW's hair for brushes and insect blood, among other materials, for paint—are a highlight. Services are held at the chapel every Sunday. Changi itself still operates as a prison. The Changi Beach Massacre Site—where sixty-six Chinese men were executed—is nearby.

25. Johore Battery ★★★

Cosford Road, just north of Changi Chapel and Museum
T: 6736-6622 (Singapore Tourism Board)

The three, fifteen-inch breech-loading "monster guns" that comprised the Johore Battery were, at the start of World War II, the largest pieces of coastal artillery in the British Empire. The original guns were destroyed, but in 2001 this replica of an original gun and the tunnels and support structures around it were opened to the public.

RELATED SITES BEYOND SINGAPORE

HMS *Repulse* and *Prince of Wales* ★★★◣

The wrecks of the ill-fated battleships lie off Malaysia's Tioman Island at a depth of about 200 feet. Dives are possible for those qualified for extended-range dives.

Trips last several days. Operating out of Singapore, divemaster Michael Lim aboard the *Mata Ikan* (773-5791) leads scheduled excursions. On Tioman Island, B&J Diving Centre (60-8-8981-3049) also operates trips.

Kota Bharu World War II Museum (aka Bank Kerapu) ★★

Corner of Jalan Sultan and Jalan Pantai Cinta Berahi, Kota Bhrau, Kelantan, Malaysia
Saturday to Thursday, 10 a.m.-6 p.m., closed Friday
2 ringgits (about fifty cents)

On December 8, 1941, Japanese invaders landed at Singora, Patani (both in Thailand) and Kota Bharu on the Malay Peninsula. On Malaysia's north-eastern coast, Kota Bharu is the most interesting to visit. Its small museum includes photographs, Japanese swords and one of the rickety bicycles Japanese troops used to advance down the peninsula. About thirteen kilometers outside of town is quiet Pantai Dasar Sabak, the beach where World War II in the Pacific commenced with the landing of Japanese forces a full seventy minutes before the attack on Pearl Harbor.

GETTING TO/AROUND SINGAPORE

Singapore's major airport is serviced by many international airlines. Daily service on several carriers departs the United States from Los Angeles and San Francisco. Taxis in Singapore are plentiful and relatively inexpensive.

Singapore's MRT (Mass Rapid Transport) subway system is the easiest, cheapest and fastest way to get around. Yusoff Mahmood (6441-2294) is an excellent, accredited local guide.

ACCOMMODATIONS

Raffles Hotel

1 Beach Rd.
T: 6337-1886 F: 6339-7650
103 suites
From $650

Near War Memorial Park, the legendary Raffles remains the city's preeminent connection to the privileged end of its colonial past. Opened in 1887, this sprawling palace of design is worth a look even for those not staying.

Pan Pacific

7 Raffles Blvd.
T: 336-8111 F: 339-1861

800 rooms
From $200

Good for both central location and comfort. Discounted internet rates are sometimes available.

Hotel Grand Central

22 Cavenagh Rd./Orchard Road
T: 737-9944 F: 733-3175
390 rooms
From $120

Clean and centrally located with good in-house restaurants and a pool.

4

Saipan

MARIANA ISLANDS

THE WAR YEARS

Of all the fighting done on fanatically defended scraps of coral in the Central Pacific, the battle for Saipan was perhaps the most decisive American blow to Japanese land and air forces. Hard-fought campaigns in the Gilbert and Marshall Islands culminated in the even bloodier, all-important siege of three Japanese strongholds in the Mariana Islands during the summer of 1944— Saipan being the first and largest invasion, followed by Guam and Tinian.

Garrisoned with 30,000 Japanese troops and a large population of Japanese civilians, the fourteen-mile-long island had been a major base within the Empire's inner-defense ring since before the war. About 1,200 miles south of Tokyo, it was a linch-pin in the U.S. Fifth Fleet's 4,200-mile westward advance across Micronesia. Taking it would put U.S. bombers within range of Japan's home islands. Aslito airfield was the biggest prize, a badly needed base for America's new heavy bomber, the B-29 Superfortress, soon to become the Pacific War's deciding factor.

On June 15, two divisions of U.S. Marines scrambled up eleven separate beachheads along the exposed, reef-infested western coast of Saipan. Japan's main defense and counterattack forces had been established on the opposite coast at Magicienne Bay, an easier entrance that Saipan commander General Yoshitsugu Saito was certain the Americans would use. As U.S. amtracs buzzed ashore from the west, Saito held his ground, believing the maneuver to be a feint.

Saito's counterattack the following day came too late to be anything short of disas-trous for his forces. U.S. Sherman tanks and artillery decimated a Japanese regiment of 100 tanks in what would be the largest (and most one-sided) tank battle of the Pacific War outside China. Large battles were interspersed with a series of nightly banzai attacks that took a brutal toll on U.S. soldiers but wiped out thousands more Japanese. Within five days, American forces occupied Aslito airfield (renamed Asley Field) and secured most of southern Saipan.

The invasion instigated the even more lopsided offshore Battle of the Philippine Sea— aka "The Great Marianas Turkey Shoot"—between the massive U.S. Fifth Fleet cover-ing Saipan and Japan's already reeling Combined Fleet. On June 19, more than 400 Japanese fighters and bombers sped off to intercept the Fifth Fleet. Five hours later, 330 of them had been shot into the sea. Two Japanese carriers were also sunk before Japan's crippled armada retreated, leaving its Marianas compatriots hopelessly isolated.

While U.S. Marines swiftly worked their ways to both ends of Saipan, reserve regi-ments from the Army's 27th Division inched up the island's rugged center, meeting heavy Japanese resistance. The unsynchronized advance led to one of the most infa-mous inter-service feuds in the Pacific. Incensed with the Army's allegedly lackluster performance, Marine commander Major-General Holland "Howlin' Mad" Smith relieved Major-General Ralph Smith of his Army command. The orders were swiftly carried out and immortalized as the "Battle of the Smiths." Less publicized than Smith's bombastic published accounts of Army "ineptitude" in the Central Pacific were the results of an official investigation concluding that his actions were short-sighted and unjustified.

No matter. By early July, American troops had captured the town of Garapan and Saipan's highest point, 1,500-foot Mt. Tapotchau. With his forces reduced to less than 5,000 beleaguered men, some armed with sharpened sticks, General Saito ordered a final mass-suicide attack. On July 7 at 4 a.m., Japanese soldiers trampled two U.S. Army battalions, flattened a Marine artillery unit and left a horrifying wake of carnage along the beaches at Tanapag Harbor. Saito wearily retreated to a cave and plunged a samurai sword into his belly.

Two days later, on July 9, Saipan was declared secure. Devastating B-29 raids leaving from Saipan would raze Tokyo and other Japanese cities within months. Airfields on Guam and nearby Tinian would follow suit.

In Tokyo, the dreaded news of Saipan's fall led directly to General Hideki Tojo's resignation as prime minister (as well as an assassination plot) and an impending sense that the war could no longer be won. Nearly 30,000 Japanese soldiers, sailors and marines were killed on Saipan—4,300 of them in the final doomed suicide mission. The American victory came at a cost of 3,119 soldiers killed and 10,992 wounded or missing.

The battle's horrific epilogue involved mass suicides of local Japanese civilians—both voluntary and forced by the remaining Japanese military. Disregarding American pleas, thousands threw their children and then themselves over north Saipan's sheer bluffs (or were pushed off) near Marpi Point. Others waded into the sea to drown rather than surrender to forces they'd been led to believe would torture them and cannibalize their children.

The most devastating Pacific battles were still to come, intensifying with each step closer to Japan. Saipan proved to be a dire forecast of what lay ahead, but its three-week siege was also an indelible turning point.

SOURCES & OTHER READING

Saipan: The Beginning of the End, Hoffman, Carl, Presidio Press, 1987

Hold the Marianas: The Japanese Defense of the Mariana Islands, Denfeld, D. Colt, White Mane Publishing Co., 1997

Saipan in Flames: June, 1944 Invasion, Stewart, William H., Saipan Economic Service Council, 1993

Oba, the Last Samurai: Saipan 1944-45, Jones, Don, Presidio Press, 1986

Howlin' Mad vs. the Army: Conflict in Command: Saipan 1944, Gailey, Harry A., Dell Publishing Co., 1987

Saipan: Oral Histories of the Pacific War, Petty, Bruce M., McFarland & Company, 2001

The Marianas Turkey Shoot, Tillman, Barrett, Phalanx Publishing Company, 1994

World War II Remnants: Guam, Northern Mariana Islands, Lotz, Dave, Arizona Memorial Museum Association, 1998

1. Airport Road
2. Obyan Beach Bunker
3. Veterans Memorial/Landing Beaches/Tanks in Water
4. War Memorial
5. Japanese Tank
6. Museum of History and Culture
7. American Memorial Park
8. Marine Corps Memorial
9. Bomb Storage Shelters
10. Korean Peace Memorial
11. Last Command Post
12. Banzai Cliff
13. Suicide Cliff
14. Golf Course Tank
15. Lau Lau Beach

SAIPAN TODAY

Population: 70,000 • Country Code: 670 • Currency: U.S. dollar

One of the war's more curious vestiges, the island of Saipan is part of the fourteen-island, U.S.-affiliated Commonwealth of the Northern Mariana Islands (CNMI). English is widely spoken, the U.S. postal system is used and Americans can live and work here without restrictions (about 3,000 do). Otherwise, from the karaoke bars to the noodle shops, Saipan is pure Asia, with an economy based almost entirely on garment-manufacturing sweat shops and Japanese tourists.

It's also one of the best Micronesian islands to visit. At fourteen miles long by six miles wide, it's compact and manageable. Activity is centered around the main city of Garapan. Saipan's beaches aren't breathtaking, but the 2.7-mile paved Beach Pathway is great for walking, running or biking. The mood is laid back. World-class resorts overlook narrow belts of clean sand and clear, open water. Well-maintained roads are lined with the island's ubiquitous red flame trees.

Though tourism boomed in the 1980s and '90s, over-development has been kept in check, in part due to a history of neglect. "Saipan was the last major battlefield of World War Two to be reconstructed," wrote Saipan historian William H. Stewart. "It was largely surplus capital from the 'recovered' Japanese economy (in the late 1970s) that provided the impetus for Saipan's economic recovery." As a result, ties to Japan appear, on the surface at least, much stronger than ties to the United States.

With its many accessible sites, small Saipan is one of the Pacific's top sites. It can be covered in one to two days.

Excluding Beach Road (the main drag running up the western coast) and Middle Road (the inland road that parallels Beach Road) most Saipan roads are unmarked. Many are unnamed.

1. Airport Road ★★

Along the main road north (toward Garapan) from Saipan International Airport is a collection of war remnants including the American Red Cross Building (formerly a Japanese power plant), earthen bunkers, concrete, oval-roofed air-raid shelters and various structures. All of this was meant to help defend the airfield, the same one in use today.

2. Obyan Beach Bunker ★★

Exit the airport to the west, find the road sign for Obyan Beach, travel 2.2 miles of rough road along the fenced southern boundary of the airport, then turn right on an unmarked, rocky road to the beach.

On the beach is a large circular bunker subdivided by concrete baffles between firing ports. One of the Pacific's more interesting bunker types, it's a German design, similar to the one described on Wotje (page 95) in the Marshall Islands. The beach is rarely visited and good for walking or wading.

3. Veterans Memorial/Landing Beaches/Tanks in Water ★★★★

Beach Road at Oleai Beach

At the roadside beach park U.S. and CNMI flags fly at a hand-painted war memorial. Near the basketball court a marker for the Saipan World War II Landing Beaches designates the area as a U.S. National Historic Landmark. The highlights are two U.S. Sherman tanks left exactly where they were stranded in the shallow surf in 1944, front cannons and turrets sticking out of the water. It's an easy swim (the water never gets above five or six feet) to the closer of the two.

A couple hundred yards down the beach, in front of the Saipan Diamond Hotel, plastic kayaks rent for $10 an hour. With the Japanese resorts in the background, the tanks present one of the more unique photo ops in the Pacific.

4. War Memorial ★★

Intersection of Beach Road and Chalan Mnsgr. Guerrero (across from Toyota dealership)

Two white columns—one built by the people of Saipan, the other by the U.S. Navy—commemorate the soldiers and 419 Saipanese who died in the 1944 campaign. Two Japanese anti-tank guns are in front.

5. Japanese Tank ★★

Beach Road, San Jose

A damaged Model 89A tank sits atop an overgrown bunker on the roadside. The corroded engine block is visible. A comparison to the tanks at Point 3 gives a good idea of how much larger and more powerful American armaments were in the latter stages of the war.

6. Northern Marianas Museum of History and Culture ★★★

Middle Road, Garapan
T: 664-2160
$3
Monday-Friday, 9 a.m.-4:30 p.m.
Saturday, 9 a.m.-Noon
Closed Sundays, holidays

The surprisingly good museum has a small collection of artifacts, including the last two Japanese rifles surrendered on Saipan. Exhibits titled "Japan in the Marianas: The Prosperous Years" and "Japanese Education for All" cast a positive light on Japanese imperialism—depicted as a benign adventure in education and economic development—an obvious result of heavy Japanese investment here and comparative American neglect. There's an interesting review of the post-war U.S. military government, but the highlight is a framed and rare Japanese children's board game from 1942 called Around the South Seas. Played with dice, the game board features children starting in Yokohama and moving through Imperial possessions in Micronesia, Indonesia and other lands collecting rubber, fish, bananas and other commodities. The museum is housed in the wartime Japanese hospital.

7. American Memorial Park ★★★★

Intersection of Beach Road and Micro Beach Road
T: 234-7207

Operated by the U.S. National Park Service, the large, beachside park's focal point is the Flag Circle and Court of Honor where the names of the 5,050 U.S. soldiers who died in battles for Saipan, Tinian and the Philippine Sea are inscribed in marble. Toward the beach are the rusting hulks of two Japanese tanks, anti-aircraft guns, assorted hardware, a pillbox and an American Battle Monuments Commission twelve-foot, rose-granite obelisk. Plans are reportedly in the works for a (much needed) major upgrade of this facility.

8. Marine Corps Memorial ★

Intersection of Beach and Capital Hill Roads

It's easy to drive past this orb on a seven-foot-tall, timeworn stone pedestal. Even the plaque commemorating the U.S.M.C. has been taken away by weather or looters.

9. Bomb Storage Shelters ★★

Along the Coast Highway (also called Marpi Road)

About two miles south of Point 10, a series of oval shelters used for bomb and equipment storage sit along the roadside.

10. Korean Peace Memorial ★★

Coast Highway, northern end of island
Often overlooked victims of the war are

Koreans who, in vast numbers, were used by the Japanese as forced "comfort women," laborers and frontline soldiers across the Pacific. Flanked by a pair of stone lions, this memorial honors Koreans who died in Saipan. Part of one translated poem reads: "Here, from Korea, the torch of Asia, the land of Morning Calm, how many people, once deprived of their fatherland, were drawn never to return!" From this moving spot it's hard to imagine that the Korean Memorial on nearby Tinian expresses even more intense emotion.

11. Last Command Post/Peace Memorials ★★★★

Coast Highway, adjacent to Point 10

At the base of Suicide Cliff (not to be confused with Banzai Cliff) sits one of the largest collections of Japanese military hardware in the Central Pacific. Most of the rusting material was relocated from points around Saipan and nearby Rota Island. A destroyed light tank, torpedo shell, seven large guns (including anti-aircraft and long-range naval cannons) and various debris are gathered beneath the cliff-side command center where General Yoshitsugo Saito made his final stand then committed hara-kiri. No flashlights are needed in the large room carved out of the rock—bomb holes opened holes big enough to let the light shine in. Original gun mounts are still embedded in the stone at the command post entrance. Painted maps show battle plans and strategies for each side. Adjacent are large Okinawan and Japanese Peace memorials.

12. Banzai Cliff ★★★

Coast Highway (follow signs from Point 10)

Dozens of stone and marble monuments stand in memory of one of the most tragic and still shocking events of the war (and one that played out less famously on Tinian and Okinawa). Here, on a bluff above jagged rocks and pounding surf, entire families lined up to leap to their deaths—parents often throwing infants and pushing children, soldiers pushing the reluctant—rather than be captured by the barbarous Americans whom they believed would torture and possibly eat them. The peaceful, windy bluff is, incongruously, one of the island's more scenic spots.

13. Suicide Cliff ★★★

Off of Coast Highway (follow signs around northern end of island 3.3 miles beyond Last Command Post)

At the top of the cliff directly above the Last Command Post is a small Peace Memorial Park for the hundreds of Japanese soldiers who, in the final days of the battle, threw themselves to their deaths down this 820-foot drop.

14. Golf Course Tank ★★
(★★★★★ for golfers)

Lau Lau Bay Golf Resort
T: 236-8888
About $100 a round

Near the fifth hole of this spectacular ocean-side course sits a badly rusted American tank, stopped just where it did in 1944, making this one of the most historic golf holes in the world. At the base of the overhanging rock behind the fifth tee is a small Japanese war graveyard. Several caves are in the area, though most of the entrances are overgrown. Greg Norman designed the thirty-six-hole course—it's one of the best in the Pacific. Nongolfers can arrange visits to the tank.

15. Lau Lau Beach ★★

Lau Lau Bay, southwest of Point 14

To access the beach, turn right on the dirt road seventy-five yards before Happy Market as you drive toward Point 14. After a little less than a mile of rough road is a beach parking area.

In the trees at the western end of the beach is a Japanese stone and concrete coastal-defense bunker. This site is recommended more for the small, quiet beach than the bunker.

OTHER AREA ATTRACTIONS

Managaha Island ◣

A short boat ride out of Tanapag Harbor, Managaha Island has Saipan's best white, sandy beach, great snorkeling and most photogenic scenes. War relics in the shallow water (twenty to forty feet) include a Zero fighter, landing craft, guns and various debris. But the island is more about the classic tropical beach setting. Strong swimmers have made the swim from Saipan, but a number local operators run day tours to the island (there are no overnight facilities). Managaha Tours (322-7734) operates four boats daily. The fares are $35 for adults, $25 for children, $70 and $65 respectively for the snorkel tour. Definitely worth an afternoon.

RELATED SITES BEYOND SAIPAN

Dive sites ★★★ ◣

Stingray Divers
T: 233-6100
rick.northern@saipan.com

For its abundance of reefs, marine life and a few war wrecks, the waters around Saipan are a popular dive destination. In Tanapag Harbor at about thirty feet is a debris field of what's likely a Japanese seaplane converted into a bomber, colloquially known as a "Bouncing Betty." Identifiable parts include a turret gun. Beneath Banzai Cliff, at depths ranging from forty to seventy feet, U.S. forces dumped mechanical refuse of war. Tank and aircraft parts can be seen here along with vehicles and heavy ordnance. More wrecks can be found around Managaha Island (see Other Area Attractions). Most dive shops on Saipan cater to the Japanese market, meaning they don't speak much English. Stingray Divers is a reliable exception.

GETTING TO/AROUND SAIPAN

Saipan is serviced daily with direct flights from Guam by Continental Airlines (800-523-3273; 671-647-6453 in Guam) and Northwest Airlines-partner, Saipan-based Pacific Island Aviation (647-3603). There are also direct flights from Tokyo/Narita and Osaka on Japan Airlines (800-525-3663).

Taxis and buses are available, but driving is easy (roads follow American rules), and a car is essential on Saipan. Rental car companies include Budget Rent A Car (234-8232; 800-527-7000 in U.S.), Hertz (234-8336; 800-654-3131 in U.S.) and Dollar Rent A Car (288-5151; 800-800-4000 in U.S.). Marianas Trekking (322-0770 ext. 7) rents bicycles by the day ($25) and half-day ($19) and leads tours that include Suicide Cliff and Last Command Post.

ACCOMMODATIONS

Aquarius Beach Tower

Beach Road, Chalan Kanda
T: 235-6025 (800-367-5004 in U.S.)
F: 235-8098
55 units
$95-$300

All rooms are suites with full kitchens (some with in-room laundry) in this converted apartment building. On the beach, but off the tourist strip, the unit feels more like a quiet home than a hotel. Price depends on ocean view.

Hyatt Regency Saipan

Beach Road, Garapan
T: 234-1234 (800-233-1234 in U.S.)
F: 234-7745
325 rooms
$158-$278

Next to American Memorial Park, this is one of the top resorts on the island. Very good restaurants (Italian, Chinese, Japanese) and bars. All rooms have gorgeous views of the ocean.

Aqua Resort Club

Beach Road, Achugao
T: 322-1234 F: 322-1220
91 rooms
$153-$220

With low-rise buildings set in an airy, tropical garden, low-key Aqua is often recognized as the classiest resort on the island. Extremely popular with Japanese tourists.

Hiroshima

JAPAN

THE WAR YEARS

L ike many Pacific War battlefields, much of the world had never heard of Hiroshima before it became associated with one of the most fateful events in human history. But prior to August 6, 1945—the day the United States dropped the world's first atomic bomb on the city—Hiroshima was well known to strategists on both sides of the war. With a population of about 250,000 civilians and 150,000 soldiers, the city was the linchpin in the defense of Western Japan, which was by then bracing for certain Allied invasion scheduled to begin in November 1945.

Ascending as an important military center during the 1904-05 Russo-Japanese War, Hiroshima by 1945 had become the Second General Army Headquarters, with the bulk of its command and troop facilities centered in or around Hiroshima Castle. Less than a mile south was Japan's naval academy on the island of Etajima. Early in the war, tens of thousands of troops had embarked through Hiroshima's *Gaisenkan* ("Hall of Triumphant Return") for stations in the Pacific.

Even with resources in short supply, many of the city's large factories—Mitsubishi, Toyo Industries, Japan Steel—maintained twenty-four-hour shifts producing weapons and vital materials late into the war. Due to regular air raids, most children had been evacuated to the countryside by spring 1945 and entire sections of the city demolished to create firebreaks. With food in desperate supply, reeds, grubs, beetles and worms were being consumed by Hiroshima's starving population.

Even with all this, no one could have anticipated the horror that swept the city at 8:16 a.m. on August 6, when the American bomber *Enola Gay* flew overhead and dropped its solitary payload. An unearthly whitish-pinkish glow engulfed the city, followed by a blast compared to a hundred simultaneous thunderclaps. "A horrible howling wind arose, succeeded by a wave of suffocating heat," wrote historian Robert Leckie. "Within a few seconds the center of the city vanished." Most of Hiroshima's buildings were made of wood and clustered together within a natural bowl of green hills—qualities that made the city a prime target for the new weapon. Of its estimated 90,000 buildings, about 62,000 were destroyed in the blast and subsequent firestorm.

Temperature at ground zero reached several thousand degrees centigrade. Those closest to the blast were incinerated beyond recognition. Unable to bear the heat, others rushed into rivers only to be boiled alive. Of the city's 200 doctors, 180 were killed or injured. Just three of its fifty-five hospitals and medical facilities remained usable. Fatality estimates range from 71,000 to 140,000. Injuries, radiation sickness and other conditions caused by the blast, likewise uncountable, continued to surface decades later.

Hiroshima's casualty figures are often used to illustrate that more destructive and deadlier bombing raids were carried out at places such as Tokyo and Dresden. While it's probably true that more people were killed in those Allied attacks, it's the ominous and revolutionary manner by which those in Hiroshima died that continues to make the event so controversial. In the words of the Hindu poem "Bhagavad Gita," recalled by Manhattan Project director Robert Oppenheimer after the first successful atomic explosion in Alamagordo, New Mexico: "I am become death, the destroyer of worlds."

"The historiography of the Pacific War has been largely undisturbed by serious controversy, except in relation to two events: the attack on Pearl Harbor and the use of the atomic bomb against Japan," wrote British historian David Smurthwaite. Historical perspective on the bombing continues to proliferate in literature as widely opposed as Paul Fussell's *Thank God for the Atom Bomb* and the growing body of work contending that the bombing was unnecessary (and/or racially motivated), based on the belief that Japan was ready to capitulate or at least thoroughly defeated long before the bomb was dropped.

From the view of the ground soldier preparing to invade Japan (as Fussell was), one can appreciate the enormous support for the decision to drop the bomb, thereby hastening the end of the war and perhaps averting the one million American deaths often predicted for the invasion. As for Japan's putative surrender, it's true that many in the Imperial government had long recognized the futility of their war. But Emperor Hirohito refused to impose his will on the country's military leaders—Hirohito was "a figurehead, but not quite a stooge," said Douglas MacArthur after the war—until after the second atomic bomb was dropped on Nagasaki on August 9. Until then, the Army remained in firm control of the government and deeply committed to continuing the war with an elaborate plan for the defense of Japan. Some Japanese officers were on the record as ready to sacrifice the lives of ten million of their own civilians in order to repel the Allied invasion. Even at this point, the popular phrase *ichioku gyokusai* ("one hundred million souls dying for honor") was on the lips of Japanese across the country.

In the end it's almost certain that many times more Japanese, American, Asian and Allied lives would have been lost had the atomic bombs not been dropped. Still, it's the appalling method and efficiency by which those in Hiroshima and Nagasaki were killed, the message of greater doom the bombs presented, that continues to mark the event for debate and grief.

SOURCES & OTHER READING

Prompt and Utter Destruction: Truman and the Use of Atomic Bombs Against Japan, Walker, J. Samuel, University of North Carolina Press, 1997

The Making of the Atomic Bomb, Rhodes, Richard, Simon and Schuster, 1986

The Decision to Use the Atomic Bomb, Alperovitz, Gar, Vintage Books, 1995

Enola Gay, Thomas and Witts, Pocket Books, 1977

Codename Downfall: The Secret Plan to Invade Japan, Allen and Polmar, Headline Book Publishing, 1995

Thank God for the Atom Bomb and Other Essays, Fussell, Paul, Summit Books, 1988

Brotherhood of the Bomb: The Tangled Lives and Loyalties of Robert Oppenheimer, Ernest Lawrence and Edward Teller, Herken, Gregg, Holt/John Macrae, 2002

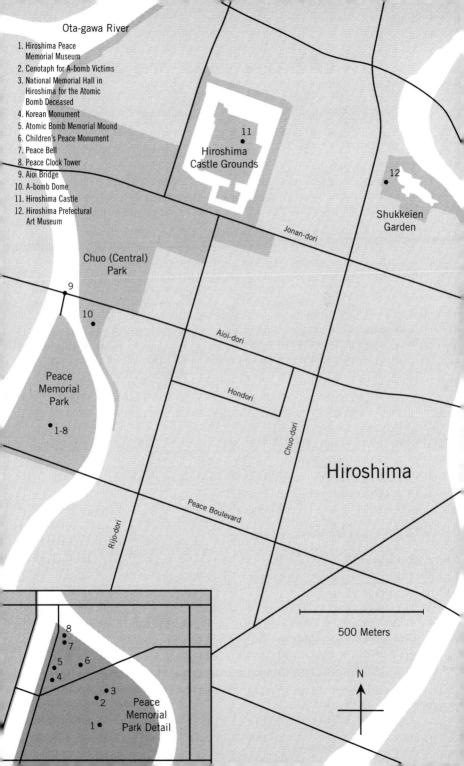

Ota-gawa River

1. Hiroshima Peace Memorial Museum
2. Cenotaph for A-bomb Victims
3. National Memorial Hall in Hiroshima for the Atomic Bomb Deceased
4. Korean Monument
5. Atomic Bomb Memorial Mound
6. Children's Peace Monument
7. Peace Bell
8. Peace Clock Tower
9. Aioi Bridge
10. A-bomb Dome
11. Hiroshima Castle
12. Hiroshima Prefectural Art Museum

Hiroshima Castle Grounds

11

12

Shukkeien Garden

Jonan-dori

Chuo (Central) Park

9

10

Aioi-dori

Peace Memorial Park

1-8

Hondori

Chuo-dori

Hiroshima

Peace Boulevard

Rijo-dori

500 Meters

N

Peace Memorial Park Detail

8
7
5
6
4
3
2
1

HIROSHIMA TODAY

Population: 1.1 million • Country code: 81 • City code: 082 • Currency: $1 = 118 yen

All but removed from the map in 1945, Hiroshima today is a thriving port city with a young (for Japan) population and what's called here an "international outlook." Like most Japanese cities quickly rebuilt after the war, it's not necessarily attractive—square concrete buildings, neon advertisements and lots of traffic are the immediate visual elements. Still, it's impossible to look around and not be impressed by the fact that virtually the entire city was built in a matter of decades and quite literally from the ashes of defeat. No place on earth offers such a striking illustration of the human facility to adapt, regenerate and prosper.

On a series of low-lying islands on the delta of the Ota River, Hiroshima fans out around three parallel east-west streets. Heiwa-O-dori (Peace Boulevard) fronts Peace Memorial Park, which contains most of the city's war-related points of interest. Several hundred yards north, Hon-dori includes a busy shopping arcade as well as restaurants and nightclubs—there are an estimated 4,000 bars in the city. North again a few blocks, Aioi-dori is Hiroshima's primary traffic artery, with the main streetcar line running through town from Hiroshima Station (located on the eastern edge of the city). This is also the area of Hiroshima Municipal Stadium, home of the beloved Hiroshima Carp professional baseball team.

With the aid of a quick taxi or streetcar ride between major points, Hiroshima is an easy and pleasant walking city. War-related attractions can be toured in a single, short day. An additional afternoon is recommended for nearby Miyajima (see Other Area Attractions).

POINTS OF INTEREST

With the exception of Hiroshima Castle and Hiroshima Prefectural Art Museum, all sites below are concentrated in or adjacent to Peace Memorial Park and easily visited on foot. In addition to highlights described here, the park is filled with many small monuments and memorials.

1. Hiroshima Peace Memorial Museum
★★★★★

1-2 Nakajima-cho, Naka-ku
T: 082-241-4004
Daily, 9 a.m.-6 p.m. (last entry 5:30 p.m.), April 1-July 31
Daily, 8:30 a.m.-7 p.m., August 1-15
Daily, 8:30 a.m.-6 p.m.,
August 16-November 30
Daily, 9 a.m.-5 p.m.,
December 1-March 31

Closed December 29-January 2
No entry from thirty minutes before closing
Adult: 50 yen
Student: 30 yen

From Hiroshima Station, take streetcars bound for Hiroshima Port (aka Ujina) via Kamiyacho. Get off at Chuden-mae. Or take streetcars bound for Eba or Miyajima-guchi and get off at Genbaku Domu-mae (A-Bomb Dome).

A three-minute film introduces visitors to this most sobering of all Pacific War sites. With English and Japanese signage, displays at the three-story, two-wing museum chronicle Hiroshima's rise as a military center, the American decision to make it a primary target for the atomic bomb, the science behind the bomb, its use, devastating effects, recovery efforts and subsequent atomic race, Cold War and global anti-nuclear movements. Relics include rocks and other heavy items distorted by the intense heat of the blast and personal items from pre-war Hiroshima. The unforgettable images, however, are provided by large before-and-after scale models of the scenic-then-obliterated city and an exceedingly graphic display titled "A-bomb Damage to Human Bodies." Grotesque photos of charred victims with faces literally melted away are juxtaposed with more poignant articles, such as a scorched tricycle along with the tragic story of the boy to whom it belonged. Films and videotaped testimonies from survivors (with English subtitles) are included, with heart-wrenching accounts of children searching for parents amid the turmoil unleashed in the city. This comprehensive treatment of history's first atomic attack leaves most visitors in a somber reflective mood.

Though politics inevitably colors every war museum, this one strives to be evenhanded. The Japanese Army's 1937 Rape of Nanjing is acknowledged to some degree (a rarity in Japan) as is the United States' calculated use of the bomb on Japanese civilians by way of blunting Soviet ambitions in Europe and the Far East. Difficult as it may be to take in, this is without question the most absorbing museum anywhere dedicated to the Pacific War.

2. Cenotaph for A-bomb Victims ★★

About 100 yards north of Point 1

In the center of the Peace Memorial Park is this large, concrete cenotaph (a memorial for the dead whose remains lie elsewhere). Through its odd, covered-wagon shape one can see the park's Eternal Flame and A-bomb Dome.

3. National Memorial Hall in Hiroshima for the Atomic Bomb Deceased ★★

About 40 yards northeast of Point 2
A large fountain is outside this modern,

gray structure, most of which is underground. It houses the Hall of Remembrance, library, seminar rooms and exhibition areas.

4. Korean Monument ★★

About 60 yards northwest of Point 2

A twelve-foot-tall stone pillar rests on the back of a large turtle, a tribute to the estimated 100,000 Korean soldiers, laborers and ordinary citizens in Hiroshima in 1945, more than 20,000 of whom, according to the memorial, died in the blast.

5. Atomic Bomb Memorial Mound ★★

Just north of Point 4

Near the bomb's hypocenter, this mound houses an underground cinerarium with the remains of tens of thousands of victims. Memorial services are held here each August 6.

6. Children's Peace Monument ★★★

About 75 yards north of Point 2

Atop a cement tower is the figure of a girl holding an origami crane, Hiroshima's ubiquitous symbol of peace. Thousands of paper cranes surround the monument.

7. Peace Bell ★★

About 100 yards northwest of Point 2

As a symbol of noble aspirations, visitors are encouraged to step forward and "toll this bell for peace."

8. Peace Clock Tower ★★

North end of Park, 120 yards north of Point 2

At 8:15 each morning, "the mortal moment of the blasting back in 1945," the clock chimes with its prayer for perpetual peace.

9. Aioi Bridge ★★

Crosses Motoyasu River at north boundary of Park

With its distinctive "T" shape, this bridge was the aiming point for the bombardier aboard the *Enola Gay*. Miraculously, the bridge survived the blast and remained in use until being replaced with this new construction at the same location in 1983.

10. A-bomb Dome ★★★

Just across north boundary of Park, next to Point 9

Gated off and surrounded by stone monuments, the former Hiroshima Prefecture Industrial Promotion Hall was the largest building near the bomb's hypocenter. The crumbling brick walls and skeletal framework of its domed roof now stand as the defining symbol of atomic devastation. The bomb exploded about 2,000 feet directly overhead.

11. Hiroshima Castle ★★★

21-1 Motoi, Naka-ku
T: 082-221-7512
Daily, 9 a.m.-5:30 p.m.,
April 1-September 30
Daily, 9 a.m.-4:30 p.m.,
October 1-March 31
Closed December 29-January 2
Adult: 320 yen
Child: 160 yen

Completely destroyed by the atomic blast, the ancient castle has been rebuilt to its former glory. Exhibitions of samurai-era Japan are displayed throughout the castle and grounds, which were used to house the Second General Army Headquarters and Fifth Army Division during the war. A plaque and foundation ruins at the entrance of the grounds note the site of the wartime headquarters building.

12. Hiroshima Prefectural Art Museum ★

2-22 Kaminobori-cho, Naka-ku
T: 082-221-6246
Daily, 9 a.m.-5 p.m. (until 7 p.m. Saturdays)
Closed Monday (except national holidays) and December 28-January 4
Adult: 500 yen
College student: 300 yen
High school and under: Free

On permanent display is Ikuo Hiriyama's well-known "The Holocaust at Hiroshima." The large, six-panel painting depicts A-bomb Dome and Hiroshima's skyline burning beneath a fiery red and black sky while a mournful deity looks down upon the destruction. Hiriyama was a teenager in Hiroshima at the time of the blast. The rest of the collection is interesting—the warped clocks of Salvador Dali's "Dream of Venus" are here along with interesting works mostly from Japanese artists.

OTHER AREA ATTRACTIONS

Miyajima

Itsukushima Shrine
T: 0829-44-2020
6:30 a.m. to sunset
May be closed January 1-5
300 yen

About fifteen kilometers southwest of downtown Hiroshima. Accessed by ten-minute ferry (many departures throughout day) from in front of Miyajima-guchi Station on the JR (Japan Railways) San-yo line. Trains from Hiroshima Station take twenty-six minutes to reach Miyajima-guchi Station. Hydrofoil ferries (Adult: 1,460 yen; Child: 730 yen) take about twenty minutes from Hiroshima's Ujina Port (Seto Inland Sea Steamer; 082-251-5191 in Hiroshima; 0829-44-0086 in Miyajima).

Miyajima Island's famed "floating *torii*" at Itsukushima Shrine—the enormous red gate made of camphor wood and surrounded by water appears in seemingly every Japan travel brochure—is one of the most photographed attractions in the country. The bright orange and white

Itsukushima Shrine, built like a series of piers, is also spectacular. There are many temples, shrines, shops and walks on the popular island of Miyajima (aka Itsukushima). Another impressive site is Senjokaku, an enormous hall built of massive timber pillars and beams in 1587. Going to Hiroshima and skipping Miyajima is like going to the beach and skipping the sand. A full morning or afternoon is recommended.

GETTING TO/AROUND HIROSHIMA

Hiroshima is served daily by domestic airlines including Japan Airlines (800-525-3663) and All Nippon Airways (800-235-9262). Flights depart from Tokyo's Haneda Airport and Okinawa, among other cities.

Hiroshima Station is a major rail junction for trains across Japan. It's best reached from Tokyo by *shinkansen* (bullet train). The express trip takes about four-and-a-half hours and travels past Mt. Fuji.

In place of a subway and local trains, Hiroshima has easy-to-use, cheap (about $1 to anywhere) streetcars, with English signage. Many streetcars stop just in front of Hiroshima Station—the ride into the city takes fifteen minutes or less. Buses and taxis are also available. Because sites are closer together than in other Japanese cities, taxis are generally affordable.

ACCOMMODATIONS

Rhiga Royal Hotel Hiroshima

6-78 Motomachi, Naka-ku
T: 082-502-1121 F: 082-228-5415
12,000-55,000 yen
491 rooms

The largest and most luxurious hotel in town, the Rhiga is located next to Hiroshima Castle, within walking distance of the Peace Park. Large rooms and stylish furniture put it a cut above most Hiroshima hotels. Executive rooms offer a high level of service and amenities.

Park Side Hotel

2-6-24 Otemachi, Naka-ku
T: 082-244-7131 F: 082-242-6071
Rooms: 92
6,400-11,000 yen

This reliable, basic business hotel on the edge of the Peace Park has typically small but comfortable rooms. Most rooms have an extra phone jack for internet access.

Hiroshima Central Hotel

1-8 Kanayama-cho, Naka-Ku
T: 082-243-2222 F: 082-243-9001
136 rooms
6,500-11,500 yen

In the center of Hiroshima on the Kyobashi River, this business hotel is minutes away from the Peace Park and downtown area. Most rooms have an extra phone jack for internet access. Japanese-style rooms available.

Peleliu/Palau

THE WAR YEARS

By historians and troops who fought there—including some who saw action on the European battlefields of World War I—the Battle of Peleliu has been characterized as the most brutal and, if such a thing can be quantified, most terrifying battle of the Pacific War. Against this claim perhaps only the veterans of Tarawa can mount an argument. As with that battle, Peleliu has been characterized as both extraordinarily violent and strategically needless, "one of the bloodiest debacles of the entire war," according to Pacific War historian Harry Gailey. Expected to last three to four days—that injudicious promise being delivered to assault troops and the media by Marine commander Major-General William Rupertus—the struggle for Peleliu would drag on for two-and-a-half shocking months.

Operation Stalemate II's objective was the neutralization of the Palau Islands in order to secure the rear flank of the October 1944 Douglas MacArthur-led invasion of the Philippines. On Peleliu's southern tail the Japanese had constructed an airbase that put its pilots within just 600 miles of the southern Philippine island of Mindanao. Despite the fact that even according to an official Marine history, "Japanese air power had been very thoroughly knocked out long before the (Peleliu) assault took place," the airfield was classified as a potential threat. The controversial operation—Admiral William "Bull" Halsey was among those who bluntly opposed it—was ultimately approved by Pacific Theater naval commander Admiral Chester Nimitz.

After five days of naval and air bombardment—the assault denuded the island of virtually all vegetation, turning it into a featureless coral moonscape—the veteran First Marine Division hit Peleliu's southern beaches on September 15, 1944. Though many units were pinned down on the jagged coral shore, advancing groups captured the southern sector of the airfield by mid-afternoon. The quick success proved illusory. Under the indomitable command of Colonel Kunio Nakagawa, Japanese forces soon began contesting ground with even more tenacity than American assault troops had seen in the past.

Temperatures rose as high as 115 degrees. For soldiers laden with heavy packs and supplies strapped across their bodies, the humidity was intolerable. Many on both sides succumbed to heat prostration, too weak even to stand.

Like the Americans, the Japanese had absorbed the lessons of vicious battles at Tarawa and Saipan. "The Japanese examined earlier American island assaults and decided that it was a wasteful proposition to resist on the beach," wrote historians James Dunnigan and Albert Nofi. Defenses were set up in the island's infinitely more defendable interior. With more than 500 caves and extensive interlocking strong points built into Peleliu's virtually indestructible rock, the Japanese were well dug in and amply fortified. Nakagawa would order no futile banzai charges that terrified the enemy, but ultimately spent valuable resources for little gain. In this way, Peleliu signaled a fundamental change in Japanese operational tactics, presaging the gruesome island-interior struggles to come on Iwo Jima and Okinawa.

"The Japanese were as dedicated to military excellence as the U.S. Marines," wrote Peleliu veteran E.B. Sledge. "The opposing forces were like two scorpions in a bottle. One was annihilated, the other nearly so."

With Japanese units infiltrating American positions at every opportunity, the entire island became a front line. Hand-to-hand fighting was occasionally so close that even bayonets couldn't be used. One Marine killed an enemy in his foxhole by gouging out his eyes with his fingers. Like most men in the battle, Sledge was exposed to atrocities such that "something in me died at Peleliu." In the words of historian Paul Fussell, "Both sides declined to take prisoners and both sides defiled enemy corpses." Malice was as much a part of Peleliu as terrifying nonstop mortar fire, insufferable heat and the inescapable stench of decomposing bodies.

With casualty rates at about fifty percent per regiment, U.S. forces slowly extended their perimeter. Aided by the introduction of a new weapon—the Navy Mark I long-range flamethrower could shoot a stream of blazing napalm up to 150 yards—the Marines and Army 81st Infantry eventually drove the last Japanese forces into a 900- by 400-yard pocket on Bloody Nose Ridge (correctly called Umurbrogol Mountain). The craggy cave-pitted rise that overlooked the airfield was the focal point of Peleliu's most terrible struggles.

Though groups of stragglers would hold out in caves until April 1947, U.S. troops finally secured the island on November 27, taking the last organized Japanese position on a height called China Wall. Of Peleliu's 10,900 Japanese military defenders, only nineteen were taken prisoner. The rest were killed or committed suicide. American casualties numbered about 1,800 killed and 8,000 wounded.

"In proportion to the number of men engaged, Peleliu was the fiercest, bloodiest battle in the Japanese war," wrote historian Robert Leckie.

The battle's cost was undeniable. Its rewards remain debatable. MacArthur's Philippine campaign began in October long before the fighting was over and succeeded with little tactical support from Peleliu. Most of Palau's other islands were bypassed, remaining in Japanese control until the end of the war.

SOURCES & OTHER READING

The Devil's Anvil: The Assault on Peleliu, Hallas, James H., Praeger, 1994
With the Old Breed: At Peleliu and Okinawa, Sledge, E.B., Presidio Press, 1981
The Assault on Peleliu, Hough, Major Frank O., Historical Division Headquarters U.S. Marine Corps, 1950
Bloodiest Victory: Palau, Falk, Stanley, Ballantine Books, 1974
Coral Comes High, Hunt, George P., Harper Brothers, 1946

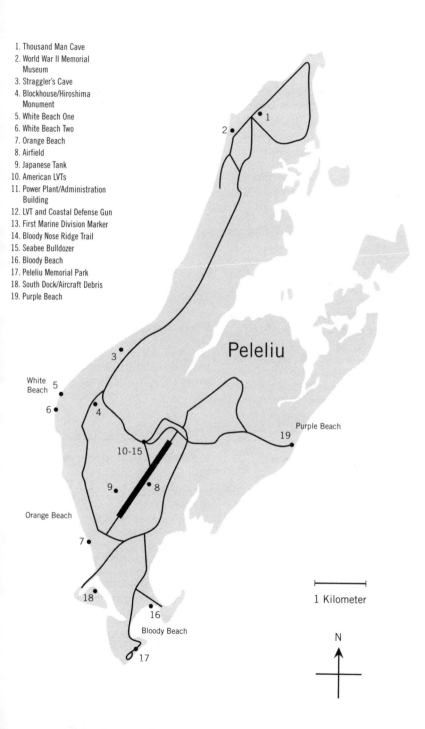

1. Thousand Man Cave
2. World War II Memorial Museum
3. Straggler's Cave
4. Blockhouse/Hiroshima Monument
5. White Beach One
6. White Beach Two
7. Orange Beach
8. Airfield
9. Japanese Tank
10. American LVTs
11. Power Plant/Administration Building
12. LVT and Coastal Defense Gun
13. First Marine Division Marker
14. Bloody Nose Ridge Trail
15. Seabee Bulldozer
16. Bloody Beach
17. Peleliu Memorial Park
18. South Dock/Aircraft Debris
19. Purple Beach

Peleliu

White Beach

Purple Beach

Orange Beach

Bloody Beach

1 Kilometer

N

PELELIU TODAY

Population: 600 • Country code: 680 • Currency: U.S. dollar

At six miles long by two miles wide, tiny Peleliu could hardly less resemble the scene of "overwhelming grayness of everything in sight," that veteran E.B. Sledge described in 1944. Reclaimed by the jungle, thick vegetation and Palau's famously clear water now greet visitors with powerful shades of green and blue.

Calling life slow paced in the main village of Klouklubed inaccurately suggests the existence of a measurable pace of any kind. Locals subsist on fishing, farming and, notoriously, marijuana cultivation. Beyond this there are a couple of nice beaches and good scuba sites nearby, but no restaurants and few services.

Rich with Pacific War sites, Peleliu's high ranking nevertheless owes largely to the breathtaking natural attractions of the 343-island Republic of Palau (population 20,000), an independent nation since 1994 in Compact of Free Association with the United States. Above and below the water, few places match the central Rock Islands—limestone, basalt and coral islets that explode with color and rise from the pristine waters of the Pacific Ocean and Philippine Sea like enormous toadstools in a tropical fairy tale. The provisional capital of Koror is the main population center and gateway to the country.

Peleliu can be toured in one or two days (depending on time spent hiking through overgrown Bloody Nose Ridge), but a week at minimum is recommended for Palau's other attractions. With numerous Japanese leftovers, touring war-related and other sites in Nikko Bay (see Related Sites Beyond Peleliu) is generally more pleasant than touring Peleliu.

POINTS OF INTEREST

1. Thousand Man Cave ★★★★

Main road, 1.3 kilometers north of Klouklubed village, directly across from North Dock ruins

Running at least seventy-five yards into the mountainside, with a series of deep laterals, this roadside cave is one of the best and most accessible Japanese caves in the Pacific. It housed about 1,400 men and is littered with hundreds of wartime beer bottles—stored for Molotov cocktails—and small relics. Most of Peleliu's 500 caves were bulldozed into oblivion, making this cave an excellent example of the complex Japanese defense system, a spot that illustrates the difficulties faced by defenders and invaders. Flashlight necessary.

2. World War II Memorial Museum ★★

North end of Klouklubed
T: 345-1036
By appointment only

This dusty one-room museum houses an interesting collection of artifacts from the Peleliu jungle—guns, shells, helmets, bottles—and post-war memorabilia donated by American veterans. Most items are badly deteriorated. Little effort is being made to preserve them.

3. Straggler's Cave ★★

Main road, 3.9 kilometers south of Klouklubed

A roadside marker tells the story of thirty-four Japanese soldiers who held out in caves about fifty yards into the marsh off the road. The stragglers surrendered to the U.S. Army on April 21, 1947.

4. Blockhouse/Hiroshima Monument ★★

Main road, 1.3 kilometers south of Point 3

On the roadside is a bomb-damaged Japanese blockhouse. Next to it, beneath a small, Roman-style pavilion, a Japanese-built memorial includes a paving stone from Hiroshima exposed to the 1945 atomic blast.

5. White Beach One ★★

At dead end, a few hundred yards toward the beach down dirt road directly across from Point 4

Japanese pillboxes and other fortifications can be seen on the dirt road leading to White Beach One, where American forces led by Marine legend Lewis "Chesty" Puller landed on September 15, 1944. Now overgrown with jungle, there's little to see. Large concrete pads in the jungle are foundations of post-war U.S. Quonset huts. About 150 yards north along a rough trail that parallels the beach is a plaque attached to a rock commemorating the heroic leadership of Marine Captain George P. Hunt, who served as managing editor of *Life* magazine in the 1960s.

6. White Beach Two ★★

Continuing on dirt road about 0.5 kilometers from Point 5

Along with shell casings still occasionally found here, a bunker and large earthen defense structure are all that remain.

7. Orange Beach ★★

Off main road (about 1 kilometer south of the point where the dirt road from Points 5 and 6 rejoins main road), follow another dirt road about 100 yards to the beach.

About 1,000 yards long and divided into three sectors (the directions above lead to the center of the beach), this landing beach across from the airfield is marked by the remains of a chapel and two stone memorials honoring the U.S. Army 81st Infantry. The site was originally an American cemetery.

8. Airfield ★★

Down dirt road heading east off main road, 0.2 kilometers beyond turnoff to Point 7

The strategic objective of the Peleliu campaign was the Japanese airstrip. It now serves as the island's airport. Visitors can drive or walk the length of the open runway.

Bloody Nose Ridge Area

With the exception of Point 9, the following sites are concentrated on the north-western side of the airfield. Jungle growth and a maze of unmarked dirt paths can make them difficult to find—locating them without a local guide generally requires a trial-and-error effort.

9. Japanese Tank ★★

Off southern end of runway—south of the small airport terminal/shelter—a dirt road veers left (northwest). Follow this dirt road a few hundred yards.

The three-man Mitsubishi light tank here is badly rusted and missing all its guns. Tires and treads remain attached.

10. American LVTs ★★

Off of runway, north of airport terminal/shelter, turn left (northwest), follow dirt road 0.3 kilometers, take hard right turn (almost a U-turn) and follow dirt road 0.2 kilometers

An American LVT (Landing Vehicle, Tracked) troop carrier sits on the roadside with its landing ramp down. About 0.3 kilometers down the same dirt road are the rusted hulks of an LVT-A4 and an

LVT2, both dragged here from the coast.

11. Power Plant/Administration Building ★★★

On dirt road, approximately north of Point 10

Though badly bomb-damaged, the concrete remains of the two-story Japanese administration building retain identifiable kitchen, toilet and soaking tub. Heavy iron blast shutters remain on the windows. The stairwell is intact. Bomb holes let in light through the roof. The nearby power plant is gutted—no generators, switchboards or large pieces remain.

12. LVT and Coastal Defense Gun ★★★

On dirt road, about 0.5 kilometers north of Point 10

An LVT with a gun still mounted sits at the base of Bloody Nose Ridge at a spot known as Hill 205. In a small cave just up the hill (visible from the LVT), a large Japanese coastal defense gun remains on its well-preserved subterranean rotating mount.

13. First Marine Division Marker ★★

100 yards from Point 12 (follow sign)

In an open grassy space, the six-foot-tall stone monument was dedicated in 1994 in this area of final Japanese resistance.

14. Bloody Nose Ridge Trail ★★★

Trailhead 50 yards from Point 12 (follow sign to "Bloody Nose Ridge U.S. Army 323rd Infantry")

After a two-minute walk, the trail forks at a stone monument erected in 1989 honoring Japanese defenders of Peleliu. To the left, a set of steep stairs ascends a short hill, at the top of which are a twelve-foot-tall stone monument to the U.S. Army's 323rd Infantry and panoramic views of the island, including landing areas and Horseshoe Valley (current site of a rock quarry), the scene of intense battles. The fork to the right of the Japanese monument leads downhill to a series of Japanese caves. Artifacts placed at cave entrances include canteens, hand grenades, mortar shells and cooking utensils. The best caves are about a half-kilometer down the trail at a small, stone marker engraved with Japanese characters. Some caves are fairly deep (flashlight needed), but even at the entrances beer and sake bottles and other small relics can be found. Beyond these caves the trail deteriorates into a sketchy jungle path marked by strips of red survey tape. The trail does pass through a hallowed battleground, albeit one thoroughly overgrown and hardly resembling its 1944 state.

15. Seabee Bulldozer ★★

Horseshoe Valley, along dirt road, 0.5 kilometers from Point 12

The rusting bulldozer sits on the road at the entrance of the rock quarry. In this area, 218 Japanese caves were bulldozed shut. Veering left along the quarry road, an American military dump is located about 0.6 kilometers from the bulldozer. In the jungle are rotting parts of various vehicles, oil drums and an LVT.

16. Bloody Beach ★★

Down a series of dirt paths about 1 kilometer southeast of the southern end of the airfield

Bloody Beach is actually a pair of attractive beaches separated by a narrow spit. American forces took the area from points inland. Today it's breezy and quiet, the most scenic spot on the island.

17. Peleliu Memorial Park ★★

From Point 16, take dirt road inland 0.5 kilometers, turn left (south) at dirt road and proceed 1.2 kilometers to end of the road

At this nicely landscaped Japanese-built park are a beach bunker and twisted remains of a U.S. pontoon causeway. Picnic shelters and pine trees line the rocky shore.

18. South Dock/Aircraft Debris ★★

About 2 kilometers (by a series of dirt roads) north of Point 17

The remains of a pontoon causeway sit at this former U.S. military harbor. On the roadside about 1.1 kilometers down the main dirt road heading north is the front half of the fuselage of a Mitsubishi Zero. The wings are gone but the cockpit canopy remains. On a dirt road directly across the small harbor from the South Dock pontoon ruins is a rusting tangle of aircraft parts—wings, engines, fuselage pieces—bulldozed into a scrap-metal pile. The pile is strewn amid the trees for 100 feet or so along the road. It includes Corsair and Betty Bomber parts, though few pieces are easily identified.

19. Purple Beach ★★

Along dirt road, about 1.5 kilometers east of northern end of airfield

Small skirmishing occurred here, but mostly this breezy, scenic beach was used as a post-battle recreation area for American troops. Northeast is a mangrove swamp reported to contain a U.S. Dauntless dive-bomber. Finding the plane requires a boat and local guide.

OTHER AREA ATTRACTIONS

Rock Islands ◤

In addition to war-related sites, the Rock Islands are famed for their aesthetic beauty, world-class diving, deserted beaches, sportfishing and unique swimming/snorkeling spots. Jellyfish Lake is a land-locked marine lake inhabited by millions of jellyfish that, after thousands of years of isolated evolution in the absence of natural predators, have lost their ability to sting. Snorkeling through this swarm of benign jellyfish ranks among the world's most surreal experiences. Nearby is the Milky Way, a small bay with aqua waters beautifully clouded by a thick, white-clay mud that lines the shallow bottom. Swimmers cover their bodies in the restorative mud and rinse in the warm bay. A short boat ride away is the shallow, color-packed Cemetery Reef which, for its rich variety of coral and fish, is among the best snorkeling sites in the entire Pacific. There are numerous world-class dive sites in the area. Sam's Tours (see above) is a first-class, English-fluent dive shop, fishing charter and tour service that puts together day (or longer) trips to the best of the Rock Islands.

RELATED SITES BEYOND PELELIU

Ngesebus Island ★★★

Across the water a few hundred yards northwest of Point 1 is small Ngesebus Island. Assaulted by U.S. forces as part of the Peleliu invasion, it's rarely visited and contains relics—possibly including at least one intact aircraft. It's a small, unexplored frontier on the war-history route, requiring a boat and local guide.

Anguar Island ★★★

A ten-minute flight southwest of Peleliu (Belau Air, 488-8090), idyllic Anguar has nice beaches, fascinating jungle, wild monkeys and limited but excellent war relics. In the jungle near an aircraft debris site—including wings and other parts of a Betty Bomber—is one of the more well-preserved Corsair wrecks in the Pacific. Sitting upright, the plane is entirely intact—prop, cockpit, fuselage, wings, tail. A few kilometers away is the gutted hulk of a U.S. Sherman tank, its guns and turret missing. A guide is needed to find these sites—roads are unmarked throughout the island. Leon Gulibert (277-1111) is a reliable local guide who rents bicycles and operates a guest house near the beach. Taking the morning flight in and afternoon flight out, Anguar can be done as a day trip from Koror or Peleliu. If rustic accommodations aren't a problem, however, a night on the peaceful island is recommended. There's no regular boat service to Anguar.

Nikko Bay/Rock Islands ★★★★◥

Part of the famed Rock Islands, Nikko Bay (accessed by boat from Koror) and the surrounding Rock Islands are filled with relics from Japanese positions built to defend against an American assault that never came. A highlight is the Pillbox, a position along a fortified gauntlet that includes original and relocated artifacts including shell casings, sake bottles and a Japanese helmet. Inside a nearby storage bunker a scrawled message from a tormented Korean laborer in part reads, "Father, Mother, my heart thinks of seeing you." Across the bay, German Lighthouse was the site of a large, Japanese encampment. It includes extensive concrete ruins and massive naval cannons in the deep jungle. At Skogie Reef, near German Lighthouse, a Japanese Zero rests at snorkel depth (from waterline to five feet). Another Zero at snorkel depth (five to ten feet) off Ngchus Island still has glass in the cockpit—the island has two concrete storage bunkers and a good beach campsite about 100 yards from the Zero. A boat and guide are essential—American expat and marine biologist Ron Leidich, owner/operator of Planet Blue Sea Kayak Tours (located at Sam's Tours in Koror), is by far the best World War II guide in Palau. Sam's Tours (488-1062; sams-tours@palaunet.com) is also excellent for wreck diving as well as arranging Rock Islands day trips or boat charters.

GETTING TO/AROUND PELELIU/PALAU

From the United States and Japan, Palau's main city of Koror is accessed via Guam on Continental Airlines (800-231-0856). From Koror, Belau Air (488-8090) flies small planes twice daily to Peleliu and Anguar. Flights take twenty-five minutes to Peleliu, ten minutes more to Anguar. Using morning and afternoon flights, Peleliu can be visited as a day trip out of Koror, though it's best done as an overnight trip.

No rental cars are available on Peleliu—the main village of Klouklubed can be walked in ten minutes. War relics are dispersed across the island, leaving one to rely on a local guide for a vehicle. One option for independent travelers is Storyboard Beach Resort, which rents bicycles for $10 a day. Storyboard owner Godwin Sadao (345-1058; PDivers@palaunet.com) is a good Peleliu-based guide. Sam's Tours (see above) of Koror can also arrange tours to Peleliu. Tengie Hesus (345-1036) is another local Peleliu guide.

Rental cars are available in Koror from Toyota Rent A Car (488-5599), Budget Rent A Car (488-6233) and King's Rent A Car (488-2964). Informal rides around town are cheap and tend to be arranged by hotels and guide/dive services.

Accommodations

Peleliu

Storyboard Beach Resort

Klouklubed
T: 345-1058
6 beach cottages
$85-$100

The only decent accommodations on Peleliu are these somewhat overpriced but comfortable (native wood floors, electric fans, no air-conditioning) beach huts in the island's main village. Divemaster/owner Godwin Sadao is knowledgeable about local war sites, but the dive shop is the main reason for the hotel's existence. The hotel serves good food to guests.

Koror

Palau Pacific Resort

Arkebesang, Koror-B
T: 488-2600 F: 488-1601
160 rooms
$210-$320

It's a few minutes from downtown Koror, but the sixty-four-acre garden setting on a Pacific-side beach helps make this one of the best resorts in Micronesia.

The Carolines Resort

Koror
T: 488-3754 F: 488-3756
7 beach cottages
$150

With decks overlooking the spectacular Rock Islands, these modern bungalows are among Palau's best.

The Guest Lodge

Ngerbeched, Koror-C
T: 488-6320 F: 488-5616
12 rooms
$45-$55

Central location near shops, stores and internet cafes make this basic but clean motel the top budget choice in town.

7

Solomon
Islands

THE WAR YEARS

"**W**ith the Japanese evacuation of Guadalcanal on February 9, 1943, the Pacific War was set to enter its third phase," wrote historian Eric Hammel in *Munda Trail: Turning the Tide Against Japan in the South Pacific.* "The defensive opening had ended and the confused stopgap initial offensive had been successfully waged. Now the organized offensive could begin."

That offensive would begin with a crawl up the Solomon archipelago, a chain of islands running roughly east-west between Rabaul in Papua New Guinea and south of Guadalcanal. The land, air and sea campaign that followed included some of the most tortuous, violent battles of the war, incongruously fought in view of some of the most gorgeous geography and undisturbed village populations on the planet.

Little about the war suggested a South Pacific idyll, particularly for participants in the New Georgia Island campaign, the land battle to capture Japan's major Munda air base, just 150 miles northwest of Guadalcanal. The rigors of that fight were so overwhelming—raw recruits and green officers subjected to some of the most horrifying jungle battle of the war—that New Georgia became the place where the debilitating mental disorder euphemistically known as "combat fatigue" first came to be defined and widely diagnosed.

Fought across obscure waterways and islands with exotic names such as Kolombangara and Kohinggo, maritime supremacy became paramount. Allied intelligence of Japanese naval movement was aided immeasurably by a network of "coastwatchers," primarily Australian, New Zealander and British land owners, traders and military personnel around the islands who escaped to the hills with the Japanese invasion of 1942. At tremendous personal risk, the coastwatchers made surveillance reports by radio from hillside hideouts. Coastwatchers were eventually elevated to mythic status, as in the character of French planter Emile De Becque from the musical *South Pacific.* But throughout the war they were a critical Allied force, nowhere more than in the Solomons where, in addition to keeping watch on Japanese ship movements, they assisted in the rescues of numerous downed airmen and sailors, including future President John F. Kennedy and his PT-109 crew.

Begun less than two weeks after the American conquest of Guadalcanal, the Solomons campaign was essentially a drive northward toward large Japanese bases at Bougainville and Rabaul. At dawn on February 21, 1943, U.S. troops landed on the Russell Islands expecting a tough fight. Unbeknownst to the Americans, the Japanese had evacuated the islands. Soon, 9,000 Allied personnel were operating out of the small islands about sixty-five miles northwest of Guadalcanal.

On June 21, a group of Marine Raiders walked unopposed onto the beaches of New Georgia Island at Seghe Point, and the fight for the Central Solomons was underway. Just over a week later, an Allied invasion force overwhelmed light opposition on Rendova Island, soon to be strengthened as support for the New Georgia force. Action on New Georgia intensified considerably with early July landings of the U.S. Army 43rd Infantry—comprised largely of green New England National Guardsmen—at Zanana Beach and Ilangana Village. Both landings were part of the bloody, disease-ridden drive to capture Munda, which finally fell on August 5. Taking New Georgia cost 1,094 Allied killed and 3,873 wounded. At least 2,500 Japanese were killed.

After New Georgia, the Solomons campaign became a series of emphatic though difficult Allied victories in which supremacy of the sea and air were decided in numerous small engagements and skirmishes. By late summer, Americans and New Zealanders had taken Kolombangara and Vella Lavella Islands (against light opposition) and the domination of the Central Solomons was complete, setting the stage for the critical invasion of Bougainville. Geographically and ethnically part of the Solomon Islands, Bougainville is today part of Papua New Guinea (see Papua New Guinea chapter for travel details).

The battle for Bougainville—its capture would complete the encirclement of Rabaul— began on October 27, 1943, with the landing of a New Zealand force on Treasury Island, just south of Bougainville. As they had throughout the campaign, Allied aircraft pounded the five Japanese airfields collected on the southern end of the 4,000-square-mile island. On November 1, 14,000 American Marines landed at Cape Torokina on Bougainville's southwestern coast, far from any concentration of Japanese troops. The Americans began constructing airfields in Empress Augusta Bay, eventually used in the advance to islands north of Rabaul. Meanwhile, the U.S. Navy sent aircraft carriers and warships to grapple with the Japanese aircraft stationed on Bougainville and Rabaul, as well as Japanese battle groups and reinforcement ships arriving from Truk. In defending their invasion beachhead, the Americans scored decisive victories, damaging three Japanese destroyers and three cruisers, and destroying fifty-five aircraft.

In March 1944, 15,000 Japanese troops launched a mass offensive against the growing American bases, but were repelled at the cost of several thousand men. From roughly this point on, isolated Japanese forces on Bougainville were hampered by dwindling supplies, disease and hunger, and ceased to be a serious threat. Nevertheless, they fought tenaciously and maintained an organized guerrilla presence on the island until the end of the war.

SOURCES & OTHER READING

The Solomons Campaigns 1942-1943: From Guadalcanal to Bougainville, Pacific War Turning Point, McGee, William, L., BMC Publications, 2002

Munda Trail: Turning the Tide Against Japan in the South Pacific, Hammel, Eric, Orion Books, 1989

Lonely Vigil: Coastwatchers of the Solomons, Lord, Walter, Viking Press, 1977

Devil Boats: The PT War Against Japan, Breuer, William B., Presidio, 1987

PT 109: John F. Kennedy in World War II, Donovan, Robert J., McGraw-Hill, 1961

Bougainville

South Pacific Ocean

Choiseul

Vella Lavella Island

Kolombangara Island

New Georgia Sound (The Slot)

New Georgia Island

New Georgia Islands

Munda

Uepi

Marova Lagoon

Seghe

Santa Isabel

50 Miles

N

Russell Islands

Solomon Islands

Florida Islands

Guadalcanal

Malaita

Rennell

San Cristobal

1. Lion's Point
2. Seabee Spigot
3. LST 342
4. *Kikutsuki*
5. Gavutu Island
6. Tulagi Island
7. B-24 Liberator
8. Seghe Airfield
9. P-38 Lighting
10. Coastwatcher's House site
11. Japanese Gun/Tank
12. Lubaria Island/Rendova Island
13. Munda Airfield
14. Japanese Memorial
15. Kia/Ilagana villages
16. American Military Dump
17. Japanese Dual-purpose Guns
18. Japanese Freighter
19. Enoughai Guns
20. Stuart Tank
21. Japanese Caves/Gun Emplacement
22. Ringgi Cove
23. F6F Hellcat
24. Kennedy Island
25. Gizo
26. Japanese Barge
27. Barakoma Airfield

To Noro

Japanese Guns

N

Not to Scale

Noro Road

American Dump

Munda

Munda Airfield

Kia/Ilagana Villages

Japanese Memorial

SOLOMON ISLANDS TODAY

Population: 480,422 • Country Code: 677 • Currency: $1 = 7.14 Solomon Islands dollars

Emerald seas surrounding jungle-covered volcanic islands. Coral reefs just below an ocean surface bursting with electric blues, neon reds and solar yellows. Palm-thatch houses on stilts dotting sandy white beaches. Islanders paddling between islands in dugout canoes suspended above crystalline waters as though floating in air. These are the enduring images of the Solomon Islands, one of the vastly under-visited treasures of the South Pacific.

Comprised of 992 islands (347 inhabited), the Solomons stretch in a double chain of islands extending 1,033 miles in a southeasterly direction from Papua New Guinea. The country achieved independence from Great Britain in 1978; the capital city of Honiara is located on Guadalcanal, the largest island in the chain. There are nine provinces, the three most important of which for war sites are the Western Province (New Georgia, Rendova, Kennedy, Gizo, Vella Lavella Islands), Central Province (Russell, Savo and Florida Islands, including Tulagi) and Guadalcanal Province (see Guadalcanal chapter). About one percent of the country's land is arable, there are less than thirty miles of paved road and more than sixty-seven indigenous languages. A premier underwater destination, the Solomons attract scuba divers from around the world.

With a military-tour service (see Getting to/around the Solomon Islands), the country's major sites can be visited in about two weeks. Given the distance between islands and sporadic nature of in-country transportation, covering the same sites independently could take a month or more. For independent travelers, pinpointing two or three sites (say Gizo, Munda and Guadalcanal) and utilizing Solomon Airlines and local tour operators is an effective way to see the country.

POINTS OF INTEREST

Visiting many of the sites listed below requires a boat, usually furnished by local dive shops or tour operators in the larger centers of Tulagi, Munda and Gizo.

1. Lion's Point ★★

Taroaniara on Port Purvis, southeast end of Nggela Sule Island

On the former site of the U.S. Navy headquarters for the Solomon Islands are a set of war-era government buildings and, up a set of stairs, a plaque dedicated to all Allied naval units in the Solomons.

2. Seabee Spigot ★

Pidgeon Point, Point Purvis Passage, about 1.5 km north of Point 1 on southeast end of Nggela Sule Island

It's not much to look at, but amazing that a fresh-water pipeline constructed by U.S. Seabees in 1942 is still pouring freshwater into the small bay north of Point Purvis. The bay was once filled with U.S. warships awaiting water.

3. LST 342 ★★★★

Taroaniara peninsula at entrance of Tokoyo Bay (aka Tokyo Bay), on southeast end of Nggela Sule Island

The LST (Landing Ship, Tank) was likely torpedoed off either Bougainville or the Russell Islands. The front section was towed here where its mammoth bulk rises like a giant monument above the mangrove shore, the white number 342 visible off its port bow. A large float for an anti-submarine net sits among the mangrove about seventy-five yards off the port bow.

4. Kikutsuki ★★★

About 1.5 km from Point 3 up the narrow channel into Tokoyo Bay, just around the first horseshoe, Nggela Sule Island

Torpedoed and abandoned, this Japanese destroyer was towed by the U.S. Navy to this secluded bay. It now sits at about the waterline with its main gun, depth-charge racks and stern gun mount visible above the water. It's possible to walk on the deck, though it's sinking more each year.

5. Gavutu Island ★★ ◣

South of Nggela Sule Island, east of Tulagi Island

Along with Tulagi Island, tiny Gavutu was stormed by U.S. troops in a supporting action for the larger Guadalcanal campaign. On the northern tip of the tiny island is a pre-war British dock at the site of a Japanese seaplane base. In the water around the dock and causeway to small Tanambogho Island are the very broken remains of three Kawanishi flying boats submerged at about thirty to sixty feet. A trail behind the dock leads past Japanese fortifications uphill to a Japanese tunnel and concrete foundation where the first American flag was planted after capture of the island. "26 CB 4/6/43" is engraved in a concrete slab at the site.

6. Tulagi Island ★★ ◣

South of Nggela Sule Island, west of Gavutu Island

This small island was the site of a Guadalcanal-related invasion against a 450-man Japanese garrison. Tulagi is about four kilometers around, and takes ninety minutes to walk on a dirt road that circumnavigates the island along the beach. In the jungle behind the main town at Sasape Wharf are Japanese pillboxes, memorials and small relics. Beginning from Sasape Wharf and walking along the road roughly southeast (away from Vanita Motel) sites include a concrete foundation (atop the dirt road) of a U.S. Quonset hut/workshop and hills above a large cricket/soccer field where intense fighting took place. About 1.5 kilometers from Sasape Wharf is Blue Beach, where Americans landed on August 7, 1942. The rusted hulk of an American pontoon sits on the beach. Tulagi's dives include the U.S.S. *Aaron Ward*, an intact destroyer with gun turrets still attached, at 230 feet; the New Zealand minesweeper *Koa* at 130 feet; and two Kawanishi flying boats, one a debris field, one intact at 100 feet. Solomon Islands Diving-Dive Tulagi (677-32144) connected to Vanita Motel leads wreck dives and can help arrange land-based tours of the island.

7. B-24 Liberator ★

Northern end of Nggatokae Island, at top of small bay formed with Tamba Island, in Marova Lagoon

The wreckage of a B-24 that ran out of fuel after a raid on Rabaul (the entire crew bailed out safely) is scattered in a small area a few feet inland and visible from the water. Props, wing pieces and fuselage are identifiable and not badly rusted, but the plane is not at all intact. A primitive guest lodge is a long swim away (see Accommodations, Tibara Lodge).

Seghe, New Georgia Island

There are several sites around part of the area where the Allied campaign on New Georgia Island was fought.

8. Seghe Airfield ★★

Just off beach at Seghe Point, southern tip of New Georgia Island

This grassy airfield was built by American Seabees in just ten days following unopposed U.S. Army landings here. About 150 yards along a wide path from the southeastern end of the runway (near ocean) is a leftover Quonset hut now used by locals.

9. P-38 Lighting ★★★ ◤

About 40 yards out to sea from southeast end of runway in Point 8

An intact P-38 aircraft sits upright and in one piece at twenty feet—props, cockpit, twin fuselages, rear stabilizer—in an area that also has decent marine life. Designed by legendary aeronautical engineer Kelly Johnson (of U2, SR-71 and Skunk Works fame), the P-38 was used as a long-range escort fighter and saw action in practically every major combat area of the world. In the Pacific Theater, Lightning pilots downed more Japanese aircraft than pilots flying any other airplane.

10. Coastwatcher's House site ★

Walk through village of Seghe along coastal path described in Point 8. About 30 yards past Seghe Hospital turn left and follow path uphill about 80 yards to a narrow trail on the left marked by two palm logs crossing a small gully. Follow this trail uphill about 300 yards to Peniel Chapel. From front door of the chapel follow narrow trail about 400 yards (past village houses) to a clearing/depression.

This clearing is the site of the former plantation house of New Zealander Major Donald Kennedy, the war's most famed and daring coastwatcher. In addition to sighting enemy sea traffic and assisting downed Allied pilots, "Kennedy's Army" of about thirty men led fatal raids on small groups of Japanese troops. Despite becoming the target of a determined Japanese manhunt, Kennedy survived the war.

11. Japanese Gun/Tank ★★

Tetemara Village, Viru Harbor, New Georgia Island

On a hill at the top of the village are the tracks and engine of a Japanese light tank and coastal gun. The picturesque village makes the site memorable.

12. Lubaria Island/Rendova Island ★

Lubaria Island is about 2.5 km off the northern end of Rendova Island

This small island—it can be walked in twenty minutes—housed the squadron where PT-109, John Kennedy and others were based. The island formerly housed the small Kennedy Memorial Hall and Museum. The one-room, thatch-hut museum was dismantled during the political turmoil of 2000. Today it's open and derelict, with a few rusting relics inside. Outside are a Japanese mountain gun and anchor.

Across beautiful Rendova Harbor, once filled with Allied warships, the volcanic Rendova Peak (3,486 feet) makes Rendova Island one of the most magical sites in the Pacific. The island was fortified with U.S. long-range guns used to pound Japanese positions on New Georgia Island. The guns were moved forward with the Allied advance. There are few war-era relics left on the scenic island.

Munda, New Georgia Island

The focal point of one of the most important battles in the Solomons can be explored by foot or vehicle. Local transportation, dive and World War II tours can be arranged through Dive Munda (677-61107) or Go West Tours (677-61133), both attached to the Agnes Lodge at Munda Wharf.

13. Munda Airfield ★★ ◥

Center of Munda, 300-400 yards inland from the shore at Agnes Lodge, New Georgia Island

Used by Solomon Airlines, it's possible to walk the runway built for Japanese fighters, then captured and expanded for Allied bombers. Fighting for the airfield was fierce—most of it took place at the end of the runway nearest to town/Agnes Lodge. The famed Black Sheep squadron flew from this field. Bob Hope once did a show here while soldiers gathered on the eastern end of the runway to watch. In the trees along a side road at the same end of the strip is a Japanese cave that goes back about fifteen yards. Wreck dives include the *Casi Maru*, a Japanese freighter sunk off Noro Island, a landing craft just in front of the anti-aircraft guns described in Point 15 and an as yet unidentified fighter plane discovered off Hopei Island in the summer of 2002.

14. Japanese Memorial ★

At Lambete Station just below (toward the ocean) the eastern end of the airstrip

This twelve-foot-tall inverted "V" has a small altar in the center. It's dedicated to the soldiers of all nations who died in the Solomons.

15. Kia/Ilagana villages ★★★

Villages along beach, about 1.5 km east of airstrip

U.S. troops landed here in July 1943. Artifacts include many U.S. pontoons on the beach and a small concrete structure (reportedly the paymaster's quarters). On the western end of the picturesque villages are two Japanese anti-aircraft guns in front of a modern, green house on stilts. In the jungle behind the house is an American military dump with enormous pieces of barges, landing craft and aircraft parts.

16. American Military Dump ★

About 2.5 km up (proceeding north) Noro Road from western end of airstrip at Point 13. A small access road wraps around the western and northern ends of the runway and connects to Noro Road.

Amid the brush on the right (east) side of Noro Road is a dull military dump site—extremely corroded vehicle parts, oil drums, gas cans, Coke bottles.

17. Japanese Dual-purpose Guns ★★★

Continue north on Noro Road about 0.5 km from Point 16. Turn right and travel along single-track logging road about 0.5 km to guns on left (north) side of road.

Two large Japanese 75mm dual-purpose guns sit side by side in a clearing in the jungle. With muzzles about eight feet long, thousands of these guns—identifiable by the waffle-iron plating on the side—were produced by the Japanese and can be found throughout the Pacific. Few are as well preserved as these two. About one to two kilometers north along the Noro Road is a small empty Japanese cave in the hill along the left (west) side of the road.

18. Japanese Freighter ★★

Mboroko Bay, northwestern end of New Georgia Island

With mast and crane sticking above the water, the remains of this Japanese ship (sunk by U.S. dive-bombers) are picturesque against the dense jungle of the nearby shore. A trailhead near here at the heart of Bairoko Harbor was a northern terminus of the infamous Munda Trail, used by the Japanese as a supply route.

19. Enoughai Guns ★★

At head of Enoughai Inlet, northwestern end of New Georgia Island

Three large Japanese naval cannons stick out of the jungle along the beach here (visible from water). "Throughout the war, Japanese coast defense batteries were strangely ineffective," according to U.S. Navy historian Samuel Eliot Morison.

20. Stuart Tank ★★★

About 300 yards up jungle trail behind Tahitu village, on the small Mukimuki Peninsula on the northern shore of Kohinggo Island. Cross the lagoon to find the trail.

In the jungle where it was stopped by Japanese fire is a U.S. Stuart light tank. Used in early-war jungle battles, the rare Stuart is in superb condition, with all cannons and guns attached, motor inside and minimal rusting.

21. Japanese Caves/Gun Emplacement ★

At Temeh village, on southeastern edge of Kolombangara Island

Less than a kilometer up a trail from small Temeh are a series of caves, including two that can be entered. A flashlight and guide (villagers are usually helpful) are both necessary. The larger one is twenty to thirty yards deep and includes sake and medicine bottles. The other includes machine gun parts, an empty magazine and unused shells. Beer and medicine bottles can be found on the trails to both caves. Uphill, about 100-200 yards southwest of the village

along a separate trail are the concrete and iron remains of a Japanese anti-aircraft gun emplacement.

22. Ringgi Cove ★

Southeastern end of Kolombangara Island, across from Kohinggo Island

At this former barge and supply station, two large Japanese cranes and associated cement and iron works sit on the beach at the harbor entrance.

23. F6F Hellcat ★★★ ◤

Between Goumu and Mandemangguta Islands

Sitting upright and intact at forty feet (machine gun barrels still on one wing) and with the cockpit accessible, this makes for a good beginner dive. The Hellcat had the highest kill/loss ratio of any American fighter plane in service during World War II.

24. Kennedy Island (aka Plum Pudding Island, Kasolo Island) ★★★ ◤

About forty-five-minute boat ride south of Gizo Island

There isn't much to see on the tiny, deserted island Lieutenant John F. Kennedy and ten other survivors swam four hours to reach after the PT-109 ship commanded by Kennedy was cut in half by a Japanese destroyer. The beautiful island is surrounded by sandy beaches and a shallow coral wall teeming with marine life—fantastic for snorkeling. Kennedy later transferred his party to Olasana Island and swam to Naru Island (just east of Olasana Island) for provisions. The two nearly adjoining islands are visible to the south. Discovered by locals in contact with coastwatchers, the entire party made it back to its base off Rendova Island. Amid great publicity in 2002, Kennedy's PT-109 was reported discovered in Blackett Strait.

25. Gizo and surrounding islands ★★★ ◤

The Solomon's Western Province has lagoon-mountain-and-islet-filled seas and picturesque villages where few travelers tread. At the southern tip of Gizo Island, the capital city of Gizo is the province's largest settlement and gateway to Vella Lavella, Kennedy, Kolombangara, Kohinggo and other nearby islands. Dive Solomon Charters (677-60324) in downtown Gizo, adjacent to the Gizo Hotel, offers day trips that include an American Stuart tank (Point 20) and Japanese relics on Kolombangara Island (Point 21). The dive highlight is the Nagasaki-built *Toa Maru*, a 446-foot-long Japanese freighter at twenty-two to 120 feet. Tanks are still in its holds. Snorkel and dive trips on aircraft in and around Gizo Harbor include a Hellcat (Point 23), Japanese Zero (at about twenty-five feet) and upside-down Betty bomber (at about sixty feet).

26. Japanese Barge ★

About 30 yards from shore in front of Liapari village, on small Liapari Island off southern tip of Vella Lavella Island

At low tide you can see and sometimes walk out to the sunken barge that could carry about twenty troops and supplies. It's just up the beach (away from village) from the large, rusted remnants of a (non-World War II) railway and docking pulley.

27. Barakoma Airfield ★★

On eastern coast between villages of Pusisama (north) and Sombuniru (south), Vella Lavella Island

From this airfield, Corsairs flew patrols and covered the invasion of Bougainville. The tent camp for pilots and crew was in the hills above the airstrip. Toward the north end of the airstrip, a solitary palm-thatch house stands on stilts. Behind this house is a very overgrown trail leading uphill about a quarter of a mile to an American military dump. Rusting and corroding remains are here—oil drums, bales of barbed wire, Coke bottles, sections of the perforated steel Marston Mats used to make runways and roads on the coral islands. Near the dump, buried beneath vines and dirt are concrete slabs poured by Marines in 1943 and engraved with names. In 1965, the last Japanese straggler came out of hiding in the thick Vella Lavella jungle. Survivors of the July 5, 1943, sinking of the light cruiser U.S.S. *Helena* paddled and swam to safety along the eastern shore of Vella Lavella Island, far north of this site.

OTHER AREA ATTRACTIONS

Marova Lagoon ◤

Isolated and largely unspoiled, the shallow, mountain-rimmed Marova Lagoon on the eastern end of New Georgia Island is the country's most well-known dive destination. Often mentioned among the most beautiful lagoons in the world—some call it the largest saltwater lagoon in the world—it's also excellent for snorkelers and swimmers. Uepi Island Resort (see Accommodations) operates a dive shop in a spectacular setting on the northern end of the lagoon.

GETTING TO/AROUND THE SOLOMON ISLANDS

Trips to the Solomon Islands generally begin with a flight into the capital city of Honiara. See Guadalcanal chapter for details.

In country, Solomon Airlines (677-36048 in Honiara; 310-670-7302 in Los Angeles; 617-3407-7266 in Brisbane, Australia) flies to twenty-three locations, including Seghe, Viru, Munda, Ringgi Cove, Gizo and Barakoma on Vella Lavella Island.

A passenger ferry runs between Honiara

and Gizo every Wednesday at 4 p.m. as of this writing. The dirty, smoke-belching *Tomoko* (677-24259) only has two private rooms (deck passage for everyone else), toilets are generally filthy and the boat can be extremely crowded. The ferry makes many stops along the twenty-four hour trip, which costs SI$130 each way. Though not recommended, it's a cheap local option. The *Uminao* (contact Wings Company, 677-22414) passenger ship may or not be making trips to the Western Solomons.

In outlying areas it's best to arrange boat trips to destinations with local guides or dive shops. Many dive shops run World War II tours that don't necessarily involve diving. Additionally, it's possible, if such is your style, to barter rides around the islands with locals, nearly all of who own or have access to a canoe or motorized boat.

Because it's an island nation with poor infrastructure, the Solomon Islands are a good destination for organized World War II tours. California-based Valor Tours (800-842-4504 or 415-332-7850) operates superb trips to the country's primary war sites (including Guadalcanal and most sites listed in this chapter) led by British World War II bomber pilot and Pacific War travel pioneer Bob Reynolds. Trips involve a week on a live-aboard dive boat cruising through some of the most atmospheric scenery in the South Pacific. Valor Tours also runs excellent trips to other destinations in this book including the Marshall Islands, Tarawa and the Philippines.

Operated by Bilikiki Cruises (677-20412 in Honiara; 800-663-5363 in the U.S. and Canada) the *Bilikiki* and *Spirit of Solomons* are twenty- and twenty-six-passenger live-aboard dive boats available for group charters. Oftentimes, groups will fill only a portion of the boat, leaving room for individual, couple or small-group bookings.

ACCOMMODATIONS

Tulagi Island

Vanita Motel

At Sasape Wharf, Tulagi Village, Tulagi Island
T: 677-32052 F: 677-32155
8 rooms
SI$50 per person, per night

Sparse backpacker-level accommodations with electricity, fans and shared bathrooms. In a central location, it has a good bar and Aussie-run dive shop connected.

New Georgia Island

Agnes Lodge

Munda Wharf
Lambete Village, Roviana Lagoon
T: 677-61133 F: 677-61230
12 rooms
SI$40-SI$250

Near the important battlefield at Munda, this inexpensive lodge has a good, seafront location and air-conditioning, as well as a restaurant, outdoor bar and attached dive and tour shops.

Marova Lagoon

Uepi Island Resort

Eastern end of 2.5-km-long Uepi Island, northern end of Marova Lagoon
T: 61-3-9787-7904 (in Australia)
F: 61-3-9787-5904 (in Australia)
6 bungalows, 2 rooms
From US$100

With a secluded, sandy beach, this is one of the better resorts in the Solomons. Unforgettable lagoon and ocean dives are the attractions. Other available activities include kayaking and fishing.

Tibara Lodge

Tamba Island, on western side of small bay formed with larger Nggtokae Island, about 400 yards south of Point 22.
Address: Tibara Lodge, Batuna P/Agency, Marova Lagoon, Western Solomon Islands
T: None F: None
2 huts (four persons each)
SI$50

Palm-thatch huts. No phone. No electricity. It does have lanterns, toilets and cheap local meals on a remote bay with good snorkeling. A rustic experience for those who truly want to leave civilization behind.

Gizo Island

Gizo Hotel

Gizo town waterfront
T: 677-60199 (61-7-3303-2900
in Brisbane, Australia)
F: 677-60137
45 rooms
SI$100-SI$450

Not luxurious, but, with central location, air-conditioned rooms, private bathrooms, good bar and restaurant, and a dive/tour shop attached, it's a good, clean place to base for Kennedy Island, Kolombangara Island and other area excursions.

Paradise Lodge

Gizo town
T: 677-60324 (book through Dive Solomon Charters)
F: None
6 units
SI$15

The fan-cooled backpacker-style hotel is in a newly constructed building on a hill with good views of the city, Gizo Harbor and Kolombangara Island.

Aleutian
Islands

(UNALASKA/
DUTCH HARBOR)

THE WAR YEARS

Bleak. Bitter. Forgotten. These are the words that arise in most accounts of the Aleutian Islands campaign, one of the most overlooked actions of World War II—and one that would have direct impact on Europe's eastern front as well as the obsolescence of the Mitsubishi Zero fighter. Stretching out as an 1,100-mile emerald causeway between Asia and North America, the Aleutian chain was feared by both the United States and Japan as the shortest invasion route to each other's territory. As early as 1935, famously foresighted aviator Billy Mitchell told Congress that the Japanese "will come right here to Alaska ... it is the most important strategic place in the world."

Forming plans for the battle of Midway, Admiral Isoroku Yamamoto sought to exploit long-standing Aleutian anxiety by sending a token force to seize the islands of Attu and Kiska. Yamamoto hoped to draw American ships away from Midway to protect Alaska. But American cryptographers had broken Japanese codes and were aware of the deceit. U.S. forces remained at Midway, crushing the Imperial Navy in what was arguably the most significant naval battle of the twentieth century.

Concurrently, on June 3 and 4, 1942, Japanese aircraft bombed the American base at Dutch Harbor, Alaska, killing forty-three and injuring sixty-four. On June 7, 8,600 Japanese invaders walked onto Attu and Kiska virtually unopposed. The United States rushed to build or reinforce bases at Kodiak, Cold Bay, Dutch Harbor, Umnak, Adak and other islands across the region.

In the words of British historian David Smurthwaite, the Aleutians were "strategically unimportant but emotionally significant." With supply lines battered—the American/Canadian naval victory at the March 22, 1943, Battle of the Komandorski Islands completed the isolation of the Japanese garrisons in the Aleutians—Japan posed no real threat to North America. Nevertheless, the U.S. media grew increasingly agitated with the enemy presence on North American soil.

A panicky public cried for action. Throughout 1942-43, Allied planes dropped 7.5 million pounds of bombs on the frostbitten Japanese occupying Attu and Kiska. Even so, winds up to 120 mph, constant fog and unpredictable storms made shipping and flying a perilous endeavor, one that contrasted sharply with the tropical image of the Pacific War. "The fight to drive the Japanese out of the Aleutians was as much a battle against the weather as it was against enemy troops," wrote Alaska historian Terrance Cole. Noncombat casualties—most attributed to exposure—greatly out-numbered combat casualties.

Along the 1,450-mile Alaska-Canada (ALCAN) Highway, construction was stepped up to frantic levels. In eight-and-a-half months, 10,607 Army engineers and support troops established the first overland link between the United States and Alaska, liter-ally paving the way for the massive influx of military personnel that would change Alaska forever.

After a brutal winter, the Allied offensive commenced on May 11, 1943, with landings of 15,000 men at Holtz and Massacre Bays on the thirty-five-mile-long by fifteen-mile-wide Attu. The Japanese fought tenaciously, holding landing forces to minimal advances. Biting cold, wind and deep mud hampered movement. Casualties were heavy on both sides, but the Americans' overwhelming man and air superiority proved too great for the Japanese to resist. On May 29, a final banzai charge broke American lines but eventually exhausted itself in an orgy of suicide, a ghastly harbinger of scenes to follow across the Pacific. All but twenty-nine of the 2,321-man Japanese force was dead. American casualties for the campaign were 549 dead, 1,148 wounded and 2,132 noncombat casualties. "In terms of numbers engaged, Attu ranks as one of the most costly assaults in the Pacific," said a U.S. Army report. "For every 100 enemy found on the island, about seventy-one Americans were killed or wounded ... second only to Iwo Jima."

Now the stage was set for the critial battle of the campaign. On August 15, 30,000 Americans and 5,000 Canadians descended on the larger Japanese base at Kiska anticipating an even tougher fight. Unbeknownst to the Allies, Japan had under cover of heavy fog evacuated all of its 5,183 troops three weeks earlier. In more enveloping fog, soldiers fumbled across the island for several days, firing at unseen enemies and wandering into booby traps. The Allies had attacked an uninhabited island—a tragic-comic operation that claimed 313 casualties, including twenty-one killed, many to friendly fire. Japan had pulled off one of the most successful and dramatic retreats of the war—but they'd been purged from the Western Hemisphere.

Foremost among the Aleutians' many back stories are the dark facts surrounding the U.S. government's forced relocation of the Unangan (Aleut) people to squalid deten-tion camps (see Point 13). The recovery of a downed Zero fighter had happier conse-quences for the United States. In near-perfect condition after an emergency landing on the island of Akutan, "Koga's Zero"—pilot Tadayoshi Koga died in the crash—was shipped to the Grumman aircraft factory in San Diego where it was reverse-engineered and used as a template for adjustments to American fighters that soon would be out-performing the once-dominant Zero. With Japanese air power eliminated from Alaskan skies, American and Soviet pilots were able to fly more than 6,000 Lend-Lease air-craft from Alaska to Siberia to aid the Soviet Union's fight against Germany.

Despite its significance, the Aleutians campaign has remained largely forgotten by historians and the public, partly because the campaign was an essential dead end for both sides—neither Attu nor Kiska were used as launch pads for further conquest.

SOURCES & OTHER READING

The Thousand Mile War, Garfield, Brian, Doubleday, 1969

The Capture of Attu: Tales of World War II in Alaska, Northern History Library, Alaska Northwest Publishing Company, 1984

The Forgotten War: A Pictorial History of World War II in Alaska and Northwestern Canada, Vols. 1-4, Cohen, Stan, Pictorial Histories Publishing, 1981-1993

Cracking the Zero Mystery, Rearden, Jim, Stackpole Books, 1990

Center of the Storm: The Bombing of Dutch Harbor, et al., Dickrell, Jeff, Pictorial Histories Publishing, 2002

When the Wind Was a River: Aleut Evacuation in World War II, Kohlhoff, Dean, University of Washington Press, 1995

The Williwaw War, Goldstein and Dillon, University of Arkansas Press, 1992

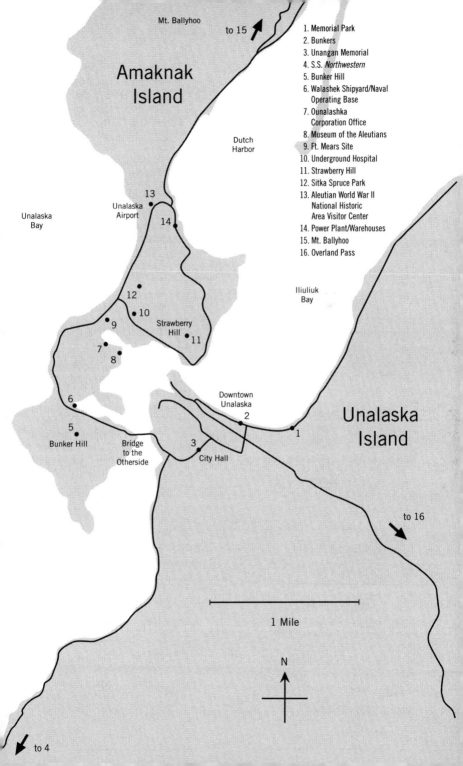

Mt. Ballyhoo

to 15

Amaknak
Island

Dutch
Harbor

1. Memorial Park
2. Bunkers
3. Unangan Memorial
4. S.S. *Northwestern*
5. Bunker Hill
6. Walashek Shipyard/Naval
   Operating Base
7. Ounalashka
   Corporation Office
8. Museum of the Aleutians
9. Ft. Mears Site
10. Underground Hospital
11. Strawberry Hill
12. Sitka Spruce Park
13. Aleutian World War II
    National Historic
    Area Visitor Center
14. Power Plant/Warehouses
15. Mt. Ballyhoo
16. Overland Pass

Unalaska
Bay

13

Unalaska
Airport

14

Iliuliuk
Bay

12

10

9   Strawberry
            Hill
7   11
8

6

5   Downtown
Bunker Hill   Unalaska
                            2
          Bridge   1
          to the
          Otherside   3   Unalaska
                    City Hall   Island

                                    to 16

1 Mile

N

to 4

ALEUTIAN ISLANDS (UNALASKA/DUTCH HARBOR) TODAY

Population: 4,000 (10,000 during fishing season)
• Area Code: 907 • Currency: U.S. dollar

With enough summer green to pave Ireland, the Aleutian gateway of Unalaska (the name Dutch Harbor is interchangeable) is one of the epic surprises in the Pacific. Surrounded by fertile ocean and a ring of contoured volcanic mountains, Unalaska Island's only settlement (Unalaska town) is home to the most profitable commercial fishing fleet in the United States. The rough-at-the-edges town—an onion-domed 1890s Russian Orthodox Church remains its major landmark—is divided into two parts. Downtown Unalaska is on Unalaska Island. The portion of town sometimes referred to as Dutch Harbor is on adjacent Amaknak Island, joined to the mainland by the short Bridge to the Otherside.

Remote location and fishing wealth make Unalaska expensive for visitors—one restaurant sells an $18.95 burrito—and the weather is often uncooperative. But wandering across this majestic far-flung island one can't help but get a sense of the grandiose ambitions for empire nurtured in both Japan and the United States. Nor can one easily blame any people for desiring to hold such a spectacular piece of real estate. More than anything, scenery propels the Aleutians near the top of the list of Pacific War sites.

Most Aleutian relics are from American defensive fortifications—somewhat the parallel of Japanese sites found throughout the Marshall Islands. Alaska's long summer hours—summer is the only reliable season for travel—mean Unalaska's war sites can be toured in a single day, but two or three days (minimum) are recommended. Charters to other islands in the chain account for additional days.

POINTS OF INTEREST

1. Memorial Park ★★

Bayview Road, east end of downtown Unalaska

Eight monuments, two bunkers and the prop from the S.S. *Northwestern* (see Point 4) honor Aleutian maritime heroes, from the old U.S. Revenue Cutter Service to World War II veterans. Several Japanese bombs fell amid the houses above the park during the June 3-4, 1942 attacks.

2. Bunkers ★★

Bayview Road between Fourth and Sixth Streets, 0.3 miles west of Point 1

There are countless bunkers around Unalaska—set in downtown, these two are among the easier to find and more interesting to photograph.

3. Unangan Memorial ★★

At City Hall on Airport Beach Road, 0.8 miles west of Point 1

This small monument is dedicated to the native residents of five villages relocated to Southeast Alaska detention camps in June 1942.

4. S.S. *Northwestern* ★★

Captain's Bay Road, 3.7 miles south
of intersection with Airport Beach Road

At the point where Captain's Bay Road
becomes a gated private road, the
rusted bow of the S.S. *Northwestern*—
a cargo and passenger ship sunk by
Japanese aircraft—can be seen sticking
out of the water near the opposite shore.
The wreck was towed to its present
location.

5. Bunker Hill ★★★

Off of Airport Beach Road, turn left
(south) on Henry Swanson Drive. After
0.7 miles, turn right on unmarked road
leading 1.1 miles to the top of the hill.
Four-wheel-drive with high-clearance
necessary. The trail to the top starts
off Airport Beach Road about 0.3 miles
beyond (west) the turnoff to Henry
Swanson Drive.

Amid metal and wood refuse stands a
double-decker observation bunker overlooking Iliuliuk and Dutch Harbors. Two
gun-turret rims remain, but the reason for
trekking up the 421-foot hill is the 360-
degree view, one of the best on the
island.

6. Walashek Shipyard/Naval Operating Base ★★

0.4 miles west of the Bridge

This still operating shipyard was used by
the U.S. Navy during the war. The split-
roofed building was and is the main dry
dock facility. The submarine dock from
Iliuliuk Submarine Base is in use on the
north side of the harbor.

7. Ounalashka Corporation Office

400 Salmon Way
T: 907-581-1276

No war significance here. It's the place
to obtain hiking permits ($6) for Bunker
Hill, Mt. Ballyhoo and Overland Pass.
The office is open Monday-Friday, 8
a.m.-5 p.m. Security personnel issue
permits on weekends.

8. Museum of the Aleutians ★★

314 Salmon Way
T: 907-581-5150
Adult: $4
Child (12 and under): Free
Monday-Saturday, 10 a.m.-5 p.m.;
Sunday, Noon-5 p.m.,
June 1-September 30
Wednesday-Saturday, 11 a.m.-4 p.m.;
Sunday, Noon-4 p.m., October 1-May 31

Dedicated to Aleutian history, this excellent museum has a small but interesting
collection of war artifacts including a
leather "teddy bear" flight suit. Traveling
down Salmon Way, jagged Army trench
lines are visible in the hill to the right.

9. Ft. Mears Site ★

Airport Beach Road, 1.2 miles from
Bridge

The flat area around the Grand Aleutian
Hotel was the site of Ft. Mears,
Unalaska's major Army installation.
Pillboxes, concrete structures and
foundations can be found in the area.

10. Underground Hospital ★★

Off Airport Beach Road, turn right (east)
and travel 0.3 miles down East Point
Road.

The large concrete structure on the left
side of the road was a military hospital
built largely underground. Entries are
sealed off. Jagged trench lines are visible
in the hill behind the hospital.

11. Strawberry Hill ★★

From Point 10, continue 0.3 miles down
East Point Road. Turn left (north) on
unmarked road at two yellow, war-era
military buildings. Continue uphill and
veer right at fork after 0.1 miles.

The large military buildup on Strawberry
Hill is evident in all manner of rusted
and cement debris. About 0.3 miles
beyond the fork, the only brick building
in the Aleutians—bachelor officers quarters during the war—sits off the right
side of the road.

12. Sitka Spruce Park ★★

From Airport Beach Road, turn right (east) on Biorka Drive and travel 0.2 miles.

A large Japanese bomb crater can be seen by following the short path around the pond. The spruce trees are not indigenous; they were planted by U.S. soldiers. Also visible are Army trenches, a pair of military warehouses and, turning left off Biorka Drive and traveling up Kashega Drive, colorful houses left over from wartime.

13. Aleutian World War II National Historic Area Visitor Center ★★★

Airport Beach Road, just
past Airport Drive
T: 907-581-9944
Tuesday-Sunday, 1-5 p.m.
and by appointment
Closed Monday
Adult: $4
Senior: $2
Veteran, Child (12 and under): Free

Opened in June 2002, this interpretive center in the war-era Aerology Building represents the largest organized effort to date to preserve the history of the Aleutians campaign. Displays include 7.7mm rounds taken from "Koga's Zero," uniforms, weaponry, propaganda leaflets and a convincing re-creation of Aerology Building activity with original maps, radios and a U.S. pilot mannequin in cold-weather flight suit. Absorbing displays tell the stories of Dutch Harbor, soldiers' battles with northern boredom, the battle for Attu and Japanese escape from Kiska. A thirty-five-seat theater shows excellent war documentaries. Even the bathrooms have exhibits.

This is also one of the few places that chronicles the U.S. government's depressing relocation of the Unangan (Aleut) natives, who had inhabited the Aleutians for at least 9,000 years. With the invasion of Attu and Kiska, the Unangan were moved to squalid intern-

ment camps—usually abandoned and decrepit fish canneries in Southeast Alaska. (Non-native residents of the Aleutians were permitted to remain on the islands throughout the war.) The overcrowded camps lacked schools, stores, medical facilities and water/sewage systems. According to some estimates, a quarter of internees died during the relocation period. (Forty-two Attuans and a female American teacher captured by the Japanese spent the war as detainees in Otaru city on the Japanese island of Hokkaido. Sixteen died there.) At war's end, many Unangan weren't allowed to return to their native islands—principally Adak—these since taken over by the U.S. military. Those who could return often found villages and homes vandalized and looted—boats, fishing and hunting gear and religious objects stolen by U.S. servicemen. On August 10, 1998, federal law gave the Unangan people financial compensation and an apology from the American people.

14. Power Plant/Warehouses ★★

Intersection of East Point Road and Biorka Drive. Or follow Airport Beach Road 2.2 miles from the Bridge.

The long wooden warehouses are probably the oldest military structures Unalaska. Across the street, five-foot-thick concrete walls mark the still-operational power plant as a major piece of war-era construction.

15. Mt. Ballyhoo ★★★★

From Bridge, follow Airport Beach Road 2.1 miles (toward airport), then turn left (north) on Ballyhoo Road. After 1.2 miles, veer left on unmarked road that leads 1.3 miles uphill—four-wheel-drive and high-clearance necessary—to the fork at base of summit of 1,634-foot Mt. Ballyhoo. Veer right and travel 0.7 miles to reach Ulakta Head National Historic Area. To reach the hiking trail up Mt. Ballyoo, travel about 0.2 miles after the turn onto Ballyhoo Road, then turn left and travel another 0.2 miles to the visible trail leading up the ridge.

The site of Ft. Schwatka is now scattered with military leftovers—crumbled buildings, bunkers, gun turrets, lots of badly rusted metal. About 0.4 miles from the fork leading toward Ulakta Head is a small wooden doorway (on the right, about halfway up the hill). The doorway leads to a subterranean tunnel that connects with the bunker at the top of the hill. It's easy to walk—flashlight helpful. The dominant structure at Ulakta Head is the Command Post, a large concrete building with a half-oval entry (flashlight necessary). An observation bunker and circular gun-turret rim flank either side of the Command Post. All of this is extraordinary, but it's the picturesque views of Unalaska's sea-torn landscape that makes the tough drive or hike worth the trouble.

16. Overland Pass ★★★

Follow Broadway through Unalaska town, turn left on Overland Drive. Follow the steep rough road (four-wheel-drive and high-clearance required) seven miles over the mountain pass and down to the T at the beach at Summers Bay. A left turn at the T leads four miles back to town. A right turn leads 2.7 miles past scenic coves before dead ending.

Scattered debris—gun turrets, bunkers, dilapidated wooden structures—from an area collectively known as Ft. Brumback sits along this old military road. Once again, it's the sweeping views that make the drive remarkable.

RELATED SITES BEYOND UNALASKA/DUTCH HARBOR

Ft. Glenn ★★★★

On the island of Umnak—a forty-five-minute charter flight from Unalaska on PenAir (907-581-1383)—is the sprawling Ft. Glenn, an Army base with a secret airfield. From here, U.S. fliers intercepted and downed four Japanese planes returning to carriers after their June 4, 1942, raid on Dutch Harbor. With hundreds of Quonset huts still (mostly partially) standing, the five-mile-long, three-mile-wide base is a monumental, surreal and largely unknown Pacific War find. Still standing is the theater where Bob Hope performed; stage, projection room and theater chairs included. Most buildings are gutted and falling apart, but the officers clubs (with fireplaces and murals on walls), commander's house, hospital and power station are in recognizable shape. The remains of what is probably a B-26 Marauder—engines, props and wings intact—sit at the end of the runway. The entire site is reminiscent of Unalaska before a clean-up effort there in the 1980s. This is a unique and spectacular site—the scenic flight alone is worth the trip. Bed-and-breakfast-style accommodations with shared bathroom ($120 a day including meals) are available at the Bering Pacific Ranch (403-931-3583 at Alberta, Canada office). The ranch also rents Honda all-terrain vehicles for $150 a day—overgrown roads crisscross the huge base, so the vehicles come in handy, especially for short visits. From Unalaska, Aleutian Adventure Sports (888-581-4489 or 907-581-4489) operates boat charters to Ft. Glenn/Umnak that can be more reliable than weather-restricted flights.

Attu ★ and Kiska ★★★

Attu is now the domain of occasional bird watchers. Military artifacts are minimal—a few dilapidated buildings. Attu's lone relic of significance—a P-38 aircraft—was moved in 2000 to Heritage Park at Elmendorf Air Force Base in Anchorage.

Kiska remains littered with Japanese artifacts—large defense guns, anti-aircraft guns, bunkers, airstrip, crumbling build-ings, shipwrecks, a midget submarine, large guns at North Head and on Little Kiska Island, and remains of the Japanese army base at Gertrude Cove. All travel is on foot, often through wet marshy ground. There are no accom-modations.

With no scheduled sea or air service, travel to Attu and Kiska is extremely dif-ficult. PenAir (907-243-2485) operates charters from Anchorage to Attu. Charters seating eleven or twelve passengers can top $26,000. Attu charters with Anchorage-based Security Aviation (907-248-2677) on an eight-passenger jet cost about $17,000.

Kiska has no operational landing strip or anchorage, so getting there is often a matter of arranging a ride with a fishing boat or other vessel from Unalaska. Weather can make the passage danger-ous. PenAir operates regular flights from Anchorage to Adak (round trip $1,210). From Adak—the former navy base there is owned by the Aleut Corporation (907-561-4300)—it may be possible to charter ships to Kiska or Attu. Typical boat passage from Adak to Kiska takes about eighteen hours. The Adak Port Office number is 907-592-0185.

The German cruise ship *Hanseatic* (booked through Radisson Seven Seas Cruises, 866-213-1272) operates trips through the Aleutians and Western Alaska in summer. Trips sometimes include stops at Attu. Arctic birding tours on the *New World Discoverer* are operated in summer by the U.K.-based Orintholidays company (44-1794-519-445). The trips, which include stops at Attu and Kiska, begin in London, set sail from Hokkaido, Japan, and end in Seattle before con-necting with return flights to London. Prices from London begin at about $8,900.

As of this writing, a U.S. Coast Guard LORAN station is still operating on Attu (907-392-3315). Attu veterans and those with U.S.C.G. contacts can some-times catch a ride on supply ships and bunk at the station.

Kodiak ★★★★

Not officially part of the Aleutians chain, 177-mile-long Kodiak Island is neverthe-less a scenic wonder with a number of war sites. The best is Ft. Abercrombie State Historical Park (907-486-6339; 1400 Abercrombie Dr., 3.8 miles north of town), a 186-acre wooded park filled with "remnants of a time that anticipated and saw an enemy invasion on U.S. soil." A 0.7-mile self-guided walking tour has eighteen points of interest, including massive coastal defense guns, bunkers and a forest with a mossy carpet so soft it feels like pillows. With five-foot-thick reinforced concrete walls, the massive War Reserve Magazine is a stark fortress in the woods. If only for sheer scenic beauty, few short hikes anywhere match this one. Within the park the Kodiak Military History Museum (907-486-7015; open Saturday, Sunday, Monday and Wednesday, 1-4 p.m. in summer, or by appointment) tells the story of Kodiak during wartime (a major supply and support base). An array of "hands-on" items includes authentic uniforms, original working Army phone system, small weapons, a Japanese fire hydrant from Kiska and bomber jackets visitors can try on. The museum is housed inside the restored and huge Ready Ammunition Bunker at scenic Miller Point. Outside is a pair of thirty-three-foot-long cannons—never fired in anger but often in practice—next to their original carriage mounts. The guns could fire a projectile twenty miles. The park has thirteen campsites.

In town, the Baranov Museum (907-486-5920; corner of Central Avenue and Marine Way) has five albums of war-era photos. Images include an Army vs. Navy tug of war on a packed Main Street, and a shot of Soviet pilots in downtown Kodiak killing time before flying Lend-Lease aircraft to the Soviet Union. On Rezanof Drive, 2.2 miles south of town, Deadman's Curve is a scenic viewpoint offering commanding views of Kodiak, Chiniak Bay and surrounding islands. The U.S. Army also liked the view—on the hill behind the parking lot is a concrete observation bunker. Most visitors never notice it amid the rocks. A mile-long trail to the Harbor Defense Command Post starts just past Boy Scout Lake (3.7 miles south of town on Rezanof Drive) on the dirt road blocked by large boulders. Walk through the boulders then veer left at fork after 0.1 miles. After about a quarter mile, fork right twice in succession to the command post near the top of the hill. The imposing concrete structure was part of the U.S. Army's Ft. Greely. The land is owned now by the Natives of Kodiak Corporation (907-486-3606) and requires a free land-use permit. A trail near the command post leads down to the shore and Iron Bottom Beach, a military dump site—corroded hardware and vehicle parts are visible at low tide. The otherwise pristine beach speaks as much about changed attitudes toward environmental protection as it does about the war. The Buskin River Inn (1395 Airport Way, about five miles south of town) has a fifteen-foot-long coastal defense cannon out front. There's also a huge war-era Navy anchor, similar to many found around town. On the site of the former Kodiak Naval Operating Base, the U.S. Coast Guard Base (main gate off Rezanof Drive, 6.5 miles south of town) has been declared a National Historic Landmark. ID is checked at the gate, and cars are waved through. Most of the housing near the entrance was built during the war, as was the Star of the Sea Chapel and crumbling dock known as Marginal Pier. The massive refurbished hangars are World War II originals. Coast Guard property extends for about fifteen miles and includes many sites—bunkers, concrete foundations, etc.—that are off-limits to most visitors. Still, the site and layout

are the same as when the U.S. Navy was here. Past Road's End Restaurant (worth a stop itself) about 43.1 miles south of town, the old Chiniak Military Runway crosses the main road. To the right (south) about seventy-five yards, sections of Marston Mat—used to construct runways and roads—still form a small portion of the airstrip. Scattered pieces lie in the brush to the side of the road. Farther up the main road are the Chiniak Bunkers, a Kodiak highlight. Spread along a spectacular bluff overlooking Chiniak Bay are six large bunkers (more exist nearby on private land) used for observation or defense guns. The most photogenic is a two-level concrete observation post, but among the many bunkers catalogued in this book, panoramic views of distant islands and mountains and soft grassy hillocks make this site memorable. To reach the bunkers continue just beyond the old Chiniak Military Runway and follow the middle path where the road splits in three directions. After 0.2 miles, bear left at fork, then proceed about one mile before bearing left again. Most people walk the remaining half-mile uphill to the central bunker. The land belongs to the Leisnoi native corporation (907-486-8191)—hikers are required to carry a free land-use permit.

Other Kodiak Attractions

Justly deserving its nickname, The Emerald Isle, Kodiak is filled with high mountains, craggy coastline and lush moss-carpeted forests. It's arguably the most scenic destination in this book. (Though admittedly, there's an apples-and-oranges element to any argument comparing palm trees and sandy beaches with pine-covered mountains and brown bears.) Most of the population is concentrated on the island's northeast corner in the town of Kodiak, a typical rough-hewn coastal Alaska town. The island is well-known for its population of 3,000 or so Kodiak bears, the largest of the grizzlies. It's also the former capital of Russian Alaska and home to one of the United

States' largest commercial fishing fleets. Despite the superlatives and quick, easy access from Anchorage, Kodiak remains surprisingly unspoiled, just off the well-trodden Alaska tourist circuit.

Almost the entire western two-thirds of the island is part of the Kodiak National Wildlife Refuge, a 1.87-million-acre area that belongs to bear, goat, deer, beavers, fox, eagles, 200 other bird species, whales, porpoise, seal, otter and salmon. The Refuge is reached by float plane or boat (Kodiak's road system ends about fifty miles outside of town). The Visitors Center (907-487-2600) is located four miles south of town on Buskin Beach Road (off Rezanof Drive). In summer, it's open 8 a.m.-4:30 p.m. on weekdays, and noon to 4:30 p.m. on Saturday and Sunday. Recreational activities include rafting, canoeing, camping, backpacking, hunting, fishing and wildlife photography. Bear viewing is among the most popular activities. Most of it's done by float plane (typically about $400 an hour). Among many established operators are Highline Air (907-486-5155), Sea Hawk Air (800-770-4295 or 907-486-8282) and Kodiak Air Service (907-486-4446). Among innumerable fishing lodges and day-trip operators are Kodiak Lodge (888-556-3425 or 907-847-2322) and Larsen Bay Lodge (800-748-2238 or 907-847-2238). Two interesting operators are Kodiak Treks (907-487-2122), which specializes in wildlife-photography excursions and Distant Loon (907-486-1789), which offers fishing and a private cabin in the rain forest for $100 a day (a deal on pricey Kodiak). The Kodiak Convention and Visitors Bureau (800-789-4782 or 907-486-4782) is helpful with literature and advice. Two days are recommended to see the war sites listed above, but one could spend weeks in Kodiak's rugged back country.

OTHER AREA ATTRACTIONS

Fishing/Hiking/Kayaking

Most visitors come to Unalaska for the extraordinary fishing—particularly the record-setting halibut and good salmon fishing. Charter fishing operations include Far West Outfitters (907-581-1647) and Shuregood Adventures (907-581-2378). Hiking across soft, open mountains or paddling through dramatic waterways offers a glimpse of a stunning part of Alaska few ever see. Aleutian Adventure Sports (888-581-4489 or 907-581-4489) leads hiking, biking and kayaking trips.

GETTING TO/AROUND THE ALEUTIANS

From Anchorage, Alaska Airlines (800-252-7522) operates flights twice daily to Unalaska and Kodiak. Both can also be reached by the Alaska Marine Highway System (800-642-0066 or 907-465-3941). The cruise takes about ten hours from Homer to Kodiak and about sixty hours from Kodiak to Unalaska. From Unalaska, PenAir (907-581-1383) operates charters ($775 per hour) to Ft. Glenn and other islands.

Unalaska has expensive taxis and no public transportation. A rental car is a must.

B.C. Vehicle Rental (907-581-6777) rents trucks (necessary for Bunker Hill, Mt. Ballyhoo and Overland Pass) for $85 a day. Cars from B.C. and North Port Rentals (907-581-3880) start at $40 a day. Both are located at the airport. Cars on Kodiak (a necessity) can be leased from Budget Car Rental (800-527-0700) and Rent-a-heap (907-486-8550).

Bobbie Lekanoff of The Extra Mile Tours (907-581-6171) leads Unalaska World War II tours that include Bunker Hill and Mt. Ballyhoo.

ACCOMMODATIONS

Unalaska/Dutch Harbor

Grand Aleutian Hotel

498 Salmon Way
T: 866-581-3844 or 907-581-3844
F: 907-581-7150
112 rooms
$160-$180

Unalaska's only business-class hotel is located on the site of the former Ft. Mears, about a mile from the airport and next to two shopping centers. The lobby, bar, restaurant and rooms are all first-rate.

Carl's Bayview Inn

606 Bayview
T: 800-581-1230 or 907-581-1230
F: 907-581-1880
35 rooms
From $100

In downtown Unalaska near the Russian Orthodox Church, Carl's is a clean modern hotel with a central location and good bar and restaurant. Suites have kitchens. The best deal in town.

Bunkhouse by the Sea

Gilman Road
T: 907-581-4357 F: 907-581-6247
20 rooms
$55

Located on the old Navy Operating Base, this cheap "bunkhouse" (with private rooms and bathrooms) caters to fishing-industry workers.

Kodiak

Best Western Kodiak Inn

236 Rezanof Dr. W.
T: 888-563-4254 or 907-486-5712
F: 907-486-3430
80 rooms
$139-$150 (summer); $89-$100 (winter)

One of Kodiak's two best hotels is located downtown and has a good restaurant and bar.

Buskin River Inn

1395 Airport Way
T: 800-544-2202 or 907-487-2700
F: 907-487-4447
50 rooms
$135-$170

Kodiak's business-class hotel is next to the small airport, about five miles south of town. It's flanked by the Buskin River and high green mountains.

Shelikof Lodge

211 Thursheim Ave.
T: 907-486-4141 F: 907-486-4116
38 rooms
$65-$75

Amenities include restaurant, bar, airport pickup, free local calls and cable TV. Central downtown location.

9

Okinawa

JAPAN

THE WAR YEARS

I n light of the atomic bombs that brought World War II to its rapid conclusion in August 1945, it's tempting to dismiss the Battle of Okinawa as yet another Pacific "meat grinder" that might have been avoided. It's important to remember, however, that when the battle was launched—Easter Sunday, April 1, 1945—the first successful nuclear explosion at the Alamogordo test site in New Mexico was still more than three months away. Thus, World War II's most costly (in terms of lives) battle was conceived as the final step in preparation for the dreaded autumn 1945 invasion of the Japanese home islands, just 375 miles from Okinawa.

With the exception of the march across the Philippine island of Luzon, Okinawa was to become the only major American land campaign of the Pacific War. Fought in villages and towns—the island's wartime population was roughly 500,000—as well as across mountain ridges and valleys, the assault on Okinawa was a backbreaking operation that foreshadowed the carnage that surely would have accompanied a conventional invasion of Japan.

The Japanese command pursued an in-depth defense of Okinawa. Troops positioned in the island's hilly interior allowed American forces to land unopposed on the western beaches near Kadena. The effortless landings were among the war's most pleasant surprises for U.S. soldiers, especially given the logistical nightmare that could easily have plagued the gargantuan landing force.

"Never before ... had there been an invasion armada the equal of the 1,600 seagoing ships carrying 545,000 American GIs and Marines that streamed across the Pacific," wrote historian Robert Leckie. "In firepower, troops, and tonnage it eclipsed even the more famous D day in Normandy."

Okinawa was a victory of logistics. The American armed force that Leckie called the "monster of consumption" had to be supplied 7,500 miles from the country's western shore. No amphibious operation in military history comes close to matching it on a scale of distance and enormity.

Even more miraculous, the soldiers remained supplied in the midst of massed kamikaze attacks, euphemistically known as *kikusui* or "floating chrysanthemum." Kamikaze attacks are regarded to have been largely insignificant in the wide scope of the war. Off the shores of Okinawa, however, missions launched against Allied naval assets—sometimes as many as 300 planes at a time—sank thirty-four ships, damaged 368 more and killed or injured thousands of sailors. Even the pride of the Japanese Navy, the super-battleship *Yamato*, was used as a kamikaze of sorts. With enough fuel for only a one-way mission, the ship was sent out to confront the American Navy. She was quickly swarmed by more than thirty planes and sunk with a crew of 2,500 off Tokuno Shima island.

On land, Okinawa quickly devolved into a sadistic killing ground. After taking control of the lightly defended central and northern sectors, Allied forces pushed south against Japanese entrenched in the cliffs and ridges running east-west across the island. On April 18, famed war correspondent Ernie Pyle was killed by a sniper during a relatively small action on nearby Ie Shima Island. Pyle had been taking part in his first-ever amphibious assault. Continuous rains began in May, turning the mountainsides and Okinawa's "excellent network of bad roads" (according to one American officer) into a quagmire of mud and decomposing bodies. Foxholes had constantly to be bailed out. Sleep was nearly impossible.

"We were surrounded by maggots and decay," wrote Marine veteran E.B. Sledge. "Men struggled and fought and bled in an environment so degrading I believed we had been flung into hell's own cesspool."

Absorbing the highest casualties they'd ever endured, Marine and Army forces closed in on Shuri Castle, the ancient command post that formed the Imperial Army's defensive spearhead. From here, through binoculars, the Japanese command had watched the American landings on April 1. The First Marines Division finally overran the castle, hoisting above it a Confederate flag in honor of Okinawa campaign commander Simon Bolivar Buckner, Jr., whose father had been a Confederate general. On June 18, Buckner was killed by shrapnel while observing the battlefield from Mezado Ridge.

The Japanese now withdrew to a final defensive line along the southern coast. With American troops barely 100 feet away, Army commanders Lieutenant-General Mitsuri Ushijima and Lieutenant-General Isamu Cho donned dress uniforms, sat on a white sheet on a ledge overlooking the sea and committed the ritual suicides befitting their samurai heritage. On June 22, the battle was officially declared over.

An estimated 100,000 Japanese soldiers were killed along with 80,000 civilians, thousands of whom committed suicide rather than be captured. In addition, the Empire lost about 7,830 aircraft and 180 ships during the battle. American casualties amounted to 12,520 killed (including 5,000 at sea, the worst losses suffered in any campaign in the history of the U.S. Navy) and 37,000 wounded. The United States lost 800 aircraft and thirty-six ships. All told, Okinawa was the bloodiest operation of the Pacific War.

By July, bombers operating out of Okinawa were pummeling the Japanese home islands. The island became a massive American base, the intended staging ground for the coming invasion of Japan that would soon be rendered needless. The accounting of the carnage on Okinawa played heavily in the decision to drop the atomic bombs just six weeks after the Battle of Okinawa had ended.

SOURCES & OTHER READING

Okinawa: The Last Battle of World War II, Leckie, Robert, Viking Penguin, 1995
The Battle for Okinawa, Yahara, Hiromichi, J. Wiley (reprint), 1995
With the Old Breed at Peleliu and Okinawa, Sledge, E.B., Presidio Press, 1981
Okinawa: The Last Battle, Appleman, Roy E. (and others), Historical Division, Department of the Army, 1948

Diamond Head, Oahu, page 7

Rock Islands, Palau, page 52

Ft. Abercrombie State Historical Park, Kodiak, page 74

Corsair, Anguar Island, Palau, page 51

Kranji Beach Battle Site, Singapore, page 22

Guadalcanal, page 109

Peace Memorial Park and A-bomb Dome, Hiroshima, page 40

Dulag, Leyte, Philippines, page 139

Wotje Island, Marshall Islands, page 94

Sherman tank, Oleai Beach, Saipan, page 32

Veteran, VFP Museum, Manila, page 173

LST 342, Tokoyo Bay, Solomon Islands, page 58

Heian Maru, Chuuk, page 165

Chuuk Photo: Kevin Davidson

Nanjing Massacre Memorial, page 192

Peace Memorial Park, Hiroshima, page 40

Ga'an Point, Guam, page 185

Diamond Passage, New Georgia Island, Solomon Islands, page 60

Nanjing Massacre Memorial, page 192

Emiej Island, page 210

B-24 wing, Majuro, Marshall Islands, page 92

Japanese dual-purpose gun, Munda, Solomon Islands, page 61

Peace Museum for Kamikaze Pilots, Chiran, Japan, page 131

Overland Pass Road, Unalaska/Dutch Harbor, page 73

Tonoas Island, Chuuk, page 163

Bataan, Philippines, page 200

Manila American Cemetery and Memorial, page 173

River Kwai Bridge, Kanchanaburi, Thailand, page 154

Bloody Ridge, Guadalcanal, page 115

Ft. Siloso, Singapore, page 25

Yasukuni Shrine, Tokyo, page 102

Beach at Klouklubed, Peleliu, page 48

Punchbowl, Oahu, page 5

Japanese torpedoes, Emiej Island, page 208

National War Dead Peace
Mausoleum, Okinawa, page 86

Suicide Cliff, Tinian, page 146

Corregidor, Philippines, page 14

Capitol Compound, Lingayen City, Philippines, page 175

Unalaska/Dutch Harbor, Aleutian Islands, page 67

Laura Beach, Majuro, Marshall Islands, page 92

East China Sea

Oku

Ie Shima

Okuma
Beach

Ie Shima
Ferry

Motobu

Pacific Ocean

Moon Beach

Okinawa

1

Okinawa
City

2

3

4

Kokusai-
dori

5

6

7

17

9

12-16

10   11

10 Kilometers

N

1. Invasion Beaches
2. Hacksaw Ridge
3. Battle of Okinawa Museum
4. Okinawa Prefectural Museum
5. Shuri Castle
6. Japanese Navy Underground
   Headquarters
7. Buckner Monument
8. Kyan Memorial
9. Himeyuri Monument/Museum
10. Konpaku no To
11. Kenji Monument
12. Peace Memorial Museum
13. Cornerstone of Peace
14. War Memorial to Koreans
15. Okinawa Peace Hall
16. Cemetery and National War
    Dead Peace Mausoleum
17. 44th Brigade Cave

OKINAWA TODAY

Population: 1.3 million • Country Code: 81 • Currency: $1 = 118 yen

With a unique and tumultuous history, this sixty-mile-long island (from two to eighteen miles wide) is still struggling to solve the fascinating puzzle of its identity. Its royal Ryukyu kingdom becoming the first victim of Japanese imperialism in the 1870s, the island remained under contentious American control from 1945 to 1972, when it was returned to Japan. Taking advantage of its southern latitude, the warm sunny island has since been recast as a domestic beachnik getaway for Japanese travelers. The American military has nevertheless retained a heavy presence—with about 50,000 soldiers and dependents, U.S. bases occupy about twenty percent of the island. Many native Okinawans have recently begun reasserting their cultural heritage vis-à-vis American and Japanese dominance of the island.

The result is a cultural mix cut into three geographic sections. The southern third of Okinawa includes the major Japanese city of Naha (population 300,000) and most of the points of interest. American bases, including the huge Kadena Air Base, are located in scenic central Okinawa, alongside the primary beach strip. Northern Okinawa is rural, rugged and lightly populated. Not counting the drab modern Japanese cities, the island of cedar trees and dramatic seaside vistas is striking in many places.

Activity is centered along Naha's International Street (Kokusai-dori), a busy mixture of small shops, modern malls, restaurants and bars that constitutes most of the island's nightlife. Limited local transportation (no trains or subways) and language barrier are drawbacks, but many of Okinawa's sites are first rate and its historical significance is unquestioned. Two days are recommended to see all the island's points of interest.

POINTS OF INTEREST

1. Invasion Beaches ★

Route 58, Central Okinawa

Though there's nothing of military nature left to see (other than a commemorative marker near Chatan-cho), the American invasion beaches run along a seven-mile stretch of public beach. Turn west off Route 58 and head for any beachfront between Bolo Point (running past Torii Station First Special Forces Camp and Kadena Air Base) to Camp Foster.

2. Hacksaw Ridge ★★★

The ridge runs across Central Okinawa roughly between the Hanby area on the western coast and Kita-Nakagusuku on the eastern coast. Traveling south on Route 58

from Kadena, turn left at the Garlic House restaurant (the wall is covered with pictures of garlic plants) and proceed to the top of the hill. Turn left again at the sign (in English) for Urasoe Castle and proceed to the top of the hill and the small Japanese military park at Hacksaw Ridge (also the site of Urasoe Castle).

Part of the forbidding Maeda Escarpment, Hacksaw Ridge was an important part of Japan's Shuri Defense Ring. On April 26, 1945, American troops launched a massive attack on the escarpment, suffering enormous casualties. The Japanese were so well dug into the slopes that at one nearby spot—Kakazu Ridge, now covered with buildings—2,500 Japanese held off three American divisions (more than 45,000 men) armed with tanks and flame throwers for ten days. The site includes Japanese caves, tunnels, small memorials and panoramic battle site views from which you can see the entire invasion beach and area of the first six weeks of American advance.

3. Battle of Okinawa Museum ★★★

Marine Corps Base Camp Kinser, Building 107, Urasoe City
Camp Kinser Main Gate off Highway 58
T: 098-936-0730 (Museum Director Dave Davenport; the Japanese voice on the answering machine instructs callers to leave a message at the tone)

This six-room exhibit includes a number of interesting battle artifacts—uniforms, weapons, a Japanese Medal of Honor found at Suicide Cliff, a flag that belonged to Vice-Admiral Minoru Ota who killed himself at the Navy Underground Headquarters—collected by the museum's director Dave Davenport and his Tunnel Rats group. In cave and mountain expeditions, the Tunnel Rats have over the years recovered the remains of more than 300 Japanese and two American soldiers. Non-military visitors must have an escort to enter the museum. Call Davenport at the number above to arrange an escort.

4. Okinawa Prefectural Museum ★

Onaka-cho, Shuri, Naha-shi
T: 098-884-2243
Daily, 9 a.m.-5 p.m. (last entry 4:30 p.m.)
Closed Monday, legal holidays (closed Tuesday if legal holiday falls on a Monday) and December 28-January 4
Adult: 210 yen
Student: 100 yen
Child (Jr. High and under): 50 yen

A five-minute walk north of Point 5, this small museum initially established by the U.S. military government is devoted almost entirely to Okinawan culture. A corner on the first floor has a very small

World War II display that includes a helmet, photos, map and a rare Axis alliance lapel pin showing the co-joined flags of Imperial Japan, Nazi Germany and fascist Italy.

5. Shuri Castle (Shuri-jo) ★★★

1-2 Kinjo-cho, Shuri, Naha-shi
T: 098-886-2020
Daily, 9 a.m.-6 p.m. (last entry 5:30 p.m.), March 1-November 30
Daily, 9 a.m.-5:30 p.m. (last entry 5 p.m.), December 1-February 28 or 29
Closed twice a year (three days each) for maintenance
Adult: 800 yen
Student: 600 yen
Child (Jr. High and under): 300 yen
Under six years: Free

Twenty-three national treasures were decimated during the Battle of Okinawa, this impressive Chinese-style fortress foremost among them. From 1429 to 1879 it served as the center of the maritime Ryukyu Kingdom. It's since been rebuilt to its original grandeur—heavy Taiwan Cypress beams, 57,900 roof tiles, lacquered red walls—and is the most popular tourist attraction in Okinawa. All displays and signage (in Japanese and English) pertain to the Ryukyu period. During the war, the castle was used as the Japanese command center. Though by then leveled, its capture by U.S. forces marked a turning point in the battle.

6. Japanese Navy Underground Headquarters ★★★★

236 Aza Tomishiro, Tomishiro-son
T: 098-850-4055
Daily, 8:30 a.m.-5 p.m.
Adult: 420 yen
Child (Jr. High and under): 210 yen

The self-guided tour begins with a descent into the dank tunnel system used as the Navy's command center during the Battle of Okinawa. Stops include the cipher, medical and commanding officer's rooms. The passageways are mostly barren (few relics) but pictures and broken English signage give a good account of the increasingly desperate end game played out within. In a small chamber with pockmarked walls hangs a typical sign: "Wall riddled with hand grenade when committed suicide." The lobby has a small museum with relics and photos. Outside is a hilltop view of southern Okinawa and a monument to Vice- Admiral Minoru Ota who killed himself here.

7. Buckner Monument ★

Maisato, Itoman-shi

A stone marker sits atop a small hill (accessed through a maze of unmarked farm roads—best to take a cab or ask locals for a lot of directions) at the spot where Okinawa campaign commander Lieutenant-General Simon Bolivar Buckner, Jr. was killed when shrapnel struck him in the chest, just three days before the island was declared secure. The man who directed the recovery of the Aleutian Islands from the Japanese became the second-highest ranking officer killed in action during the war. U.S. Army Brigadier-General Claudius Easley was killed on the same spot the day after Buckner.

8. Kyan Memorial (Kyan Misaki Enchi) ★★

Kyan, Itoman-shi

Just south of Point 7 and also difficult to find on unmarked back roads, this large blue monument with a black orb in the center overlooks dramatic ocean cliffs where many civilians jumped to their deaths to avoid capture.

9. Himeyuri Monument and Museum (Himeyuri no To) ★★★

Route 331 (4 kilometers west of Point 12), Aza-Ihara, Itoman-shi
T: 098-997-2100
Daily, 9 a.m.-5 p.m.

This popular attraction tells the story of one of the war's countless "small" tragedies largely unknown outside the local area. In March 1945, 222 high school girls and eighteen teachers were mobilized to work in a Japanese field hospital. Their duties included serving meals and disposing of amputated limbs, but they were left behind to be killed or commit suicide as the Japanese retreated south. "The Japanese military forbade surrender while it deserted defenseless girls in the midst of battle, regarding them as a hindrance," reads one sign. The excellent, sobering museum recounts the effects of the battle on civilians.

10. Konpaku no To ★★

Komesu, Itoman-shi
About 1 kilometer down a marked road (then a short trail) that turns off Route 331 about 0.2 kilometers south of Point 9

A number of elaborate stone monuments mark the area where at least 35,000 unidentified victims of the battle were buried.

11. Kenji Monument ★

About 1 kilometer down a marked road that turns south off Route 331 about 1 kilometer west of Point 12

The stone monuments and elevated statue of three high school boys is a sort of companion to the Himeyuri Monument. It commemorates local schoolboys killed during the war.

17. 44ᵗʰ Independent Mixed Brigade Cave ★★

Off Route 331, about 5 kilometers north of Point 12

In turning a hole in the mountain into a headquarters, the Japanese reinforced and extended this natural cave with a sizable tunnel system. There are no signs marking the route to the cave—the best way to go is with a guide (see Getting to/around Okinawa).

Peace Memorial Park

Route 331, southeastern end of Okinawa. All sites included below are located within the sprawling grounds of the park. The park collectively merits a ★★★★★ rating.

12. Peace Memorial Museum ★★★★

614-1, Aza-Mabuni, Itoman-shi
T: 098-997-3844
Daily, 9 a.m.-5 p.m.
(last entry 4:30 p.m.)
Closed Monday (open if Monday is a holiday) and December 29-January 3
Adult: 300 yen
Child: 150 yen

This huge two-story museum is filled with excellent displays chronicling the "typhoon of steel" that raged for ninety days, disfiguring mountains and killing about 200,000. Augmented by remarkable battle footage, a twenty-foot-long relief map connected to lights and video screens provides an extraordinary visual outline of the campaign. Graphic photos include a fly-covered corpse of a child who apparently had been shot in the head. Exhibits, life-size models, relics, and inventive presentations (in Japanese and English) are state of the art.

The politics are heavily tilted, outdistanced in the Pacific perhaps only by the Nanjing Massacre Memorial. As presented on interpretive signage, the 1930s economic crisis forces Japan "to send many emigrants to Manchuria" (overlooked is the fact that many of these "emigrants" were part of the notorious Kwantung Army). The rise of European fascism is noted, though Japan's alliance with Hitler and Mussolini is ignored. One tellingly incomplete though not exactly inaccurate sign reads, "Japanese Forces lost control over the rapidly spreading Pacific War that broke out on December 8, 1941." The museum is a major education center and destination of many school field trips.

The post-war American period in Okinawa is depicted in the forms of a replica of a lusty Yankee "hostess bar," documentation of the suppression of human rights by the U.S. military government, a large photo of U.S. troops repelling Okinawan protestors at gunpoint in 1957 and a display chronicling the 1995 gang rape of a local girl by American servicemen, and the 85,000 people who attended a subsequent rally calling for the removal of U.S. bases.

Located on the site of the final battle for the island, the museum's coverage of the Battle of Okinawa is thorough and unequaled. Politics aside, this is one of the Pacific's top war museums and the best attraction in Okinawa.

13. Cornerstone of Peace ★★★

Directly in front of Point 12

The area outside the museum is covered with hundreds of large black marble "cornerstones," upon which are inscribed the names of all who died in the battle, regardless of nationality.

14. War Memorial to Koreans ★★

Outside, directly behind Point 12

Made up of thousands of small black stones, this large monument in the shape of a turtle shell recalls the death and hardships suffered by conscripted Korean soldiers and laborers.

15. Okinawa Peace Hall ★★

150 yards behind Point 12, 448-2 Mabuni, Itoman-shi
T: 098-997-3011
Daily, 9 a.m.-5:30 p.m.,
April 1-October 15
Daily, 9 a.m.-5 p.m.,
October 16-March 31

Adult: 500 yen
Student: 350 yen
Child: 250 yen

This white tower houses a spectacular forty-foot-high praying Buddha covered with 3.5 tons of lacquer. There's also a collection of sacred stones from various countries, twenty "War to Peace" paintings, an art museum, Peace Bell, Peace Monument and small meditation forest.

16. Cemetery and National War Dead Peace Mausoleum (Mabuni no Oka) ★★★

Along a marked path (almost a mile long) southeast of Point 12

Stone monuments from every prefecture in Japan dot the walk along Memorial Path through landscaped gardens. Thousands of Japanese soldiers died on this hill, which overlooks the dramatic cliffs and roiling surf. The scenic uphill walk to the observation deck takes twenty to thirty minutes.

RELATED SITES BEYOND OKINAWA

Ie Shima Island ★★

Ferries from Motobu Port (on Okinawa's northwest coast along Route 449) to Ie Shima depart four times a day (five times daily in summer)
T: 098-49-2255 (Ie Mura Public Office)
Round trip: 1,100 yen

On April 16, 1945, American forces invaded Ie Shima island, a few miles off Okinawa's western shore. Ie Shima was secured within days, but not before beloved war correspondent Ernie Pyle—taking part in his first amphibious assault—was killed by sniper fire on April 18. A few minutes walk south of the main pier is a monument to Pyle. Visitors can walk forty-five minutes to the top of Mt. Gusuku for wide views of the entire area.

OTHER AREA ATTRACTIONS

Beaches

Most of the pristine beaches featured in Okinawa tourist brochures are actually on the many nearby islands, such as gorgeous Tokashiki and Kumejima Islands—both are surrounded by clear, aqua water. The islands are serviced daily by ferries.

The Okinawa Convention and Visitors Bureau (098-862-3061) has schedules and information in English. On Okinawa, Route 58 runs along the western shore past tourist areas such as Moon Beach (decent) and Turtle Beach (better).

GETTING TO/AROUND OKINAWA

Okinawa is served daily from many cities in Japan by domestic airlines including Japan Airlines (800-525-3663) and All Nippon Airways (800-235-9262). Direct flights are also available from Hong Kong, Shanghai, Seoul and other Asian cities on a number of airlines.

With attractions spread far apart and no train or subway, a rental car is a necessity (buses and taxis are plentiful; the first are slow, the second expensive). Avis (800-331-1084), Budget Rent A Car (800-472-3325) and Mitsubishi Rent A Car (098-867-3234) are three of many choices.

Dave Davenport (098-936-0730; the Japanese voice on the answering machine instructs callers to leave a message at the tone) is a retired Air Force officer and leading local authority on World War II sites. His eight-hour Battle of Okinawa Tour ($90) is booked through Schilling Tours (098-938-1111, then 634-4322 at the dial tone) and includes Hacksaw Ridge, Battle of Okinawa Museum at Camp Kinser, lunch at Naha Port, Japanese Navy Underground Headquarters, Suicide Cliff and Peace Memorial Park. Davenport also leads customized tours and Tunnel Rat tours through a number of Okinawa's thousands of deep caves used by the Japanese. With limited public transportation and mostly Japanese road signs on Okinawa, Davenport is a valuable asset for visitors.

Accommodations

Busena Terrace

1808 Kise, Nago City (off Route 58)
T: 098-51-1333 F: 098-51-1331
401 rooms, 18 cottages
33,000 to 51,000 yen

The question of where to stay boils down to beaches of the central coast (pretty, but an hour or more from most historic sites) or Naha City (not scenic but nearer to restaurants, shops and nightlife). On one of the better beaches, the Busena Terrace—seven restaurants, two pools, tennis, golf—is the island's top resort. Its sister hotel, Naha Terrace (2-14-1 Omoromachi, Naha City; 098-864-1111), is 1.5 kilometers from the central Kokusai-dori.

Okinawa Oceanview Hotel

1-5 Kume, 2-chome, Naha City
T: 098-853-2112 F: 098-862-6112
207 rooms
12,000 to 26,000 yen

It's miles from any decent beach, but the Oceanview is within walking distance of the Kokusai-dori entertainment strip. Large rooms for a Japanese hotel.

Hotel Yagi

1-16-10 Izumizaki
T: 098-862-3008 F: 098-862-3028
22 rooms
4,800 to 9,000 yen

This small, serviceable hotel doesn't take credit cards, but the staff is friendly, the small rooms are comfortable and the prices are low. Watanji, a great Okinawan-style pub/restaurant, is across the street.

Marshall Islands

THE WAR YEARS

To the casual observer, the Marshall Islands might appear to represent simply another obscure stepping stone in the inexorable American advance across the Pacific. For the U.S. military, however, Operation Flintlock was far from being a settled matter. It would ultimately prove that costly lessons learned at Tarawa only a few months before had been absorbed and that amphibious assaults could be executed with a minimum of casualties. It also would provide an early demonstration of a lesson soon to be accepted as irrefutable—the aircraft carrier had replaced the battleship as the world's dominant seaborne weapon.

Taking military possession of the Marshall Islands from Germany at the outbreak of World War I (Japan was awarded Micronesia by a League of Nations mandate following the war), Japan spent the years leading to World War II developing and fortifying primary atolls and islands of Majuro, Wotje, Maloelap, Jaluit, Kwajalein, and later Mili and Eniwetak. Mili Atoll briefly gained fame as one of many places Amelia Earhart was supposedly shot down by the Japanese in 1937. Because the Japanese were so guarded about their Micronesia activities between the two world wars, speculation ran rampant that Earhart's 1937 attempt to fly around the world at the equator was merely the cover for a spying mission backed by the American government.

Either way, by early 1944, the Marshall Islands stood at the easternmost perimeter of Japan's ring of defense in the Central Pacific. They guarded all westbound sea routes to Tokyo. But in the islands, Allied war planners saw mostly airfields that, if taken, could put the monster Japanese air-sea base of Truk within air range.

Amid great controversy within the U.S. command, Admiral Chester Nimitz forced the selection of the relatively obscure island of Kwajalein as the point of main attack on the Marshalls. His plan meant to achieve two goals—bypass the majority of Japan's Marshall Islands forces massed on other islands, and surprise the Jaluit Atoll-based Japanese command, which fully expected the amphibious invasion to fall upon its more important bases.

Before assault troops landed on Kwajalein and the neighboring islands of Roi and Namur, an unprecedented 15,000 tons of bombardment plastered the islands for two months. Commanded by the irascible Marine Major-General Holland "Howlin' Mad" Smith and backed by 297 ships, the first wave of troops (including an eighteen-year-old Marine named Lee Marvin), hit the beaches of Roi and Namur on January 31 and Kwajalein on February 1. Simultaneously, U.S. forces occupied Majuro, since abandoned by the Japanese. Majuro thus earned the distinction of becoming the first American conquest of a piece of Japan's colonial empire, meaning a territory formally held by Japan before 1931.

Unlike the disaster at Tarawa, the "attack on Kwajalein was a model amphibious operation in which there were no hitches," according to the West Point Military Academy's *The Second World War: Asia and the Pacific*. Almost 50,000 invaders were matched against 5,000 defenders. On the first day, resistance was comparatively light. Americans poured onto the beaches, but resistance stiffened and combat turned gruesome as fighting moved inland and enemy lines blurred. Concrete blockhouses and pillboxes—sturdy enough to survive the pre-invasion bombardment—had to be dealt with point by point. The stench of burning bodies soon overwhelmed combatants on both sides. The Japanese fought with suicidal zeal, but they were simply outnumbered. By the time Kwajalein was secured on February 4, 4,938 Imperial troops had been killed compared to 142 Americans (some sources claim fatality numbers as high as 8,000 Japanese and 350 Americans).

"The enemy had ripped the heart out of the Japanese defenses in the Marshall Islands," wrote Mark Peattie in *Nanyo: The Rise and Fall of the Japanese in Micronesia, 1885-1945.* "(It was) a setback so severe that the Japanese high command in Tokyo decided to keep it a secret from the public."

With their air forces crushed, now neutralized strongholds of Jaluit, Wotje, Mili and Maloelap would remain in Japanese hands until the end of the war, isolated and, in the argot of Pacific War historians, "left to wither on the vine."

Isolated from supplies, many Japanese and Marshallese starved. Those who survived did so by foraging, fishing and gardening. As conditions worsened Japanese abuse of the locals—not common before the war—became extreme. Tortures and beheadings destroyed whatever goodwill the Japanese had managed to build during colonial times. In stealthy U.S. nighttime operations using rubber boats, many islanders were rescued from Japanese-held islands, depriving the Japanese of an important labor supply and providing the Americans with valuable intelligence.

The Japanese garrison on Wotje learned of the end of the war via an Australian radio broadcast. In Jaluit, an American B-24 dropped a copy of the surrender document issued by the high command in Tokyo. Thoroughly emaciated and shell-shocked, no Japanese unit defied the surrender order, though some officers opted for suicide over surrender. On August 22, 1945, the Mili garrison became the first Japanese Pacific command to capitulate, eleven days before the formal surrender in Tokyo Bay on September 2.

SOURCES & OTHER READING

The Archaeology of World War II in the Marshall Islands, Christiansen, Henrik, RMI Historic Preservation Office, 1994.

Storm Landings: Epic Amphibious Battles in the Central Pacific, Alexander, Joseph H., Naval Institute Press, 1997

Nanyo: The Rise and Fall of the Japanese in Micronesia, 1885-1945, Peattie, Mark R., University of Hawaii Press, 1988

Island Victory: The Battle of Kwajalein Atoll, Marshall, S. L. A., Infantry Journal, 1945

The Pineapple Air Force: Pearl Harbor to Tokyo, Lambert, John W., Phalanx Publishing, 1990

Breaking the Outer Ring: Marine Landings in the Marshall Islands, Marine Corps Historical Center, 1994

The Reluctant Raiders: The Story of the United States Navy Bombing Squadron VB/VPB-109 in World War II, Carey, Alan C., Schiffer Publishing Company, 1999

For the Good of Mankind: A History of the People of Bikini and their Islands, Niedenthal, Jack, Bravo Publishers, 2001

Marshall Islands

Bikini

Kwajalein

Wotje

Maloelap

Majuro

Pacific Ocean

Jaluit

Mili

Emiej Island

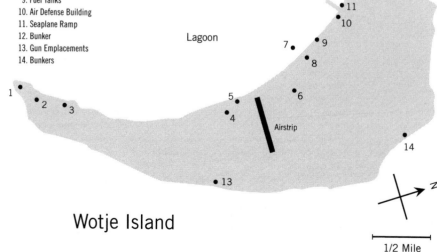

1. *Goyotsu Maru* marker
2. Communications Building
3. Dual-purpose Guns
4. Power Plant
5. Oil Tank
6. Kate Prop
7. Japanese Dock
8. *Goyotsu Maru* Deck Gun
9. Fuel Tanks
10. Air Defense Building
11. Seaplane Ramp
12. Bunker
13. Gun Emplacements
14. Bunkers

Lagoon

Airstrip

Wotje Island

1/2 Mile

MARSHALL ISLANDS TODAY

Population: 60,000 • Country Code: 692 • Currency: U.S. dollar

There are signs that point to the Marshalls as an emerging travel destination. Perfectly clear waters hover around eighty-one degrees all year, the stars in the dead of the Pacific shine impossibly bright, little-visited wartime relics litter the jungles and surrounding sea floor. Visiting atolls and islands such as Emiej, Mili, Wotje and Maloelap is like visiting the unexplored Stone Age of World War II. Debris and intact relics are easy to find.

Through the 1986 Compact of Free Association, the Republic of the Marshall Islands (RMI) changed its status from U.S. Trust Territory to self-governing democracy affiliated with the United States. The U.S. dollar is the official currency, English is spoken and many customs and laws are the same.

There are obstacles. Made up of five main islands and twenty-nine coral atolls (containing a total of 1,225 islands and 870 reef systems), the RMI's mere seventy square miles of pancake-flat land are spread across 75,000 square miles of ocean. Infrastructure is poor. There are only two cities of any significance (the capital of Majuro and the U.S. military base on Kwajalein), neither of which possess a wealth of relics. Tourism is in its infancy, meaning flights between islands are limited. Majuro and Kwajalein excepted, accommodations are largely substandard. Logistically, the RMI can be daunting to visit, a country with primarily backpacker-level tourist services and mainland U.S. prices.

Thus the tradeoff of the Marshalls—a high investment of time and money for a high return of unique sites amid remote tropical beauty. If flights are coordinated properly (see Getting to/around the Marshall Islands), one or two atolls and islands can be visited in a few days. To see the rest of the country, one to two weeks is recommended.

POINTS OF INTEREST

Because the sprawling RMI has a thousand or more identified World War II sites, this chapter deviates from form. Below is an overview of the atolls and islands with the most to offer in terms of sites and relics. For additional information regarding outer-island excursions ("outer islands" usually meaning anywhere beyond the main entry port of Majuro), see Getting to/around the Marshall Islands. For the best RMI destination, see the chapter on Emiej Island.

Majuro ★★ ◥

The center of Marshallese government, culture and population is the starting point for nearly all trips to the RMI. There are only a few wartime points of interest on the island, but the well-preserved wing of a B-24 (with four engines and three props still attached) at a depth of two or three feet provides a unique snorkel experience. The wing was part of the "Baby Sandy 2," shot down by Japanese Zeroes after a bombing raid on Maloelap on December 28, 1943. The wing is about two miles offshore from Laura Beach, so a boat ride out is necessary. Nearby is a large shallow reef teeming with marine life, making this a highly worthwhile snorkel trip. Majuro's offshore dive sites include a TBF/TBM Avenger aircraft, an F6F Hellcat and the Parking Lot, where departing U.S. forces dumped a pile of equipment and vehicles (mostly trucks and jeeps) into the sea rather than sell them cheap to the Marshallese.

Majuro's limited land-based war sites include a Peace Park donated by Japan, about three miles from the airport along the main road toward Laura Beach. The Alele Museum and Library (Monday-Friday, 9 a.m.-noon, 1-4 p.m.; 625-3372) has two or three interesting photos from the war—the Murderer's Row lineup of five aircraft carriers anchored in Majuro Lagoon is impressive—but is otherwise uninteresting. The library does have writings and reports by Matt Holly and Henrik Christiansen cataloguing World War II sites throughout the Marshalls. Christiansen's multivolume series *The Archaeology of World War II in the Marshall Islands* is especially helpful for serious jungle-stompers.

Kwajalein/Roi-Namur ★ ★ ★ ◤

Leased by the United States from the RMI, Kwajalein Island is used as a missile test site officially known as the U.S. Army Kwajalein Atoll Reagan Test Site. Operated mostly by American civilians who live permanently on the island, the site performs a number of functions, including firing missiles that intercept other missiles launched from as far away as Vandenburg Air Force Base in California.

Visits to Kwajalein are officially prohibited. However, requests for access and information can be mailed to the U.S. Army Space and Missile Defense Command Public Affairs Office, P.O. Box 1500, Huntsville, AL 35807-3801 (256-955-2171). Preference may be given to U.S. military veterans, families and groups with a specific reason to visit.

Essentially an American military town, little of Kwajalein looks as it did during the war. There is, however, a guided or self-guided World War II Battlefield Tour that's been designated as a National Historic Landmark. The ten stops on the tour include a Japanese air-raid shelter; site of the first day's fighting; Japanese Memorial; landing beaches with Japanese pillbox; first night battle site; Japanese ammunition bunker; Japanese concrete rifle pit; third day fighting and admiralty site; Island Memorial Chapel; command buildings; and Bunker Hill, where terrible fighting took place on the final day of battle.

Roi-Namur is accessible only via U.S. Army flights originating from Kwajalein. Its seventeen-stop Battlefield Tour (also encompassing a National Historic Site) is more interesting than Kwajalein's. Sites include landing beaches, Japanese cemetery, Japanese five-inch guns and fortifications including air headquarters and the line of Marine advance.

There are many good wreck dives in Kwajalein Lagoon, all accessible to the general public. A Kawanishi Mavis seaplane rests in several sections at fifty-five to seventy-five feet, but the prize is the *Prinz Eugen*, a 654-foot-long World War II German heavy cruiser that's been called one of the best wreck dives in the world. The ship was brought to Bikini Atoll for tests after the war and later towed to Kwajalein and sunk. The rudder and propeller are now visible above the waterline. The bow rests in 110 feet of water. The ship is located in the lagoon waters off Kwajalein near Ennubuj Island. For dive trips, see Getting to/around the Marshall Islands.

The adjacent island of Ebeye is used as a base for divers interested in the wrecks of Kwajalein Lagoon. Known as the "slum of the Pacific" for its densely populated squalor in the shadow of shiny "Kwaj," Ebeye is a small depressing bedroom island of 12,000 Marshallese mostly employed or otherwise dependent on the American facility across the water. The contrast in living standard between the two islands is the subject of occasional media scrutiny and a point of embarrassment for both sides. Still, it's the only place to stay near Kwajalein.

Mili Island ★★★ ◤

There are a number of Japanese aircraft on Mili in various stages of decomposition. One of the best is a Zero fighter sitting upright on its struts (very rare) about 250 yards into the jungle off a trail that runs south, and then forks right, below the west end of the main runway. Broken in half at the fuselage, its cockpit canopy and front end remain intact. It's covered with bright green moss. Mili trails are tricky to find and follow without assistance. Other sites include a completely destroyed hangar with extremely mangled remains of a Val dive-bomber and another Zero visible through the twisted debris. Wreckage of a Betty bomber and two P-39s (one in reasonably decent shape) are also in the jungle and, again, tough to locate. Dive sites include a B-25 bomber.

Taroa Island, Maloelap Atoll ★★★ ◤

The most primitive and least visited of the Marshall's primary atolls is also a place in the Pacific with good potential for new discoveries. Taroa Island includes a Japanese aircraft boneyard with parts of numerous Zeroes and a few Bettys, large concrete structures, vehicles, air-raid shelters, bunkers, pillboxes, coastal guns and small debris. Taroa's total area is less than a square mile, so sites are fairly compact. Dive sites include the freighter *Torishima Maru*, whose two main cargo masts stick out of the water about 200-300 yards offshore.

Bikini Atoll (for divers only) ★★★★★ ◤

Following World War II, the U.S. government brought 242 ships to Bikini—including many obsolete American, Japanese and German warships—to use in atomic and hydrogen bomb tests conducted at the atoll. Opened for recre-

ational diving in 1996, Bikini's "nuclear fleet" contains "no radiological risk" (according to a 1996 International Atomic Energy Agency report) and rests at a challenging depth of 170-190 feet. Wrecks include the 880-foot-long U.S.S. *Saratoga*, the world's only diveable aircraft carrier. One of the world's best wreck dives, the *Saratoga* is legendary among divers—numerous dives are needed to see all of it. Admiral Isoroku Yamamoto's Pearl Harbor command ship, the *Nagato*, is here, along with the U.S.S. *Apogon* submarine, which saw action in the Marshalls.

Wotje Island ★★★★

Flights to Wotje land on the old Japanese airfield. The large upright prop in front of the makeshift terminal is from a Kawanishi Emily flying boat, only 167 of which were built. The huge concrete pad here is from an old Japanese hangar. From the airfield, a wide easy-to-follow path parallels the approximately three-mile-long lagoon coast. With the exception of (Point 13) some large gun emplacements (★★) and (Point 14) bunkers (★★), most of Wotje's sites are placed along the scenic lagoon. A good way to get around is to rent a bike from locals or catch a ride on one of the island's few vehicles to one end of the lagoon and walk up the path. There's no formal service for bike loans or car rides, but the locals meeting planes are generally willing to do either for $10 or so.

1. *Goyotusu Maru* Marker ★★

On the southern end of the lagoon are a pair of tough-to-find (off the trail in thick brush) Japanese bereavement markers commemorating the sailors who died on the *Goyotsu Maru* cargo ship, destroyed by U.S. Navy fire on February 1, 1942. The stone markers are about five-feet tall but only just visible through the overgrowth about forty yards off the side of the road. The ship is still beached on the shore of Kimejo Island about six miles away.

2. Communications Building ★★

A few hundred yards north up the path is the former communications building. In addition to sustaining heavy bomb damage, it's being taken over by aggressive jungle.

3. Dual-purpose Guns ★★★

Two Japanese 127mm dual-purpose guns—used for firing at naval and sea assets—are still mounted on their turrets and facing out to sea. Both are in good shape. The ruins of a fire-control building are between the guns.

4. Power Plant ★★★

In the central area of the lagoon shore is a large bombed-out Japanese power plant. The building is collapsing—the brilliant coral-plaster columns leaning—but massive engines, generators, pistons and connecting rods inside are easy to access. Behind the main building are oil and water storage buildings. Six-inch-thick iron blast shutters still hang on the windows.

5. Oil Tank ★★

Just north of the power plant, a large oil tank with a perfectly placed bomb hole in the side and a tree growing through the middle makes for an interesting photograph.

6. Kate Prop ★★

Off the beach a couple hundred yards are the remains of an unusual four-bladed propeller from a Nakajima Kate bomber. But for one version, Kate propellers had three blades. Small aircraft debris is scattered in the general area.

7. Japanese Dock ★

The crane that was once at the end of this dock is now wreckage in the water alongside it. The dock itself is not spectacular, but it reaches about 200 yards into the lagoon, providing a picturesque view of the beautiful blue lagoon.

8. *Goyotsu Maru* Deck Gun ★

Across from the entrance to the dock, a gun from the ill-fated *Goyotsu Maru* is mounted, oddly enough, next to a church.

9. Fuel Tanks ★★

Three mammoth Japanese fuel tanks sit in the brush along the beach, about halfway between the Japanese dock and seaplane ramp.

10. Air Defense Building ★★

Near the seaplane ramp, this camouflage-painted building sustained heavy bomb damage.

11. Seaplane Ramp ★

Used now by fishermen, the ramp is a reminder that Wotje was once an important Japanese seaplane base. Off the ramp are the concrete ruins of an anti-aircraft gun platform.

12. Bunker ★★★

At the northern tip of the island is a German-style concrete bunker overlooking one of the prettiest beaches in the Marshalls. This is also one of the more interesting bunkers in the Pacific. Concrete baffles between firing ports subdivide the large circular housing. In the center is a self-contained concrete box—a bunker within a bunker, most often used for ammo storage. Machine gun mounts are still attached to the walls beneath firing slits.

OTHER AREA ATTRACTIONS

Diving and Fishing ◣

With only 1,800 tourist visits per year, the tropical RMI is one of the least exploited water-sports destinations in the world. The country counts more than 1,000 species of fish, 800 reef systems and a typical water visibility of 100-plus feet. Abundant trophy fish include yellowfin tuna, wahoo, bonefish and Pacific blue marlin (a 719-pounder won a 2001 tournament here). Wind and sea conditions are pleasant all year, but the most favorable fishing season is May-October.

For diving contact Marshalls Dive Adventures (625-3483; marshall@nta-mar.com) or Bako Divers (at the Outrigger Hotel in Majuro; 247-7254; jerryr@nta-mar.com).

Numerous charter fishing vessels of all sizes are available. Call MIVA (Marshall Islands Visitors Authority) at 625-6482 for booking information.

GETTING TO/AROUND MARSHALL ISLANDS

Continental Micronesia (800-231-0856) operates nonstop flights between Honolulu and Majuro several times a week. The flight takes about four hours. After stopping in Majuro, the same flight continues on to Kwajalein, Kosrae, Pohnpei, Chuuk and Guam. Kwajalein visitors staying in Ebeye fly into Kwajalein then take a short boat ride to the island.

Majuro is a strip of an island, about thirty miles long and, in most places, narrow enough to throw a rock from one coast to the other. A two-lane road runs from one end of the island at Laura Beach (named by U.S. troops after Lauren Bacall and mispronounced by locals) to the other end at Rita (named for Rita Hayworth). Most of the population is collected at Rita. Rental cars are available for about $40 a day from RRE Hotel Car Rental (625-5131), VIP Auto Rentals Executive (625-6669), Cari's Scoot Cars (625-3064) and a number of other agencies. Taxis are plentiful. All rides are shared—meaning your taxi may pull over to pick up another rider—and typically cost between fifty cents and $1.50 to anywhere around the main population center, making rental cars mostly unnecessary.

Air Marshall Islands (625-3733) flies small commuter planes from Majuro to the outer islands. Additional help with excursions to the outer islands can be provided by MIVA (625-6482). Marshall Islands Aquatics (625-3669; aquamar@ntamar.com) is operated by Matt Holly, the preeminent local World War II authority. A dive instructor, he leads excellent dive or land-based trips around the islands. Other good guide services include Wildfire Charters (692-7112; ccctim@hotmail.com) and Marshall Dive Adventures (625-3483; mmarshall@ntamar.com). Weeklong dive tours on Bikini Atoll's nuclear fleet are operated by Bikini Atoll Resort (626-3177; saratoga@ntamar.com).

ACCOMMODATIONS

Majuro

Outrigger Marshall Islands Resort
Main Road, Majuro
T: 625-2525 F: 625-2555
150 rooms
$125-$235

By far Majuro's best hotel, all rooms over-look the picturesque lagoon. The hotel also has internet service, a salt-water pool, good bar and restaurant.

Golden Hotel

Main Road, Majuro
T: 625-8388 F: 625-4759
20 rooms
$55

This beachfront hotel isn't luxurious, but it has air-conditioning, restaurant, bar, and the rooms have refrigerators.

Flame Tree Backpacker's Hostel

Main Road, Majuro
T: 625-4229 F: 625-3136
13 rooms
$25

The cheapest place in town has one of the island's better restaurant/bars upstairs.

Kwajalein

Anrohasa Hotel
Ebeye Island
T: 329-3161 F: 329-3248
22 rooms
$93-$156

Virtually all nonofficial visitors to restricted Kwajalein must stay on nearby Ebeye Island. The Anrohasa has seen better days, but it's as good as it gets here.

Mili Atoll

Primitive thatch guest houses (no electricity or running water) on Mili Island can be reserved through MIVA (625-6482). On Mili Atoll's Wau Island, Wau Cottages (625-3250) operates nine primitive beach cottages on an island noted for clam farming.

Bikini Atoll

Bikini Atoll Resort
Office in Majuro
T: 625-3177 F: 625-3330
3 four-plexes

Price based on customized dive packages.

11

Tokyo

JAPAN

THE WAR YEARS

Entering the war with an Emperor's guarantee and a 2,000-plus-year winning streak, Tokyo residents had reason to feel optimistic and secure in 1941. With one erratic exception, Japan's political and military hub remained unscathed until late 1944—its ten million residents anticipating inevitable victory long after the Empire's fortunes had irreparably turned throughout the Pacific. Through most of the war, the cataclysmic fate awaiting Tokyo in the final months was as inconceivable as surrender.

Tokyo took its first hit four months into the war. While Japanese forces rolled unstoppably through the Pacific, Lieutenant-Colonel James "Jimmy" Doolittle led a rogue U.S. air strike over the home islands on April 18, 1942, that caught the capital by surprise. The Doolittle Raid was the war's mission impossible—the brainchild of a short, unassuming man in his mid-forties who was also the most gifted American aviator of his time. A fleet of sixteen B-25 bombers headed by Doolittle was launched off the aircraft carrier *Hornet*, 650 miles east of Honshu, Japan's largest island. Most of the bombs were dropped on Tokyo factories and docks before the dauntless "Tokyo Raiders" continued toward China. Low on fuel, every B-25 was lost in the raid—fifteen crash-landed in or off the coast of China. Three men died during bailouts or crashes, one wayward plane and its crew were impounded in the Soviet Union and another eight men were captured by Japanese forces in China. Three of these men were later executed, one died in a Japanese prison. All the others, including Doolittle, survived.

"Either I would be court-martialed or the military powers that be would see to it that I would sit out the war flying a desk," was Doolittle's post-raid comment. He was welcomed home a legend, awarded the Medal of Honor and promoted to brigadier-general. Hailed the most audacious air strike in American military history, Doolittle's raid barely scratched Tokyo. But it provided a desperately needed U.S. morale boost after a succession of early-war defeats.

When America's air assault on the home islands resumed with a vengeance in the fall of 1944, Tokyo was in an incomparably precarious position. The U.S. now occupied the nearby Mariana Islands and was armed with a lethal new instrument of mass destruction—the B-29 Superfortress, a longer range aircraft that carried up to ten tons of bombs.

The first B-29 fleet left Saipan on November 24, 1944, completing a "precision" strike on the Nakajima aircraft factory in the outskirts of Tokyo that mainly missed the mark. Subsequent daylight raids above the capital's cloudy, turbulent skies proved equally disappointing. The city's vast cottage industry of small war factories woven into dense residential areas eluded them entirely.

Arriving in Saipan in early 1945 to take over the 21st Bomber Command and the 20th Air Force, Curtis E. LeMay devised a devastating new strategy. An autocratic thirty-nine-year-old major-general called "iron ass" behind his back, LeMay was a student of British low-flying, night-time incendiary raids in Europe. Fire, he believed, would quickly drive Japan's largely wooden capital city to its knees.

LeMay's bombers hit Tokyo with its first napalm "test" raid on February 23, 1945—a 172-plane mission that incinerated one square mile of the city. It was by far the most destructive raid on Japan yet. LeMay earned his title, "the Executioner of Tokyo," on May 9 and 10, when more than 300 B-29s firebombed a four-square-mile zone populated by about half-a-million civilians. The resulting inferno rapidly consumed fifteen square miles of central Tokyo, boiled rivers, melted windows, turned the sky a blazing red, cremated a quarter of the city's buildings, officially killed 83,000 people (probably far more), injured more than 100,000 and left a million homeless. Tokyo's March firebombing took an unimaginable toll on civilian life that, most historians agree, exceeded even Hiroshima.

Equally numbing was the Japanese government's myopic reaction to the incineration of its capital. While Tokyo burned, Imperial General Headquarters responded by calling up the last of Japan's doomed reserves to meet an expected U.S. ground invasion of the home islands. The invasion, of course, never happened and the burning of Tokyo has largely been relegated to the war's back pages, even in Japan.

As a result of mass evacuations, Tokyo's 1945 population had dwindled to about 3.5 million, half of its 1940 level. On September 2, Tokyo Bay became the site of Japan's official capitulation to the Allies in a ceremony aboard the U.S.S. *Missouri* presided over by General Douglas MacArthur. Following the tense ceremony, the Japanese were piped off the ship with salutes, signifying that they were no longer enemies.

Contrary to widespread fears, the Japanese were cooperative in defeat. Invigorated by his new title of SCAP (Supreme Commander of Allied Powers), MacArthur set up headquarters in the Dai-Ichi Building—referred to as The Big Number One—directly across from Emperor Hirohito's Imperial palace. From here MacArthur spearheaded a revolutionary occupation of Japan that included a new constitution and thoroughly reformed social and economic systems. The Allied occupation of Japan lasted until 1952.

SOURCES & OTHER READING

Eagle Against the Sun: The American War With Japan, Spector, Ronald H., Free Press, 1984

Flames over Tokyo: The U.S. Army Air Forces' Incendiary Campaign Against Japan, 1944-1945, Kerr, Bartlett E., Donald I. Fine, 1991

Blankets of Fire: U.S. Bombers Over Japan During World War II, Werrell, Kenneth P., Smithsonian Institute Press, 1998

Iron Eagle: The Turbulent Life of General Curtis LeMay, Coffey, Thomas M., Avon, 1988

The Doolittle Raid: America's Daring First Strike Against Japan, Glines, Caroll V., Orion Books, 1988

No Surrender: My Thirty Year War, Onoda, Hiroo, Kodansha International, 1974

Thirty Seconds Over Tokyo, Lawson, Ted, W., Random House, 1943

American Caesar: Douglas MacArthur 1880-1964, Manchester, William, Little, Brown and Company, 1978

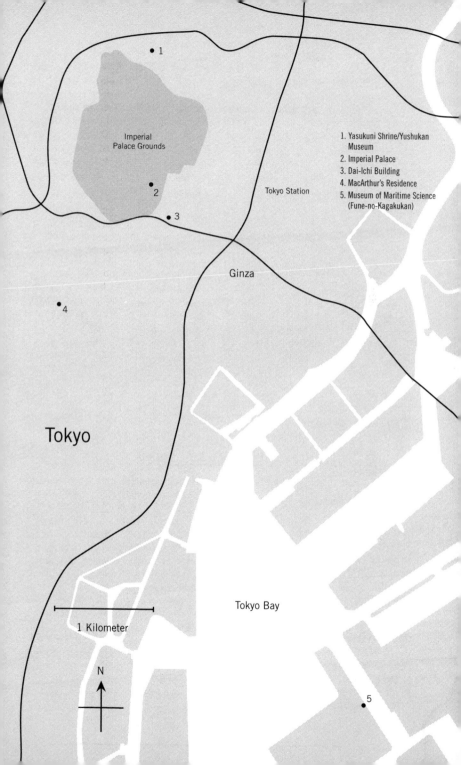

1. Yasukuni Shrine/Yushukan Museum
2. Imperial Palace
3. Dai-Ichi Building
4. MacArthur's Residence
5. Museum of Maritime Science (Fune-no-Kagakukan)

Imperial Palace Grounds

Tokyo Station

Ginza

Tokyo

Tokyo Bay

1 Kilometer

N

TOKYO TODAY

Population: 8.9 million • Country Code: 81 • Currency: $1=118 yen

Literally and figuratively one of the most electric cities in the world, Japan's capital city is still the undisputed champ of eating, drinking and nightlife in Asia. From five-star French restaurants to greasy ramen shops, tea ceremony on tatami to 2 a.m. beers out of vending machines, Tokyo's never-say-sleep ethic assaults the newcomer with visceral sensations (not all pleasant) that come and go faster than the packed commuter trains rolling through Tokyo Station.

With no recognizable skyline or single downtown area, the city is often disorienting, even for return travelers. Spreading across the Kanto Plain from Tokyo Bay, Tokyo is actually a collection of twenty-three wards *(ku)* and twenty-seven cities *(shi)*. Even with its super-efficient subway system, getting around can eat large chunks of time. Most streets aren't marked. Many aren't

named. No Westerner yet has published a convincing account of how the Japanese successfully navigate this concrete hydra. For the visitor, it usually comes down to trial and error. Time may be of the essence in any big city, but losing it is an inevitable part of the Tokyo experience.

Among Tokyo's more well known areas are Ueno (parks and museums), Asakusa (Senso-ji Temple), Shinjuku (business and entertainment), Harajuku (photogenic Meiji-jingu shrine), Roppongi (bar scene, lately overrated) and Akihabara (electronics center). Tokyo Station is within long walking or short riding distance of most of Tokyo's few wartime sites. It's also near the lively restaurants and shops of Ginza, not all as expensive as the area's ritzy reputation would suggest. Tokyo sites can be covered in a single, long day, or two easy ones.

POINTS OF INTEREST

The suffix "dori" means street or avenue.

1. Yasukuni Shrine/Yushukan Museum
★★★★★

Yasukuni-dori
Take Tozai Line to Kudanshita Station.
Depart at Exit 3 to Yasukuni-dori and walk east 200-250 yards.
T: 3-3261-8362
Shrine: Daily, 9 a.m.-5 p.m. for Main Hall (shrine always open and free)
Museum: Daily, 9 a.m.-5:30 p.m. (March-October); Daily 9 a.m.-5 p.m. (November-February)
Closed December 28-31
Adult: 800 yen
Student: 500 yen
Child (Jr. High and under): 300 yen

Without question this is the most controversial World War II site in the Pacific. Incited in part by official visits from every Japanese prime minister since Takeo Miki in 1975, Yasukuni Shrine and adjacent Yushukan Museum have been loudly and bitterly denounced by China, South Korea, the Philippines and other countries. Critics maintain that Yasukuni/Yushukan glamorize sadistic war criminals, an indication of the tacit or explicit denial with which Japan's government tends to regard (or disregard) the atrocities committed across Asia and the Pacific by the Japanese military. To those Japanese who even think about Yasukuni, it's simply a place where patriotic sacrifice is honored—of the 2.5 million souls enshrined here, 2.3 million died in the Sino-Japanese War (1937-1945) and World War II.

Constructed in 1869, the Shinto shrine was run by military authorities as a place for war dead to be exalted as national heroes and venerated as gods. During the Pacific War, Yasukuni and Yushukan (which opened in 1879) played an important propaganda role in rallying the Japanese populace around the war and military. Following the war, state Shinto was abolished and Yasukuni's government affiliation ended. Operated today strictly as a religious property, the shrine continues to exalt the war dead as heroes—included among these heroes are former prime minister Hideki Tojo and thirteen others classified as Class A war criminals in post-war tribunals conducted by the Allies. It's the perceived homage to these war criminals that ignites the most turgid protests.

The shrine itself is impressive, with massive 150-foot-tall steel *torii* gates at either end and heavy wooden doors leading to a stately courtyard lined with endless rows of yellow boxes upon which are inscribed the names of the dead. At the main altar, the shrine's 1,000 or so daily visitors can be seen offering silent prayers to the fallen patriots.

Reopened in July 2002 following a four-billion-yen refurbishment, the large modern Yushukan Museum includes numerous fascinating relics. These include personal effects and letters from kamikaze pilots, small weaponry, large guns, various artillery pieces, Long Lance torpedo, *kaiten* manned suicide submarine, a reconstructed Mitsubishi Zero fighter plane painted green and marked as it was during the war and the first locomotive to cross the infamous Burma-Siam Death Railway on October 25, 1943.

What Westerners learn about the war at Yasukuni and Yushukan "will contrast sharply with their history books at home," according to an August 2002 article in Tokyo's English-language *Asahi Shimbun* newspaper. "Japan's march into the southern city of Nanking in December 1937, which most war historians agree resulted in a huge massacre of civilians, is described as follows: General Iwane Matsui 'warned Chinese troops to surrender, but Commander-in-Chief Tang Shengzhi ignored the warning. Instead he ordered his men to fight to the death and then abandoned them. The Chinese were soundly defeated, suffering heavy casualties. Inside the city, residents were once again able to live their lives in peace.'" Such events as the Bataan Death March and biological experiments conducted on humans by Japan's notorious Unit 731 are not mentioned.

Whether a celebration of terror and inhumanity, or a sober commemoration of patriotic duty and wish for world peace (the mission of the shrine and museum, according to its directors), this is as close as Japan comes to a national museum for a war that is more often brushed under history's carpet. Because or in spite of the politics, it's a unique and fascinating place, apparently even for those eternally stationed there. As Japanese officer Hiroo Onoda reflected before going into battle in the Philippines in 1944, "If I get killed I'll be enshrined as a god at Yasukuni Shrine, and people will worship me. That isn't so bad."

2. Imperial Palace ★★★

Uchibori-dori, Chiyoda-ku
From Tokyo Station take the Marunouchi Central Exit and walk east about five minutes to the main bridge across Babasaki Moat at the corner of Hibiya-dori and Babasakimon.

Although officially off-limits to American bombers from early in the war, Emperor Hirohito's palace—the scene of increasingly desperate meetings and internal plots within the Japanese government and military as the war wound down—was nevertheless destroyed during Allied bombing raids. Rebuilt in the 1960s, the palace itself is closed to the public for all but two days of the year—January 2 and the emperor's birthday, currently December 23. It's possible, however, to walk around the massive grounds and beautiful gardens. For the best photo of the palace, cross the Babasaki Moat at Babasakimon and walk across the wide Imperial Plaza to the spot where the famed Niju-bashi Bridge (actually two parallel bridges) is in the foreground.

3. Dai-Ichi Building ★

Hibiya-dori, Yuraku-cho, Chiyoda-ku
T: 3-3216-1211 (Dai-Ichi Mutual Life Insurance Company)
From Point 2, walk to southeastern corner of palace grounds along Hibiya-dori to the building at the corner of Harumi-dori. Or, take the Mita Line to Hibiya Station and depart from exit B2, which exits onto the street in front of the building's main entrance.

Inside this building, once known as The Big Number One, Douglas MacArthur established his headquarters and reigned over one of the most surprisingly peaceful and productive military occupations in history. The six-story structure, one of the few to survive the Tokyo bombings, was chosen for its location overlooking the Imperial Palace and Plaza, the traditional military parade ground where Tokyo Rose had promised throughout the war that MacArthur would be publicly hanged. "The symbolism was not lost on the Japanese," wrote MacArthur biographer William Manchester. Now officially called the Dai-Ichi Mutual Life Insurance Company Building, it was refurbished in 1995 and appears as it did during the occupation (1945-1952), with imposing pillars and a bland stone-and-marble corporate austerity. It looks more like a faceless bank than an imperial dwelling, an apt portent of things to come for Japan. Public access to the sixth-floor MacArthur Memorial Room—which includes the General's original desk and other preserved items—was "suspended temporarily" in 2002 by the Dai-Ichi Mutual Life Insurance Company's General Affairs Division. If reopened, this site will merit a ★★★ rating.

4. MacArthur's Residence ★

U.S. Embassy, 1-10-5 Akasaka, Minato-ku
From Tameike-sanno Station on the Ginza Line, walk five-to-ten minutes southeast, across the Metropolitan Expressway
T: 3-3224-5000

Though the interior is no longer painted in the Army green he ordered, the house where MacArthur lived and often worked during the occupation is just behind the American Embassy. It's now the U.S. Ambassador's residence.

5. Museum of Maritime Science (Fune-no-Kagakukan) ★★

3-1 Higashi-Yashio, Shinagawa-ku
From Shimbashi Station take the Yurikamome Line (aka New Transit Yurikamome) to the Fune-no-Kagakukan Station. Starting from Tokyo Station, the trip takes about forty-five minutes.
T: 3-5500-1111
Daily, 10 a.m.-5 p.m. (until 6 p.m. weekends and holidays)
Closed December 28-31
Adult: 700 yen
Child (Jr. High and under): 400 yen

This large ship-shaped museum covers nautical history from native canoes to oil tankers to Jet Skis. The second-floor Security of Maritime Safety exhibit has a small display of Warships of the Japanese Imperial Navy. There's little English signage, but the large scale-models of World War I and II ships include the battleships *Mikasa* and *Mutsu*, cruiser *Myoko* and two submarines. The centerpiece is the almost-fifteen-foot-long, meticulously handcrafted model of the *Yamato*, the largest battleship ever built. The ship bristles with well more than 100 heavy guns and three scout planes ready to launch off its aft deck. The museum's top-floor observatory offers a commanding view of smoggy, industrial Tokyo Bay, where the Japanese formally surrendered aboard the U.S.S. *Missouri* on September 2, 1945. But the best items are outside. Behind the main building sits the monstrous main battery from the *Mutsu*—sixty-one-feet long, it could fire shells up to twenty-three miles. In front of the building is a rare mint-condition Kawanishi H8K2 "Emily" Flying Boat, painted and marked in original wartime colors. It's one thing to see broken pieces of this hulking machine scattered across various Pacific islands. It's quite another to walk around its staggering girth (entry is not permitted) and appreciate that this wasn't simply a large float plane, it really was a boat that flew.

Called "one of the finest Japanese warplanes to see operational service" by aviation historian William Green, the Emily functioned in many roles—reconnaissance aircraft, bomber, torpedo plane and anti-submarine aircraft. Though only 167 were produced (including thirty-six "Seiku" transport variants), the Emily was widely used and—despite its girth and 124-foot wing span—earned a reputation among Allied pilots for being difficult to attack and shoot down. Maximum speed was 290 mph with a maximum range of 4,445 miles. The plane carried an impressive array of nine defensive guns and a crew of ten.

OTHER AREA ATTRACTIONS

Nikko and Kamakura

Since Tokyo is diverse enough to offer everything from high-end jazz clubs to the sweaty spectacle of sumo wrestling, it's tough to make a single choice. Two of the more worthwhile day trips outside the city are to Nikko (north of Tokyo) and Kamakura (southwest of Tokyo). Crowded with spectacular ancient temples, shrines and pagodas in a lush wooded area, Nikko has been a sacred site since at least the eighth century—numerous

structures of the Tosho-gu shrine are a focal point. Kamakura's most well-known attraction is the thirty-seven-foot-tall, 850-year-old bronze Buddha (*Daibutsu*). There are several famous shrines and temples in the pleasant rural area (a break from busy Tokyo), which is also known as a place to buy crafts from local artisans. Regular trains run frequently to Nikko and Kamakura. English-speaking tours can be arranged through Tokyo-based Sunrise Tours (3-5796-5454).

RELATED SITES BEYOND TOKYO

Hotel New Grand ★★

10 Yamashita-cho, Naka-ku, Yokohama
T: 045-681-1841

About an hour south of Tokyo, Yokohama is Japan's second-largest city and the port where nervous U.S. troops and then General Douglas MacArthur entered the main island of Honshu to officially begin the Allied occupation. "Preceded by truckloads of American paratroopers, MacArthur and his party traveled slowly toward Yokohama," wrote U.S. Army his-

torian John Bradley of the General's first hours on Japanese soil. "Along the way, two divisions of Japanese troops stood guard. They turned their backs toward the Supreme Commander, just as they always had for the Emperor. It was a fitting display for the new blue-eyed shogun." MacArthur spent his first few nights in Japan and established temporary headquarters in this hotel. The four-star property has been modernized, but its appearance is largely unchanged from its wartime look. MacArthur's meticulously preserved Suite 316—where he penned original drafts of the address he delivered at the official surrender ceremony—can be rented for 60,000 yen per night. Standard rooms start around 10,000 yen.

Maizuru Repatriation Memorial Museum ★★

Taira, Maizuru-shi, Kyoto Prefecture
T: 0773-68-0836
400 yen
Daily, 9 a.m.-5 p.m.
Closed Monday, days following national holidays and New Year's holiday

Ninety minutes by train from Kyoto—it's not worth the all-day trip from Tokyo—is the port of Maizuru, known throughout Japan as the main point through which some 665,000 soldiers and civilians on foreign soil were repatriated between 1945 and 1958, many after grueling years in Siberian internment camps. Opened in 1988, the museum displays personal items donated from across Japan. Vantage points offer sweeping views of the sea and surrounding mountains. The scenic port serves as the setting for the legend of *Gampeki no Haha,* a grieving mother mythologized in song and story who for endless years patiently but vainly awaits the return of her MIA son.

GETTING TO/AROUND TOKYO

Dozens of airlines fly nonstop to Tokyo's Narita International Airport from many U.S., Canadian and other international cities.

From Narita airport, Japan Railways (JR) Narita Express runs nonstop to Tokyo Station (fifty-three minutes, 2,940 yen). Also from Narita airport, Keisei Railways Skyliner runs to Keisei-Ueno Station (fifty-six minutes, 1,920 yen). Trains around Tokyo and Japan can be expensive. The best strategy is to purchase a JR Japan Rail Pass before arrival (they can't be purchased in Japan). Ordinary one-week passes, which include the *shinkansen* (bullet train), cost 28,000 yen and can be purchased through most travel agents, including JTB USA in San Francisco (415-986-4764). In Tokyo, JR offers telephone information in English from 10 a.m. to 6 p.m. (3-3424-0111).

Renting a car in congested Tokyo is pointless. The city's subway and train network is breathtakingly complete. Though expensive (meters usually drop around $5), taxis can be found almost anywhere at any time. Wandering Tokyo's unmarked streets looking for sites or restaurants can be frustrating. The fastest way to reach a given destination is to take a subway or train to the nearest station (much faster than crossing town in a car), then grab a taxi for a short ride.

Most Japanese speak little or no English, even though it's taught as a compulsory subject in public schools. Outside of major hotels, routine communication—especially directions—can be daunting to non-Japanese speakers. Even so, almost all Tokyo subways, trains and many restaurant menus include English signage. Among the world's mega-city inhabitants, Tokyo's might be the most courteous. Getting by is a challenge, not impossible.

ACCOMMODATIONS

Four Seasons Hotel

10-8 Sekiguchi, 2-chome, Bunkyo-ku
T: 3-943-2222 (800-332-3442 in
U.S., Canada)
F: 3-943-2300
282 rooms
From 40,000 yen

The Tokyo branch of the celebrated hotel chain offers the expected ultimate luxury and price tag. The opulent bathrooms and guest rooms are among the largest in Tokyo, where hotel rooms are typically small. One drawback—guests may not want to leave the building.

Yaesu Fujiya Hotel

2-9-1 Yaesu, Chuo-ku
T: 3-3273-2111 F: 3-3273-2180
377 rooms
From 12,000 yen

This business hotel with typically small Japanese rooms is immaculate and operated by an English-fluent staff. It's recommended for its location reasonably close to most of the city's wartime points of interest as well as its proximity to central Tokyo Station and many good restaurants in adjacent Ginza.

Tokyo Prince Hotel

3-1 Shibakoen, 3-chome, Minato-ku
T: 3-3432-1111 F: 3-3434-5551
467 rooms
From 20,000 yen

Five minutes by car from Ginza and fifteen minutes by car to Tokyo's domestic Haneda airport, this excellent hotel overlooking Shiba Park has eleven restaurants and occasional internet specials as low as 13,000 yen.

12

Guadalcanal

SOLOMON ISLANDS

THE WAR YEARS

By the summer of 1942, the Japanese soldier was viewed in Allied quarters as nothing less than the greatest jungle fighter the world had ever seen. "An imperial warrior could presumably swim for miles underwater, booby-trap the bodies of his fallen comrades, and scamper up to the tops of trees," wrote historian Robert Smith Thompson. This was the mythology against which American troops prepared to invade Guadalcanal in the first U.S. land offensive of World War II.

Prompting the attack was aerial reconnaissance of the Solomon Islands—British-administered territory occupied by Japan in the spring of 1942—showing Japanese construction of an airfield on the island of Guadalcanal. If completed, the airfield could potentially be used in an invasion of Australia. At the least, a fortified Guadalcanal would interdict the vital Allied supply link between Hawaii and Australia.

On August 7, 1942, in conjunction with smaller assaults on nearby Gavutu, Tanam-bogo and Tulagi Islands, a U.S. invasion force of 10,000 men, spearheaded by the First Marine Division, waded ashore on Guadalcanal at Red Beach. The landing met virtually no resistance—upon sight of the attackers, the Japanese battalion at the unfinished airfield fled into the jungle. By nightfall, the airstrip had been captured and renamed Henderson Field in honor of a Marine aviator killed at Midway.

The Japanese struck back, launching air raids against Henderson and shipping rein-forcements south from Rabaul. Japan routed the U.S. Navy in the Battle of Savo Island on August 9, forcing American supply and cover ships into retreat. The sud-denly isolated U.S. garrison on Guadalcanal was backed into a corner, left with two impossible objectives: hold the perimeter around Henderson against fierce attacks, and complete the airstrip so that American fighters could land to support them.

On August 18, the same day a Japanese detachment led by Colonel Kiyono Ichiki landed on both sides of the perimeter, Henderson Field was declared operational. Ichiki's forces attacked on August 21, but determined resistance with fighter, tank and artillery support tore apart the 1,000-man force. Ichiki burned his regimental colors and committed hara-kiri.

Now the Battle of Guadalcanal devolved into a protracted, six-month series of rein-forcement landings, gory attacks and counter attacks. The worst fighting was waged amid the razor-sharp kunai grass of Mt. Austen and Bloody Ridge, strategic heights overlooking the airfield. Action at Bloody Ridge was typified by fervid frontal assaults that left the ridge "littered with Japanese bodies sprawled in the pitiful and repulsive attitudes of death," according to U.S. Navy historian Samuel Eliot Morison. Making it even worse, tropical diseases—malaria, dengue fever—ravaged both sides.

With two armies operating at the end of their supply lines, Guadalcanal's seven epic sea battles played a critical role in the outcome of the battle. The Battles of the Eastern Solomons and Santa Cruz Islands were two of the great carrier fights of the war. The naval Battle of Guadalcanal ended with the first battleship-to-battleship engagement since Jutland in World War I.

The Japanese Navy dominated the seas at night, transporting reinforcements from Rabaul down "the Slot," the channel running between the Solomons' two main parallel island chains, on runs dubbed the "Tokyo Express." The body of water between Guadalcanal and the Florida Islands would eventually earn the moniker Iron Bottom Sound for the number of Japanese and American ships sunk there (thirty-five from each side, according to one of many estimates).

In November, ferocious offensives launched by both sides ended in virtual stalemate. The Americans were drained, mentally and physically. But the Japanese, with their supply lines finally cut by Admiral William "Bull" Halsey at the naval Battle of Tassafaronga, were starved, diseased and in worse condition. During the first week of February 1943, 10,000 to 13,000 Japanese troops—the remnants of about 36,000 sent there—evacuated the island undetected. On February 9, Lieutenant-General Alexander Patch radioed Halsey: "Tokyo Express no longer has terminus on Guadalcanal."

Guadalcanal cost the Allies about 5,000 dead and many more wounded. The First Marines alone recorded 8,500 cases of malaria. More than 14,000 Japanese were killed, with at least 9,000 more perishing from disease. The U.S. Navy lost two fleet carriers, six heavy cruisers and fourteen destroyers. Japan lost two battleships, one light carrier, three heavy cruisers, one light cruiser, eleven destroyers, six submarines and some 600 airplanes.

Guadalcanal remains of intense historical interest for a number of reasons. For the first time in history, it demanded large-scale "three-dimensional warfare"—continuous integration of air, land and sea operations. It matched relatively equal forces (a rarity in the Pacific). It included an unusually large number of surface-to-surface naval engagements, more than the British Royal Navy fought in all of World War I. Finally, this arduous, lengthy campaign halted the Japanese advance across the Pacific and crushed its aura of invincibility. The stunning American victory at Guadalcanal joined early 1943 Russian and British victories in Stalingrad and North Africa in the pantheon of critical Allied triumphs—in Europe and now the Pacific, World War II had finally turned irrevocably against the Axis.

SOURCES & OTHER READING

History of United States Naval Operations in World War II, Volume V: The Struggle for Guadalcanal, August 1942-February 1943, Morison, Samuel Eliot, Little Brown and Company, 1949

Bloody Ridge: The Battle That Saved Guadalcanal, Smith, Michael S., Presidio Press, 2000

Classic Battles, Guadalcanal 1942: The Marines Strike Back, Mueller, Joseph N., Osprey, 1992

Carrier Clash: The Invasion of Guadalcanal and the Battle of the Eastern Solomons, August 1942, Hammel, Eric, Pacifica Press, 1997

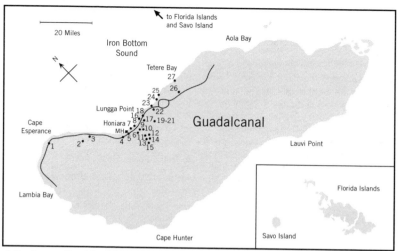

1. Cape Esperance Memorial
2. Vilu Museum
3. Sherman Tank
4. Allied Memorial
5. Tree Soldiers Monument
6. American Memorial
7. Goettge Patrol Site
8. Tanks/Hospital
9. Paige Hill
10. Japanese Memorial
11. Wright Road Marker
12. Final Destruction Star
13. Gifu
14. Japanese Observation Post
15. U.S. Mt. Austen Monument
16. Fighter 2 Airstrip
17. Betikama Museum
18. "Original" Foxhole
19. Bloody Ridge
20. Japanese Monument
21. Vandergrift's Post
22. Henderson Airport
23. U.S. Cemetery
24. Hell's Point
25. Red Beach
26. Carney Field/Koli Airfield
27. Amtrac wrecks
■ Mendana Hotel (MH)

GUADALCANAL TODAY

Population: 88,000 • Country Code: 677 • Currency: $1 = 7.14 Solomon Islands dollars

Almost 100 miles long and thirty miles wide, Guadalcanal is the largest of the Solomon Islands, the seat of its government and the usual entry point into one of the most beautiful and overlooked countries in the Pacific. Equatorial Guadalcanal's countryside is often breathtaking, characterized by jagged mountains, meandering rivers and plunging ravines. Covered with waving kunai grass, the wild green hills look much the way they did in 1942.

The exception is Honiara, the capital city where most of the island's population is concentrated. The main strip of the dirty town runs along the northern plain, abutting the Coral Sea and Iron Bottom Sound. With the island's only decent hotels and stores, as well as a central position for getting to wartime points of interest, the city is unavoidable. Few

Pacific War sites carry as much historical significance as Guadalcanal, but the area suffers as a whole due to Honiara, the least attractive—might as well say ugly—destination city covered in this book.

The political turmoil that divided Guadalcanal in the late 1990s, 2000 and beyond was characteristically exaggerated in the Western press. A peace treaty was signed in 2002, but it should be noted that some local villages still are occasionally considered off-limits due to local squabbles.

Most visitors come to walk the island's hallowed battlefields—the most moving in the Pacific—and get a sense of the island's rugged terrain and epic sweep. Sites require two to three days to cover, particularly for those wishing to spend time wandering the battlefields.

Most kilometer readings use downtown Honiara's Solomon Kitano Mendana Hotel (hereafter MH) as the 0.0 kilometer starting point to sites along or off the Main Road (aka Mendana Avenue and Prince Philip Highway). Most island roads are unmarked. While many of the sites are easy to find, local guides are affordable (see Getting to/around Guadalcanal) and worth considering.

1. Cape Esperance Evacuation Memorial ★

Off Main Road, on beach behind Tambea Resort at Cape Esperance, about 40 kilometers west of MH

A stone memorial behind the old Tambea Resort (now out of business) commemorates the point of the mass Japanese evacuation from Guadalcanal that went undetected by the Allies in February 1943.

2. Vilu Museum ★★

Off Main Road, about 22 kilometers west of MH, a side road turns left (south) and runs 1 kilometer to Vila
SI$10

The highlight of this ragged outdoor collection—mostly rusted weaponry—is a beat up Grumman F4F Wildcat fighter. Hours are irregular. Guides listed in the Getting to/around Guadalcanal section can arrange visits.

3. Sherman Tank ★★

Off Main Road, about 15 kilometers west of MH, just west of Bonegi II and 0.3 kilometers east of Tasivarongo Point (between Bonegi Creek and Umasani River), a trail leads about 300 yards to the tank

The U.S. Sherman tank named *Jezebel* was brought to this spot after the war and reportedly used for target practice. All things considered, it's in decent shape.

4. Allied Memorial ★★

Main Road, about 1 kilometer west of MH

Also called the Solomon Islanders Vouza

Memorial because its central feature is a large sculpture of the machete-wielding Sergeant Sir Jacob Vouza, a Solomon Islander who fought heroically alongside Allied soldiers. The roadside park honors all Solomon Islanders who resisted the Japanese occupation.

5. Tree Soldiers Monument ★

Main Road, across the street (just west) from MH

On the roadside are a large U.S. field artillery piece and stone monument to "America's Tree Soldiers," 1930s U.S. Civilian Conservation Corps employees in the Solomons swallowed into the armed forces after war broke out.

6. American Memorial Guadalcanal ★★★★

Skyline Drive. Off Main Road, a little more than 1 kilometer east of MH, turn right at traffic circle/Catholic Church onto Skyline Drive. After 0.1 kilometer follow sign pointing left (uphill) to memorial

The most elaborate and moving memorial on Guadalcanal recounts the battle's many elements—including the naval battles—with lengthy narratives engraved on massive marble slabs. The slabs point in the precise direction of five crucial battle sites—Bloody Ridge (aka Edson's Ridge), Iron Bottom Sound, New Georgia Island (representing the Solomon Islands campaign), Cape Esperance and Mt. Austen.

Located atop the first hill occupied by U.S. forces west of the Matanikau River battle perimeter, the site was chosen for its panoramic views of Iron Bottom Sound and Mt. Austen. The grassy valley below provided the setting for *Into the Valley: A Skirmish of the Marines*, the popular 1943 book by *Life* magazine battle reporter John Hersey. The memorial was opened in 1992 by the private Guadalcanal-Solomon Islands War Memorial Foundation and is now maintained by the American Battle Monuments Commission. It's the site of annual August 7 ceremonies commemorating the start of the battle.

7. Goettge Patrol Landing/Ambush Site ★

Main Road, 1.2 kilometers east of MH, on beach behind Sea King Chinese restaurant

Lieutenant-Colonel Frank Goettge was an intelligence officer who led a patrol to pick up a group of Japanese soldiers he believed wanted to surrender. The story was a set-up—Goettge and most of his twenty-five men were slaughtered by a Japanese ambush. Alternate accounts claim there were Japanese troops willing to meet Goettge, but that his patrol simply stumbled onto a separate Japanese shore patrol. Goettge's patrol landed on the beach behind the restaurant.

8. Tanks/Number Nine Hospital ★

Main Road, 2.1 kilometers east of MH, Kukum village. Turn left (south) into hospital parking lot just after Matanikau River Bridge and pedestrian overpass

From the parking lot of Honiara's central hospital—built by the U.S. Army as "Ninth Station" and known locally as "Number Nine"—visitors can access the beach through a hole in a fence. About 100 yards west, in front of a fantastically filthy community, the remains of three Japanese tanks sit in the water near

shore. At high tide, the top turret of only one (sans guns) is visible.

9. Paige Hill ★★

Kola Ridge Road. About 2.5 kilometers east of MH on Main Road, turn right (south) at the Anglican Cathedral and follow road uphill another 2.2 kilometers

Where the roadside sign for "Mount Austen Kingdom Hall of Jehovah's Witnesses" now stands, Marine Sergeant Mitchell Paige earned the Medal of Honor. His citation reads: "When the enemy broke through the line directly in front of his position, Platoon Sergeant Paige, commanding a machine-gun section with fearless determination, continued to direct fire of his gunners until all of his men were either killed or wounded. Alone, against the deadly hail of Japanese shells, he manned his gun, and when it was destroyed, took over another, moving from gun to gun, never ceasing his withering fire against the advancing hordes until reinforcements finally arrived. Then, forming a new line, he dauntlessly and aggressively led a bayonet charge, driving the enemy back and preventing a break through in our lines."

16. Fighter 2 Airstrip/Golf Course ★

Main Road, about 7.5 kilometers east of MH

Mt. Austen Road (aka Vura Road)

Sites on this historic road merit a collective ★★★★ rating.

10. Japanese Memorial (Solomon Peace Memorial Park) ★★

Mt. Austen Road. Off Main Road, about 4.5 kilometers east of MH, turn right (south) at Didds Service Station. Fork left twice in succession shortly after getting on this road (called Vura Road here), then fork right onto a dirt road after 2.2 kilometers (from Main Road) and proceed 1 kilometer uphill.

The central feature of this Japanese-built park on the slopes of Mt. Austen is a set of concrete pillars symbolizing love, trust, bravery and wisdom presenting equal faces to the North, South, East and West. With commanding views of Iron Bottom Sound, the park hosts annual August 7 commemoration ceremonies. Intense fighting took place on the site.

11. Wright Road Marker ★

0.5 kilometers past Point 10

A roadside sign tells the story of this narrow road—called Wright's Road during the war—built in December 1942. Along this route, supplies were trucked into Mt. Austen battlefields and injured were brought out.

12. Final Destruction Star ★★

1.3 kilometers past Point 11

In the center of a large, white American star is a plaque noting the scene of "The Final Destruction of Organized Japanese Forces, 10 January to 9 February 1943."

13. Gifu ★★★

Turn right onto the narrow dirt road at Point 12 and travel 0.8 kilometers to the open field area of Barama village

Originally named for Japan's Gifu prefecture—an apocryphal legend claims the name stood for "G.I. F— You"—the area of Barama village was a greatly feared Japanese stronghold. A road on the south side of the open field turns into a 300-yard uphill trail to a small marker noting the position of the Oka Force, which fought a lengthy battle with U.S. Army infantry regiments. Small holes in the ground, particularly on the south side of the hill, indicate dugout defensive positions. The hill commands superb views of the battlefields.

14. Japanese Observation Post ★★★

Mt. Austen Road (not Gifu side road), 2.3 kilometers past Point 12

A nondescript dirt path (a few hundred yards before and within site of Point 15) leads roughly northeast about 300 yards downhill to a metal marker (no inscription on it) and small underground cave. This is the site of the Japanese observation post that controlled many battles before being abandoned in December 1942. Like the Japanese commanders, visitors here get one of the best views of the battlefields. The dark brown section of the runway at Henderson International Airport below marks the extent of Japanese construction of the airstrip there. Savo and the Florida Islands, including Tulagi Island, are visible across Iron Bottom Sound.

15. U.S. Mt. Austen Guadalcanal Campaign Monument ★★

Mt. Austen Road, 2.4 kilometers past Point 12

A plaque on a small monument tells the story of military operations on Mt. Austen.

On the left (north) side of the road, a golf course and buildings occupy the former area of the Fighter 2 airstrip.

17. Betikama World War II Museum ★★★

From Main Road, 8.3 kilometers east of MH, turn right (south) and continue 1.5 kilometers along narrow road
Sunday-Friday (closed Saturday)
8 a.m.-Noon; 1 p.m.-5 p.m.

The site of a U.S. Army encampment, Betikama is now a Seventh Day Adventist school. Behind a fence are the wrecked remains of several aircraft, notably the front section of a P39 Bell Aerocobra, with its engine still characteristically behind the cockpit. A Dauntless dive-bomber—banged up, prop missing—sits next to a Japanese light tank. The one-room collection of war debris includes the hatch cover from a Betty bomber, with faded but original angry-red-meat-ball paint still visible.

18. "Original" Foxhole ★

Main Road, at 8.8 kilometers east of MH turn left (north) immediately after Lunga Bridge

The term "foxhole" probably originated on Guadalcanal with a Marine colonel named Fox who ordered his men to dig out defensive positions with entrenching tools. Contrary to local claims perpetuated in published guides, this concrete-lined bunker is not the "original foxhole" (which by definition isn't made of concrete, anyway). Across the Main Road, a roadside cave (a solitary tree stands at its entrance) was a U.S. communications bunker. A famous photo of First Marine Division commander General Alexander Vandergrift and staff was taken in the left-hand-side clearing about fifty yards down the small road in front of the cave.

22. Henderson International Airport ★★★

Main Road, 11.2 kilometers east of MH

Still the country's main airport, Henderson Field, as it was known during the war, was the focal point of the Battle of Guadalcanal. In front of the main terminal are a Japanese 75mm dual-purpose gun and memorial plaques to the American Seabees, Fiji Guerrillas, Solomon Islander South Pacific Scouts and Coastwatchers. A Memorial Garden has monuments to the First and Second Marine Divisions. ("The world is free because of you.") Trees can be sponsored in the name of veterans or others. Sponsorship costs US$130, including a small engraved plaque (Memorial Gardens, Box 439, Honiara, Guadalcanal, Solomon Islands).

Bloody Ridge Road

Sites in this historic area merit a collective (★★★★) rating.

19. Bloody Ridge/Edson's Ridge ★★★

Off Main Road, 10.1 kilometers east of MH, turn right (south) on unmarked road. The turn is about 1.1 kilometers before (west of) Henderson International Airport; the landmark is a set of small derelict shelters. Travel 0.4 kilometers on this unmarked road before veering right onto a dirt road. This road veers left and passes the end of the runway. After passing a Quonset hut, veer left at the fork, travel about 1 kilometer and veer right at the next fork. After about 1 kilometer the road becomes a dirt track. At this point, a white conical concrete monument should be visible next to the road.

The plaque on the conical monument is missing—it gave a brief description of events here—but this detracts little from the visceral punch of one of the most storied battlefields in American history. The hill with the conical monument is one of the places on the ridge where Colonel Merritt Edson rallied his Raiders in a superhuman defense of the ridge and Henderson Field behind it—the ridge is now known as both Bloody Ridge and Edson's Ridge. Village houses are nearby, but unlike most World War II battlefields, Bloody Ridge has remained largely undisturbed, eerily similar to its wartime state. The proximity of Henderson Field below reinforces the importance of the sacrifices made here.

20. Bloody Ridge Japanese Monument ★★

Along visible trail, 300-400 yards south (and visible from) Point 19

Visible from the conical monument is a small memorial honoring the many Japanese who died on Bloody Ridge. It's an easy walk roughly south along the ridgeline.

21. Vandergrift's Command Post ★

From Point 18, back down the road (north) about 0.5 kilometers is the head of a brushy path leading east about 1.1 kilometers to a concrete pillar.

The plaque is missing from the pillar noting the location of First Marine Division General Vandergrift's second command post. The actual post was down the hill just behind the pillar. About fifty yards farther along the path are concrete slabs poured by the Japanese, likely in preparation for the defense of the airfield they never completed.

About 200 yards west of the terminal, down a service road parallel to the runway, is the original, 1943 scaffold-style control tower. The road past the tower was the old taxiway and site of artillery units that fired on Bloody Ridge. On the right (north) side of the road, about 300 yards beyond the tower, is the site of the infamous Pagoda, a landmark torn down by the Americans after they realized the Japanese were using it as an aiming point for the bombardment of Henderson. The road leads to the end of the runway, hooking up with the Bloody Ridge road described in Point 19.

In the small terminal, the propeller from an American Navy dive-bomber is mounted on the south wall. The Heroes Wall includes plaques for the U.S.S. *President Jackson* ("First ship to land combat troops in the first offensive amphibious expedition, World War II."), Guadalcanal Medal of Honor Awardees (twenty-two men), Medal of Honor and Victoria Cross Awardees for the Solomons campaign (including Gregory "Pappy" Boyington) and others. As a plaque on the sidewalk in front of the terminal attests, Henderson was "one of the most famous airfields of World War II."

23. U.S. Cemetery ★

Main Road, 11.3 kilometers east of MH

This clearing along the left (north) side of the road just beyond Henderson International Airport was the site of an American cemetery for Guadalcanal casualties. By 1948, nearly all remains had been returned to the United States or Manila American Cemetery.

24. Hell's Point/Alligator Creek/Ichiki Monument ★★

Off Main Road, at 12.9 kilometers east of MH, turn left (north) and proceed

200-300 yards to ocean shore at mouth of Ilu River (aka Alligator Creek).

This is the site of an important early victory won by U.S. Marines, stationed on the western bank of the river, fighting the determined Ichiki force coming from the east. Walk around the beach to the eastern bank of the river, then follow a grassy, overgrown trail about fifty yards behind the beach. In a clearing where Ichiki committed hara-kiri following his defeat, a seven-foot-high marble marker tells the story (Japanese and English) of the battle.

25. Red Beach ★★

200-300 yards down beach (east) from Point 24

The rusted wreckage of several U.S. pontoons sits on the beach where Americans landed without a fight on August 7, 1942. The largely empty beach is significant as the place where the U.S. ground offensive began in the Pacific.

26. Carney Field/Koli Airfield ★★

Main Road, about 25 kilometers east of MH, turn left (north) on side road toward the end of the abandoned airstrip

Most of the old airfield was on the right (south) side of the Main Road. Along a small road running left (north) are a Seabee Memorial, site of a wartime hospital and small bunkers.

27. Tetere Beach/Amtrac wrecks ★★★

Off Main Road, about 30 kilometers east of MH and just past Tetere village, a rough road leads left (north) to the beach

The rusting hulks of about thirty American amtracs—amphibious vehicles with tractor treads used in many World War II sea-to-shore operations—sit near the beach, many covered in brush.

OTHER AREA ATTRACTIONS

For information on world-renowned Marova Lagoon, see same section in

Solomon Islands chapter.

Related Sites Beyond Guadalcanal

Dive sites ★★★ N

Aqua Action Diving

In Honiara Hotel, Chinatown, Honiara
T: 677-21737

Though most of the wrecks in Iron Bottom Sound are too deep to access, there are several good wreck dives around Guadalcanal. Just west of Honiara at Bonegi I, the *Hirokawa Maru* is a 508-foot Japanese transport attacked by dive bombers and beached in November 1942. It rests at a depth of ten to 140 feet and is one of the better wreck dives in the Solomons. At Bonegi II, the 436-foot *Kinugawa Maru* transport sits partially above the waterline down to ninety feet. Both wrecks are close to the beach and done as shore dives. The front section of a B-17 Flying Fortress (machine guns attached, cockpit accessible) rests roughly fifty feet down about 100 yards from shore near Ndoma village. The U.S.S. *John Penn* is an American troop/cargo ship lying at 120 to 140 feet off Henderson Field.

Getting To/Around Guadalcanal

Guadalcanal is reached by Solomon Airlines (677-36048 in Honiara; 310-670-7302 in Los Angeles; 617-3407-7266 in Brisbane, Australia) via Brisbane (Australia), Nadi (Fiji) and Port Morseby (Papua New Guinea). From the United States the easiest routes are with Air New Zealand (800-262-1234) departing from Los Angeles and traveling via Auckland and Brisbane or Nadi with transfers on Solomon Airlines purchased through Air New Zealand.

Cramped mini-buses service Guadalcanal's main roads and taxis are available. Honiara can easily be covered on foot. That said, a car is essential for independent travelers. Options include Economy Car Rentals (677-27100) on Mendana Avenue in Honiara and Avis (800-331-1084) at Henderson International Airport and in the Quan Chee Building in Honiara's Chinatown.

Dennis Anii of Guadalcanal Historical Tours (677-39757 or 677-27896) is a knowledgeable guide who specializes in battlefield tours. John Innes (677-38339) is a local Australian who also leads informative military tours. For full-package Guadalcanal World War II tours originating from the United States, see listing for Valor Tours in Getting to/around section of Solomon Islands chapter.

Guadalcanal Travel Service (677-22587) on Mendana Avenue can help arrange outer island trips.

Accommodations

King Solomon Hotel

Hibiscus Avenue, Honiara
T: 677-21205 F: 677-21771
58 rooms
SI$431-$605

The King Solomon has a nice pool, and the Leaf Haus restaurant is worth a stop even if you aren't a guest.

Solomon Kitano Mendana Hotel

Mendana Avenue, Honiara
T: 677-20071 F: 677-23942
96 rooms
SI$280-$750

The Mendana Hotel has a pool, good restaurant and central location. Many rooms have a view of Iron Bottom Sound.

Honiara Hotel

Off Chung Wah Road, Chinatown, Honiara
T: 677-21737 F: 677-23412
48 rooms
From SI$200

A bit out of the way, this mid-range hotel has a pool, restaurant and bar.

13

Tarawa
REPUBLIC OF KIRIBATI

THE WAR YEARS

Following the attack on Pearl Harbor and Japan's lightning thrust through the Pacific and Southeast Asia, Allied war planners devised a sweeping, two-pronged strategy to dismantle the Imperial Empire piece by piece. One arm of the attack, under the command of General Douglas MacArthur based in Brisbane, Australia, would push northward toward Tokyo through the Southwest Pacific Area. The other arm, directed by U.S. Navy Admiral Chester Nimitz based in Pearl Harbor, would drive westward on the Japanese capital through the Central and South Pacific Areas.

Seized by the Japanese from its British administrators on December 10, 1941, the Gilbert Islands (Tarawa being the primary atoll) are located about 2,000 miles south-west of Honolulu, nearly halfway between Hawaii and Australia. From here, land-based Japanese aircraft would be able to harass Allied communications, supply and troop advances. Tarawa thus became the first obstacle in the path of the juggernaut with which Nimitz intended to cross the Pacific.

Following a daring but limited U.S. Marine raid at the Japanese seaplane base at the nearby island of Makin in October 1942—the attack was meant to draw Japanese forces away from the Battle of Guadalcanal—Tarawa's commander Rear-Admiral Keiji Shibasaki busied his men by turning Tarawa's main island of Betio into one of the most heavily armed and shrewdly defended fortresses in the Pacific. About half the size of Central Park, Betio's 4,836 defenders could turn more than 100 large emplaced guns and fourteen tanks against any invasion force. Below ground, an interlocking series of bunkers allowed soldiers to crisscross the island, firing at opponents without exposing themselves to enemy fire. Coconut log bunkers and rifle trenches lined the beaches.

"A million men cannot take Tarawa in a hundred years," Shibasaki boasted to his men.

On November 20, 1943, the Allies launched Operation Galvanic against Tarawa. Relatively quick battles secured Makin and Abemama Atolls, though the escort carrier U.S.S. *Liscombe Bay* was sunk off Makin killing 860 sailors and airmen. By contrast, the primary assault on Betio was chaos. Landing at low tide, slow-moving American amtracs (amphibian tractors) were blasted in the water—only fifty-three of the first 125 launched made it to the beach. Higgins Boats (troop and supply transports) grounded on the shallow reefs up to 800 yards from shore. Many of the 5,000 attacking Marines were forced to wade to the beach through waist-high water against a curtain of Japanese fire. The invaders made easy targets, and the sea quickly churned red with blood.

Those who reached the beach faced more problems. Carefully placed mines and barbed wire funneled soldiers directly into the line of Japanese machine guns. Close-quarters combat made air cover impossible in areas. Explosions, fire and noise turned the beaches into scenes of impossible bedlam.

"Our casualties are heavy," Marine Colonel David Shoup radioed his flagship. "Enemy casualties unknown. Situation: We are winning."

Shoup's men—only thirty percent of whom made it to Betio unharmed—had reached the 500-yard-long pier that separated Red Beaches Two and Three. After being pinned down throughout the first morning, Shoup charged toward shore, took a bullet in the leg, but kept moving. Inspired troops and tank units followed. His assault ultimately knocked out a critical pillbox. Shoup won the Medal of Honor on Tarawa, ended his career in 1963 as commandant of the Marine Corps and was later ostracized by the Corps for becoming an outspoken critic of the Vietnam War.

Day Two brought a higher tide and fresh troops. One by one the Marines—still taking heavy casualties—destroyed fortifications through terrifying frontal assaults. Deep within the island, Japanese troops were becoming unnerved by the continuous assault, the terrifying whoosh of flamethrowers and sickening thud of hand grenades dropping into their concrete strongholds. Shibasaki radioed Tokyo for help, but Allied air strikes at Rabaul held reinforcements in check. After seventy-six near-continuous hours of battle, Betio fell to the Americans. Only seventeen wounded Japanese soldiers and 129 Korean laborers survived the assault. The United States suffered 900 killed and more than 3,000 wounded.

Photographs of dead Marines in the surf and reports of the operation at "Bloody Tarawa" outraged the American public. The media compared the battle to the Charge of the Light Brigade. General Holland Smith, overall Marine commander of the operation, later said that Tarawa had been strategically unimportant and the terrible carnage there unnecessary.

Tarawa today is generally regarded as a strategically needless battle, but one that taught the United States lessons in amphibious warfare that undoubtedly saved countless lives in island assaults to come. After Tarawa, pre-invasion naval bombardment would be heavier and more effectively directed. Small-unit operations, flamethrower techniques and tank-infantry coordination were improved.

Though Tarawa was used as a base in support of the Marshall Islands offensive, its lasting legacy nevertheless remains one of unremitting horror. "This was not the bloodiest of the Central Pacific assaults, nor the largest," wrote historians James Dunnigan and Albert Nofi. "But as far as intense fighting in a short time, Tarawa was the worst."

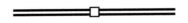

SOURCES & OTHER READING

Line of Departure: Tarawa, Russ, Martin, Doubleday and Company, 1975
The Pacific War Encyclopedia, Dunnigan and Nofi, Checkmark Books, 1998
Tarawa: The Story of a Battle, Sherrod, Robert, Duell, Sloan and Pearce, 1944
Tarawa 1943: The Turning of the Tide, Wright, Derrick, Osprey Publishing, 2000
Utmost Savagery: The Three Days of Tarawa, Alexander, Joseph H., Naval Institute Press, 1995
Tarawa—the Aftermath, Allen, Donald K., Publishers' Graphics, 2001

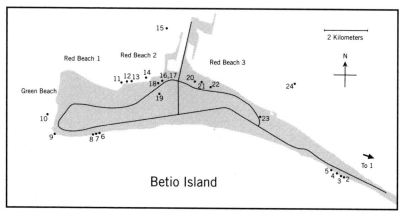

Betio Island

1. Tarawa Airport
2. Searchlight/AAA Bunker
3. Steel Pillbox
4. 8-inch Vickers Gun
5. 8-inch Vickers Gun with Broken Barrel
6. Coastwatchers Memorial
7. Dual-purpose Gun
8. Searchlight/AAA Bunker
9. 8-inch Vickers Guns
10. Green Beach LVTs

11. Red Beach One LVTs
12. Sherman Tank
13. Japanese Tank
14. Higgins Boat
15. Original Pier
16. Japanese/Korean Memorial
17. Japanese Tank Turret
18. Quonset Huts
19. Inland LVT
20. Marine Corps/Navy Memorial

21. Generator/Bunker
22. Shibasaki's Headquarters
23. Bomb Shelter
24. Wing Spar/Aircraft Engines

T A R A W A   T O D A Y

Population: 41,194 (Tarawa Atoll), 12,268 (Betio Island) • Country Code: 686 • Currency: Australian dollar

The Republic of Kiribati (population 94,149) is comprised of thirty-three low-lying coral atolls that stretch almost 2,000 miles and are sub-divided into three main groups known as the Gilbert, Phoenix and Line Islands. Not a single town but a group of small islands surrounded by a coral atoll, the capital of Tarawa is divided into North and South Tarawa. Linked by a causeway, South Tarawa includes the airport on Bonriki, government offices on Bairiki and, at the end of the chain, Betio, site of most war relics. English is spoken around Tarawa, less so on other atolls.

One of the most densely populated areas in the Pacific—rivaling even Hong Kong—Tarawa offers visitors a mixed experience. The wartime artifacts and

opportunity to visit the hallowed beaches make Betio something of a grail for those tracing the footprints of history. Many of those same beaches, however, are lined with garbage and other evidence of a country that relies on foreign aid for much of its welfare.

In swaying palms, colorful flora and friendly locals, one can occasionally see through the modern malaise to the tropical paradise islanders here once knew. But piles of trash and the Americanization of the islands, which runs the gamut from Spam to hip-hop music, is a fact of life that many visitors find incongruous with a remote, equatorial island.

Interior sites can be visited in one day. Add another to walk Tarawa's perimeter.

With the exception of Point 1, all sites are located on Betio Island.

1. Tarawa International Airport/Bomber Airstrip ★

Bonriki Island

Built by U.S. Seabees, Tarawa's main airfield was named Mullinix Field after Rear Admiral Henry M. Mullinix, who died in the sinking of the U.S.S. *Liscombe Bay*. The airfield was built to accommodate B-24 and B-25 bombers. Fighters and Ventura bombers also operated from Betio.

2. Searchlight/AAA Bunker ★

Off main road after crossing Nippon Causeway from Bairiki to Betio, on left (south) about 0.5 miles west from toll booth

Searchlights were once mounted atop this Japanese anti-aircraft/artillery (AAA) bunker. It can be entered from the top—a ladder is needed—where stairs lead to a steel door that opens into a single room.

3. Steel Pillbox ★★

Left (south) side of main road just beyond Point 2

Several of these sturdy pillboxes—constructed of two walls of heavy-gauge sheet steel with sand filling between—served as Japanese observation posts. A cupola or small turret once sat on top.

4. 8-inch Vickers Gun ★★★

Left (south) side of main road just beyond Point 3

Once believed to have been captured by the Japanese at the fall of Singapore, this gun and the one near it (Point 5) were actually purchased from Great Britain in the 1900s (four remain on the island). The breech blocks lie in the ocean beyond the reef.

5. 8-inch Vickers Gun with Broken Barrel ★★

Visible on beach just west of Point 4

This Japanese gun received a direct hit by a bomb or large-caliber shell. The impact blew off half the barrel. Tidal erosion threatened to destroy it—and the nearby companion gun—until cement-bag seawalls were constructed around their bases. Far from the invasion beaches, these two guns on the southeast beach never fired a shot during the battle.

6. Coastwatchers Memorial ★★

In the cemetery (sometimes called Protestant Cemetery) about three-fourths the way across the island west of Point 5

In the early stages of the war a number of young Australian and New Zealander coastwatchers across the atoll secretly observed Japanese plane and ship traffic, then filed reports by radio to Allied command. Many were eventually captured by the Japanese, transported to Betio and forced to work building defense fortifications. According to reports, some of the prisoners, unable to mask their satisfaction during an American bombing raid, were shot or beheaded by their incensed captors. The coastwatchers' burial site has never been located. This is their memorial.

7. Dual-purpose Gun ★

Behind cemetery on beach, near Point 6

A large crumbling mount for a 127mm, dual-purpose gun—used for firing at air and naval units—rests with the gun's twin barrels dropped into the beach.

8. Searchlight/AAA Bunker ★

Behind cemetery near main road, just west of Point 7

This is a duplicate of the bunker described in Point 2.

9. 8-inch Vickers Guns ★★

Along main road, southwest corner of island

These two tandem eight-inch guns were mounted to fire south, the expected avenue of assault. During the early hours of the invasion the upper gun was fired on U.S. troop transports. A barrage of battleship counterfire immediately silenced the gun. One round hit the guns' magazine, apparently killing the gun crew. The lower gun couldn't be trained on ships to the north—it's since deteriorated allowing the visible gun barrel to slide into the beach below.

10. Green Beach LVTs ★★

On reef northwest of Point 9

In the center of Green Beach, about 150 yards from shore, rest the remains of two LVTs that were part of the second-day landings. Both struck underwater mines and were torn apart by the explosions.

11. Red Beach One LVTs ★★

Junction of Red Beaches One and Two

The track cleats identify these as an LVT-2 (on the left/west) and an LVT-1 (on the right/east). They lie at the west end of Red Beach 2 and are possibly the units seen in a widely circulated battle photo (the LVT-1 being Number 49, *My Delores*).

12. Sherman Tank ★★★

Red Beach Two, just east of Point 11

This Sherman M4A2 was named *Cecelia* after the daughter of its driver. After landing on the beach, the tank and its crew encountered a Japanese tank, which fired a 37mm round directly into the Sherman's gun tube. The Sherman's breech was open and the shell bounced inside the turret without causing injury. Watching the action, a second American tank, *China Gal*, offered supporting fire and dispatched the Japanese tank. *Cecelia*'s cannon was damaged, but her machine guns were used to fire into enemy emplacements until the tank fell into a bomb hole on the beach, where it rests today.

13. Japanese Tank ★★

Red Beach Two, just east of Point 12

There were fourteen Japanese Type 95 light tanks on Betio during the battle. Seabees relocated this one here following the battle. Its armor is relatively thin and saltwater corrosion has destroyed much of the body.

14. Higgins Boat ★

Red Beach Two, just east of Point 13

Little remains of this light-skinned craft after nearly sixty years of erosion. Higgins boats were used to bring men and supplies to shore. Designed by Andrew Jackson Higgins—a maverick boat builder who'd gained fame designing racing boats and rum-runners during Prohibition—the early Higgins Boat was fast but lacked a bow ramp, forcing troops to disembark by jumping over the gunwales or bow.

15. Original Pier ★

Between Red Beaches 2 and 3

Tarawa's original pier was constructed of palm log pilings with a cement apron at the edge of the reef. It was heavily damaged during the battle. Seabees built a new pier just east of the original. The old pier is collapsed and best seen from the air or underwater. Several LVTs and other landing craft lie on the sea floor near the end of the pier.

16. Japanese/Korean Memorial Garden ★★

About 100 yards inland due south from the "new" Seabees Pier in Point 15

Many Japanese and Korean laborers killed in the battle were buried in this area. Family members from both countries periodically visit Betio to honor ancestors—past visits have been led by Admiral Keiji Shibasaki's son.

17. Japanese Tank Turret ★

Outside fence, south of Point 16

The turret from a Japanese light tank rests just outside of the Memorial Garden. Spared from saltwater damage, it's in relatively good condition.

18. Quonset Huts ★

Inland south of the "new" Seabees pier in Point 15

These original Quonset huts from World War II are showing their age. A number of larger huts were erected around the island after the war.

19. Inland LVT ★★

Inland about 200 yards (amid housing) south of Point 16

Workers laying a water line in 1974 discovered this buried LVT-1. When uncovered, the remains of three men—two identified as American Marines—were found in the cargo area.

20. Marine Corps/Navy Memorial ★★★

Inland about 200 yards from Red Beach Three

In front of the Betio Town Council building is a memorial to Marine and Navy servicemen who died during Operation Galvanic. A 1988 gift from the people of Long Beach, California, this monument replaced a pylon monument previously erected on the end of the Seabees pier.

21. Generator Building/Bonnyman's Bunker ★★

Inland from Red Beach 3, behind the new Betio Police Station

A Japanese bunker sits mostly underground. The large room was for a generator and the two smaller rooms for equipment. Nearby is a bombproof shelter that was assaulted by thirty to forty Marines led by Lieutenant Alexander Bonnyman, Jr., who died in the action and was posthumously awarded the Medal of Honor.

22. Admiral Shibasaki's Headquarters ★★★

Inland about 200 yards southeast from the pier area

The largest Japanese structure on Tarawa is this two-story double-walled building. The men inside held out until being burned to death. Enclosed by a chain-link fence, it can be entered with a guide (see Getting to/around Tarawa). The outer walls were heavily damaged, but the inner walls are relatively unscathed. The structure is intact, but saltwater used in making the cement has caused steel reinforcing rods to rust. As a result, some of the ceiling has separated.

23. Bomb Shelter ★

East end of Red Beach 3, near Marine Training Centre

This yellow underground bomb shelter was Admiral Shibasaki's personal refuge. Nearby is a dual-purpose gun and destroyed concrete bunkers.

24. B-24 Wing Spar/Aircraft Engines ★★

On reef about 100 yards from shore, east of boat channel at Marine Training Centre

A B-24D Liberator crashed on takeoff for a bombing run to the Marshall Islands. After many years of salt corrosion, storms and scavenging, all that remains are the heavy wing spar and engines. Also nearby are engines from single-engine fighters. Empty shells from the battle can be found on the reef in this area.

GETTING TO/AROUND TARAWA

Tarawa is served once a week by Air Marshall Islands (692-625-3733) flights departing from Majuro. The Marshall Islands can be reached daily via Continental Micronesia (800-231-0856) from Honolulu. Air Nauru (686-26567 in Tarawa; 310-670-7302 in Los Angeles) flies to Tarawa twice weekly from Nadi, Fiji. Nadi can be reached from Los Angeles via Air New Zealand (800-262-1234) and other airlines.

Because flight schedules can leave visitors in Tarawa for several days up to a week—far too long for most travelers—

it's worth considering visiting the island with a charter service such as Valor Tours (800-842-4504 or 415-332-7850), which specializes in World War II tours.

Transportation around Tarawa is available on mini-buses that operate daily, 6 a.m.-9 p.m. Rental cars are available through Otintaai Hotel (686-28084) or other hotels.

John Brown, a local guide and Tarawa battle authority, leads excellent military tours (686-26409; jaybe@tskl.net.ki). Dive operators for Tarawa and the Gilbert Islands include Mauri Paradise Divers (686-21646) and the Betio Diving Club (686-21255).

All travelers planning a trip to Kiribati should contact the Consulate of the Republic of Kiribati (808-834-6775) in Honolulu for current information on ever-changing visa regulations. Regional airlines don't often make a point of informing travelers of visa requirements before issuing tickets.

ACCOMMODATIONS

Otintaai Hotel
Bikenibeu Island

T: 686-28084 F: 686-28045
40 rooms
A$70-$130

Located on the lagoon side of Bikenibeu Island, the Otintaai is Tarawa's only modern hotel. Amenities include air-conditioned rooms, restaurant and bar. International direct-dial phones are in every room. Built by an Australian company, this is by far the best option on Tarawa.

Lagoon Breeze Motel
Eita Island

T: 686-28942 F: 686-28942
8 rooms
A$65-$75

About halfway between the airport and Bairiki Island, this motel has a park close to the lagoon. Facilities include shared kitchen and office service with internet.

Mary's Motel
Government Administrative Centre, Bairiki Island

T: 686-21164 F: 686-21362
8 rooms
From A$50

Located just off the Nippon Causeway on Bairiki, Mary's has a restaurant, bar, air-conditioned rooms and little else.

14

Nagasaki/ Kyushu

JAPAN

THE WAR YEARS

T hree days after the *Enola Gay* dropped its infamous payload on Hiroshima on August 6, 1945, Nagasaki became the target of the world's second atomic attack. History has since consigned the follow-up atomic event to the back pages of a story owned by its more prominent precursor. It's the Nagasaki bomb, however, that ultimately convinced the Japanese emperor and military government to lay down its arms. In this sense, it was the Nagasaki bomb that ended the war and supercharged the subsequent debate: Even if the United States "needed" to drop the first bomb, was a second one necessary?

Following Hiroshima, President Harry Truman's second demand for unconditional surrender, lest Japan suffer "a rain of ruin from the air, the like of which has never been seen on this earth," forced a nearly impossible timeline upon Japan's divided Supreme Council. Prime Minister Kantaro Suzuki and Foreign Minister Shigenori Togo—moderates compared to most of the cabinet—awaited hopes that neutral Soviet influence might soften America's unconditional surrender terms and, most importantly, preserve Emperor Hirohito's position as head of state. These hopes were dashed on August 8 when the Soviet Army marched into Manchuria and declared war on Japan. The next morning an atomic bomb was dropped on Nagasaki, the date being pushed ahead two days from August 11 due to unfavorable weather forecasts. An industrial port city dominated by the Mitsubishi Corporation's empire of shipyards, steel mills, electrical equipment works and arms plants, Nagasaki had until then barely been touched during the war.

On August 9, 1945, at 2:56 a.m., Major Charles W. Sweeney and his crew left Tinian Island in *Bock's Car,* a B-29 loaded with a five-ton, plutonium-implosion bomb nick-named "Fat Man." The mission was bound for Kokura, on the northern tip of Kyushu, homeland Japan's southernmost island. Sweeney circled Kokura three times, facing overcast skies, heavy flak and fuel shortage, before redirecting to the nearest second-ary target, Nagasaki. It too was covered in clouds and haze. Three times Sweeney cir-cled Nagasaki before the skies momentarily opened on a viable target in the Urakami Valley three miles north of the city center. The bomb was released at 11:01 a.m., exploding in the air less than a minute later. *Bock's Car* retreated to Okinawa, barely making it back on its remaining fuel.

"We watched a giant pillar of purple fire, 10,000 feet high, shoot upward like a meteor coming from the earth instead of from outer space," wrote *New York Times* journalist William L. Laurence, who witnessed the explosion from the mission's lone escort plane.

The bomb obliterated everything within a half-mile radius of ground zero—swallowing a hospital and medical school, ripping apart several Mitsubishi plants, killing every living thing within its scope. The blast, residual heat, fires and radiation destroyed one-third of the city and, from a population of 240,000, left an estimated 73,884 dead and 74,909 injured. On August 10, in one of the war's most unsynchronized blunders, U.S. planes dropped thousands of belated warning leaflets over Nagasaki, urging citizens to evacuate before a devastating bomb was dropped.

Any suspicions that the United States had used up its only atomic weapon on

Hiroshima were dispelled by this second mission—a fact presumably not lost on the charging Soviets. Fears that several more would be falling in short order were too tenable for the Emperor to bear. In an unprecedented act of direct arbitration, Hirohito's pronouncement to his torn cabinet on that same day was uncontested and effectively ended the war.

"I cannot bear to see innocent people suffer any longer," the Emperor proclaimed.

If the bomb saved the lives of hundreds of thousands of Allied and Japanese soldiers, it also likely saved the lives of countless civilians on Kyushu, which was scheduled to be invaded by Allied troops in the autumn of 1945. Kyushu had become increasingly vital as the war dragged on and Allied forces, with victory in Okinawa, closed within 375 miles of its shores. Military buildup on the island grew to massive proportions. For just one example, the Tachiari Joint Service Flight Training School was established in 1942 in the small town of Chiran. By 1945, the school had become the main training ground of Japan's Special Airforce Attack group—popularly known as the kamikaze force—and was the launching point for many of the fatal missions flown during the Battle of Okinawa.

Farther north, the island's primary city of Fukuoka had become a major center for POW camps. One of the most notorious incidents of the war occurred when surgeons at Fukuoka Imperial University completed the only documented vivisection of the Pacific War. Eight captured crewmen of an American B-29 were dissected alive to determine the effects of partial organ removal, saltwater injected into the blood stream and various other bodily traumas. Among other factors, the city's known population of POW camps kept Fukuoka—located between Hiroshima and Nagasaki—off the list of primary targets for atomic bomb missions.

SOURCES & OTHER READING

Prompt and Utter Destruction: Truman and the Use of Atomic Bombs Against Japan, Walker, J. Samuel, The University of North Carolina Press, 1997

The Last Act: The Atomic Bomb and the End of World War II, Smithsonian Institution Press, 1995

The Last Bomb: A Marine Remembers Nagasaki, Milam, David, Eakin Publications, 2001

The Atomic Bomb: Voices from Hiroshima and Nagasaki (Japan in the Modern World), Selden, Kyoko, M.E. Sharpe, 1997

Nagasaki: The Forgotten Bomb, Chinnock, Frank W., World Publishing Company, 1969

Disgrace: The Truth of the Kyushu University Vivisection Incident (Omei: Kyudai Seitai Kaibo Jiken no Shinso), Tono, Toshio, Bungei Shunshu, 1979 (Japanese only)

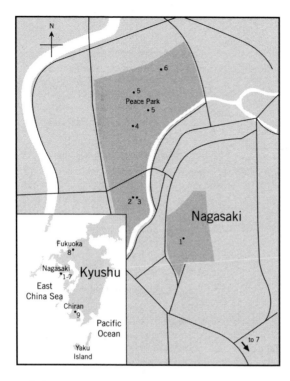

1. Atomic Bomb Museum
2. Atomic Bomb Hypocenter
3. Urakami Cathedral Ruins
4. Peace Fountain
5. Peace Monuments
6. Peace Statue
7. One-legged *Torii*

Nagasaki/Kyushu Today

**Population: 450,000 (Nagasaki) 13.4 million (Kyushu Island) •
Country Code: 81 • $1 = 118 yen**

Fronted by the sea and surrounded by a ring of forested mountains, Nagasaki is built into one of the most scenic settings of any large Japanese city. Like Hiroshima, its post-war rebirth appears to the visitor as nothing short of miraculous.

Portuguese ships arrived here in 1542 bringing trade and Catholicism—Nagasaki prefecture's estimated 68,801 Catholics gives it by far the largest percentage of Catholics in Japan—lending the city a cosmopolitan history in which it still revels. Though the wartime points of interest are in the Urakami-area's hypocenter, most of the city's attractions are found a few miles south along the harbor in the Hamano-cho and Shian-bashi districts.

The rest of Kyushu includes some of the best untrammeled territory in Japan. Fukuoka has been described by one magazine as "if not the Paris, at least the Seattle of the East," for its relaxed feel and variety of restaurants and clubs. The port city of Kagoshima (near the kamikaze museum at Chiran) is the gateway to breathtaking islands, mountains, bamboo groves, ancient forests and the majestic Sakurajima volcano, which dominates the city, visually and spiritually.

Nagasaki's points of interest can be visited in a short afternoon. Attractions in Fukuoka and Chiran can likewise be covered in a few hours, though travel time adds an extra day to each.

POINTS OF INTEREST

With the exception of the one-legged *torii*, all points below are concentrated in Nagasaki's compact Peace Park area and can be easily covered on foot.

1. Nagasaki Atomic Bomb Museum ★★★★★

7-8 Hirano-machi
T: 095-844-1231
Daily, 8:30 a.m.-5:30 p.m.
(last entry at 5 p.m.)
Closed December 29-31
Adult: 200 yen
School children: 100 yen
Under school age: Free

In a modern building, the large museum includes a number of excellent exhibits ranging from a timeline of the war to the bomb's devastating effects, Nagasaki residents' desperate efforts to deal with the tragedy, subsequent nuclear arms race and international efforts to abolish nuclear weapons. As in Hiroshima, large scale models of the city and graphic photos (naked bodies charred black by the blast) provide indelible images. Various relics bear witness to the bomb's otherworldly power—melted bottles, ruined parts of buildings and a steel helmet with remains of a skull embedded inside. A replica of the Fat Man bomb with a cutaway cross-section shows the surprisingly small plutonium core. The second floor includes films and videos featuring bomb footage and heart-wrenching testimonials from Nagasaki's A-bomb survivors. For obvious reasons, the museum often draws comparisons with the Hiroshima Peace Memorial Museum. Though not as large or elaborate, the Nagasaki museum is as engrossing and unsettling. Behind the museum, the Nagasaki City Peace Hall houses a small museum of Japanese art unrelated to the blast.

2. Atomic Bomb Hypocenter ★★★

About 150 yards north of Point 1
From the museum, a walkway and stair-

case descend through a number of memorials and sculptures, including shrieking figures and a mother embracing her stricken child. A black monolith marks the point where, 1,640 feet above, the atomic bomb exploded.

3. Urakami Catholic Cathedral Ruins ★★

Located at the Hypocenter
Relocated here are the broken pieces of a brick wall, all that remains of what was at the time of the blast the largest Christian church in East Asia. Sculptures of Jesus Christ and one of the apostles remain on the wall.

4. Peace Fountain ★★

About 200 yards north of Point 2
The Peace Fountain marks the entrance to the upper section of the Peace Park (a block north of the first section, along the main road and up a set of stairs). With a diameter of about sixty feet, the fountain shoots water twenty feet into the air in the shape of a pair of wings.

5. International Peace Monuments ★★

Lining the short walk between Points 4 and 6
Flanking the courtyard between both ends of the upper section of the park are twenty or so peace monuments donated by various countries. The variety of national styles and themes is interesting. One example: Turkey's elegant "Infinity" is a simple sculpture of a man and woman holding hands. The courtyard also includes the foundation-stone ruins of the Urakami Branch Prison, the closest public facility to the hypocenter. All 134 prison inmates and employees were killed in the blast.

6. Peace Statue ★★

75 yards north of Point 4
Erected in 1955, the thirty-two-foot tall bronze statue of a muscular male figure is Nagasaki's most recognizable monu-

ment to the bomb. An elevated right hand points toward the threat of nuclear weapons from the sky while an outstretched left hand symbolizes world peace. The superhero-style figure has been described as everything from beautiful to awful.

7. One-legged *Torii* ★

750 yards southeast of Point 1

About ten blocks from Point 1 stands one leg and part of the flared top section of a large, stone *torii* (gate) that only partially survived the blast. The gate to the Sanno Shinto shrine, it remains standing as a testament to Nagasaki's resolute character.

Fukuoka

8. Anchor ★★★★

Towada Building, 4th floor, 3-3-4, Nakasu, Hakata, Fukuoka
T: 092-291-1657
Daily, 5:30 p.m. to late evening
Closed Sundays

The most surreal Pacific War attraction, Anchor is a small bar hidden amid the Nakasu nightclub district that celebrates the glory days of the Japanese Imperial Navy. Patrons watch black-and-white videos of the Navy in action, circa 1942, sing patriotic songs from the period and occasionally dress in Navy costumes (provided by the bar) ranging from admiral dress whites to kamikaze coveralls. Thusly outfitted, customers pose for photos before various backdrops, including a Rising Sun flag, Zero fighter and tropical fleet anchorage. Small relics, photos and Imperial Navy war flags provide additional atmosphere. Regulars say they come to connect with Japan's mythic Bushido ethos and the legacy of fathers and grandfathers who fought in the war. Unlike many Japanese, most customers are candid about the war, calling it a grave mistake. For those who can get beyond the political dementia of it all (the alcohol helps immensely), Anchor provides a unique, strange and irresistible portal into the days of the Pacific War.

Chiran

9. Peace Museum for Kamikaze Pilots ★★★★

17881 Kohri, Chiran-cho
T: 0993-83-2525
Daily, 9 a.m.-5 p.m.
(last entry at 4:30 p.m.)
Adult: 500 yen
Child: 400 yen

From Fukuoka's Hakata Station, take the train to Nishi-Kagoshima Station (about three hours and forty-five minutes). Directly in front of Nishi-Kagoshima Station, air-conditioned buses depart for Chiran at 9:07 a.m., 9:57 a.m., 11:17 a.m. and 12:47 p.m. from in front of the Chiyoda Seimei Building on Naples-dori Avenue. The ride takes about eighty minutes and ends at the museum. More buses for Chiran depart throughout the day from Kagoshima's Yamakataya Bus Center.

One of Japan's most thorough and unforgettable museums memorializes the 1,036 kamikaze fliers who "all departed knowing there was no chance of return." The multiroomed museum, opened in 1975, contains six fighter planes, including a Zero, Heian Type-3 Flying Swallow and Hayabusa Type-1. Most captivating are the military mug shots of all 1,036 members (including eleven Koreans) of the Special Airforce Attack Group. Many look like the adolescents they were, but the letters, poems and diaries they left behind suggest a poignant maturity. It's not uncommon to see Japanese visitors moved to tears by the patriotism, valor and sacrifice of the young pilots. Of the more than 1,000 items on display are personal effects including flags, uniforms, scarves, watches, sake sets and a bamboo flute. The temple next door has a replica of the corps' Spartan living quarters. English interpretation is limited, though a short cassette-tape guided tour is available. Though much of the detail is incomprehensible to the non-Japanese speaker, the museum is wholly worthwhile.

OTHER AREA ATTRACTIONS

Samurai Houses, Chiran

6204 Kori, Tiran, Kawanabe, Kagoshima
(administration office)
T: 0993-83-2511
Daily, 9 a.m.-5 p.m.
Adult: 500 yen
Child: 400 yen

Five minutes down the road from Chiran's Peace Museum for Kamikaze Pilots (and served by the same buses from Nishi-Kagoshima and Kagoshima) are seven ancient samurai houses, some dating to the mid-1700s. The stone walls, gates and rock and shrubbery gardens offer a unique look at feudal Japan. Though not often seen by tourists (who rarely venture this far south) "Samurai Street" is renowned throughout Japan.

Yaku Island

About forty miles off the southern tip of Kyushu is Yaku Island *(Yaku-shima),* one of the most extraordinary places in Japan. Designated a UNESCO World Heritage Site, the mountainous island is renowned for its natural beauty and enormous Yakusugi cedar trees which, many between 3,000 and 3,500 years old, are some of the planet's oldest living trees. The easiest place to see and hike around the trees is Yaku-shima Cedar Land (also called Yakusugi Land). Outside this area, a tree known as Jomon-sugi has a girth of fifty-three feet and is said to be 6,300 to 7,200 years old, making it the oldest cedar in the world. It's reached after a four-to-five-hour mountain hike.

Transportation to the island is via airplane (Japan Air System, 0120-5-11283 in Japan; Japan Airlines, 800-525-3663) or ferry *(Yakushima 2,* 099-226-0731). The ferry takes a little less than four hours from Kagoshima. Buses regularly run the small island's main roads, but rental cars (Nakashima/Suzuki Rent A Car, 09974-2-1772) are recommended. Hotels (Yakushima Iwasaki Hotel; 09974-7-3888; from 20,000 yen) and less-expensive ryokans (Japanese-style inns) are available. For more information contact the Yakushima Tourist Center (09974-2-0091).

GETTING TO/AROUND NAGASAKI/KYUSHU

Airports in Nagasaki and Fukuoka are served by several Japanese domestic carriers, including Japan Airlines (800-525-3663) and All Nippon Airways (800-235-9262).

Fukuoka is on a main *shinkansen* (bullet train) line originating from Tokyo Station. The trip from Tokyo takes five to six hours but passes by a good stretch of the country, including Mt. Fuji. From Fukuoka, regular trains serve Nagasaki (about a two-hour trip) and Kagoshima (about three-and-a-half hours to the main station, called Nishi-Kagoshima Station).

Cheap transportation is available in Nagasaki via easy-to-use streetcars. From Nagasaki Station, English signs mark the streetcars going to the Atomic Bomb Museum and Peace Park. Taxis are plentiful and because of the city's size and compact layout, they're generally affordable. A taxi to the Peace Park from Nagasaki Station costs about 1,200 yen. Fukuoka has an extensive and easy-to-use subway system. The Anchor Bar is in the Nakasu area, but it's tricky to find—best to give the address to a cabbie.

The combined train and bus ride to Chiran (via Nishi-Kagoshima Station) from Fukuoka takes five-and-a-half hours, making beautiful but largely rural southern Kyushu one of the few places in Japan where a rental car makes sense. Fukuoka is the best starting point for drives to Kagoshima or Chiran—Hertz (800-654-3131), Avis (800-331-1212) and other large car rental companies operate out of Fukuoka—which can shave about two hours off the train/bus time.

ACCOMMODATIONS

Nagasaki

Nagasaki Park Side Hotel

14-1 Heiwa-machi
T: 095-845-3191 F: 095-846-5550
61 rooms
12,000 yen to 18,000 yen

One of Nagasaki's top hotels is the only one just a block from Nagasaki Peace Park. Rooms are large (for Japan) and the restaurants (Japanese and continental) are good.

Nagasaki I.K. Hotel

Ebisu-machi
T: 095-827-1221
28 rooms
7,000 to 12,000 yen

Located in the heart of downtown, the I.K. emphasizes a "calm atmosphere" with a subdued staff and unique Western/Japanese combo rooms—Western beds with Japanese tatami mats and other touches. The Park Side Hotel is more convenient for touring the Peace Park. The I.K. is closer to city attractions.

Fukuoka

Grand Hyatt Fukuoka

1-2-82 Sumiyoshi, Hakata-ku
T: 09-2282-1234 F: 09-2282-2817
370 rooms
From 14,000 yen

Fronting the Naka River as part of the Canal City Hakata complex (a multipurpose center with 150 shops and restaurants), this four-star hotel is near the city center and next to the entertainment and business districts. The bars and dinner buffet are so good they draw as many locals as guests.

Kagoshima/Chiran

Kagoshima Tokyu Hotel

22-1 Kamoikeshin-machi
T: 099-257-2411 F: 099-257-6083
206 rooms
From 8,400 yen

Next to the Nishi-Kagoshima Station and across the bay from the huge Sakurajima volcano, the Kagoshima Tokyu Hotel has comfortable rooms, three restaurants, tea lounge, bar, pool and spa.

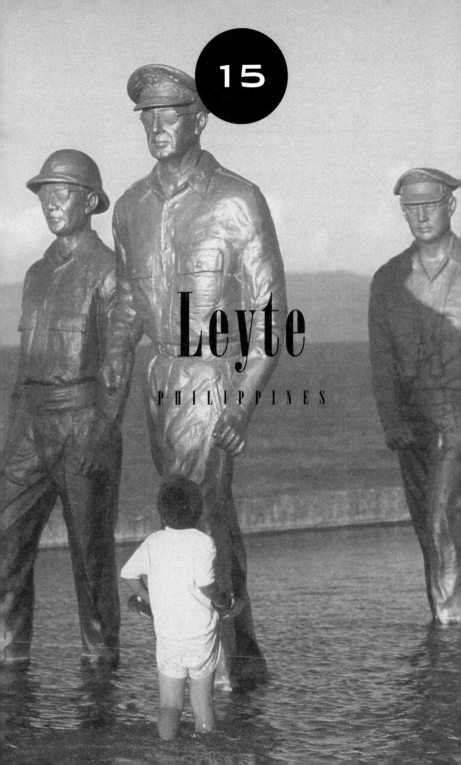

15

Leyte

PHILIPPINES

THE WAR YEARS

I n terms of ships and men, it was the largest naval battle ever fought. It featured the two most powerful maritime forces ever assembled and marked the first-ever appearance of the kamikaze fighter. The battle destroyed, with epic finality, any logical hope for the Japanese Imperial Command that it could win the war.

A series of five naval engagements, the Battle of Leyte Gulf, took place October 23-26, 1944. The battle was precipitated on October 20, when 200,000 Allied troops, under the command of General Douglas MacArthur, landed on the shores of Leyte Island with the aid of 738 vessels of the U.S. Seventh Fleet. This was the return of the American military MacArthur had promised following his ignominious departure from Corregidor Island in 1942.

Though Japanese defense of the island would grow increasingly stiff, the American landings met comparatively little resistance. Within hours of the initial landing, MacArthur waded ashore at Red Beach near the town of Palo, grasped a radio microphone and delivered his now famous speech: "People of the Philippines, I have returned. Rally to me. Let the indomitable spirit of Bataan and Corregidor lead on."

History's greatest naval battle was set to begin across an expanse of ocean roughly the size of Texas. The details are complex, but these are the essentials: Arriving from the east, the U.S. Seventh Fleet, commanded by Vice-Admiral Thomas Kinkaid, was charged with delivering the landing force to Leyte. Air cover for the beaches would be provided by three escort-carrier task forces—known as Taffy One, Two and Three—but otherwise, the bulk of Seventh Fleet defenses would be provided by the massive Third Fleet, commanded by William "Bull" Halsey.

The Japanese command had developed an intricate plan (Operation Sho) to thwart the anticipated American invasion. Arriving from points roughly west, two battle groups would attempt to catch the Seventh Fleet in a pincers movement. A third battle group, largely comprised of Japan's once formidable though lately ineffective aircraft carriers, would arrive from the north as a decoy, with the gambler's hope of luring Halsey's Third Fleet away from the main action.

The gambit worked. Sensing a crushing defeat of Japan's carrier force, Halsey left his defensive position to pursue Admiral Jisaburo Ozawa's carrier fleet far to the north at Cape Engaño, nearer to Luzon than Leyte. The Third Fleet would eventually rout Ozawa's sacrificial lambs, which included the *Zaikaku*, the last remaining veteran of the Pearl Harbor attack. But the Seventh Fleet and 200,000 amphibious soldiers were suddenly left without adequate defense, certain to be annihilated by Japan's Central Force, commanded by the able Admiral Takeo Kurita.

"Taffy 3 was all that stood between Kurita's guns and MacArthur's defenseless Leyte Gulf beachhead," wrote historian Kenneth Friedman in his comprehensive *Afternoon of the Rising Sun: The Battle of Leyte Gulf*. Thoroughly inferior in strength to Kurita's mighty Central Force, Taffy 3 was commanded by Rear-Admiral Clifton Sprague, the only major commander at Leyte Gulf to have seen action at Pearl Harbor. Executing a series of daring offensive and elusive maneuvers, and launching a swarm of aircraft,

Sprague managed a miraculous victory over Kurita, neutralizing the "super battleship" *Yamato* and saving the Allied invasion forces. Sprague's command has been called "the crowning achievement for the United States Navy in World War II" and is studied to this day at the U.S. Naval Academy in Annapolis. Among naval historians, "Halsey's Blunder" remains a hotly debated point of contention.

More than 2,000 aircraft and 244 ships engaged in the Leyte Gulf battle. The United States lost one light carrier, two destroyers, a destroyer escort and two escort carriers, one being the U.S.S. *St. Lô,* sunk on October 25 by the war's first recorded kamikaze attack. Japan lost one battleship, one fleet carrier, three light carriers, six heavy cruisers, four light cruisers and nine destroyers. As an effective fighting force, the Japanese Imperial Navy died at Leyte Gulf.

Japan's tenacious ground defense on Leyte eventually led MacArthur to commit 250,000 troops to the operation. Japan poured reinforcements through Leyte's "back door" port of Ormoc, but its mostly isolated soldiers were doomed. Advancing across the island, American soldiers found this letter written by an unknown Japanese soldier on December 21:

> "I am exhausted. We have no food. The enemy is now within 500 meters from us. Our end is near. What will be the future of Japan if this island shall fall into enemy hands? Hundreds of pale soldiers of Japan are awaiting our glorious end and nothing else."

The island was secured by the end of December. The Japanese lost 56,263 on Leyte. American casualties were 2,888 killed, 8,422 wounded. "The fortunes of war had shifted decisively at Leyte," wrote Louis L. Snyder in *The War: A Concise History 1939-1945*. "Whatever chance Japan might have had of winning the war in the Pacific was irretrievably lost."

SOURCES & OTHER READING

Afternoon of the Rising Sun: The Battle of Leyte Gulf, Friedman, Kenneth I., Presidio Press, 2001

The Battle of Leyte Gulf, 23-26 October 1944, Cutler, Thomas J., HarperCollins, 1994

Decision and Dissent: With Halsey at Leyte Gulf, Solberg, Carl, Naval Institute Press, 1995

The Little Giants: U.S. Escort Carriers Against Japan, Youngblood, William T., Naval Institute Press, 1987

Memoirs, Halsey, William F., Naval Historical Center, 1947

The End of the Imperial Japanese Navy, Ito, Masanori, Orion Press, 1956

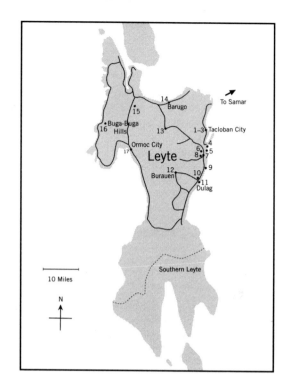

1. CAP Building
2. Philippine-Japan Peace Park
3. Hotel Alejandro
4. Japanese Pillboxes
5. MacArthur Landing Memorial
6. Hill 522
7. Bernard Reed Bridge
8. Palo Cathedral
9. Valeriano Abello Marker
10. Hill 120
11. Dulag Liberation Marker
12. Japanese Cemetery
13. Jaro Library
14. Battle of Baluarte Marker
15. Breakneck Ridge
16. Buga-Buga Hills
17. Philippine-Japan Memorial

LEYTE TODAY

Population: 2 million • Philippines Country Code: 63 • $1 = 50 pesos

Aside from its unattractive capital of Tacloban City (population 179,000), Leyte Island is a spectacular example of the beauty of the Philippine countryside. Divided into two provinces—Leyte and Southern Leyte—the roughly ninety-mile-long and thirty-mile-wide island is typified by heavily forested mountains and broad green agricultural plains. Farmers with caribou cultivating rice, corn and sugar cane remain typical. Tropical winds blow through much of the year, especially on the coasts. Life in general moves slowly.

At the main airport in Tacloban City, planes still land on the runway first laid out by American Seabees during the war. Plans are in the works for a modern airport, but outside the capital there has been little development. Southern Leyte has one of the country's lowest standards of living. The land looks much as it did when Liberation forces rolled through in 1944. Even more so than in the rest of the country, white males are still greeted with an enthusiastic "Hey, Joe," a leftover from the war years.

Short distances take a long time to cover via narrow roads. Four-star restaurants are nonexistent. Modern tourist services are limited. For some, this makes Leyte a discouraging place to visit. For others, it makes the island special. The MacArthur Landing Monument and sites along the eastern shore can be visited in a single long day. Including the scenic interior and West Coast, three days are recommended for the whole island.

1. CAP Building ★★★

Justice Romualdez Street, Tacloban City
T: 53-325-5693
Monday-Friday, 9 a.m.- 5 p.m.
(Closed noon-1 p.m.)

This colonial mansion served as MacArthur's residence and headquarters in 1944. It's now operated by the College Assurance Plan (CAP) insurance company. The General's second-floor bedrooms have been turned into a museum featuring photos, replica furniture and a preserved hole in the wall caused by an undetonated Japanese bomb. As the rooms are usually kept locked, visitors must ask permission to enter.

2. Maria Kannon Garden/Philippine-Japan Peace Commemorative Park ★

Magsaysay Boulevard, Tacloban City

The statue of an Asian Madonna was a gift from the Japanese people.

3. Hotel Alejandro photo exhibit ★★

P. Paterno Street, Tacloban City
T: 53-321-7033

Upstairs from the lobby is an extensive collection of rare photos and newspaper clippings from the 1944 campaign. Included are shots with semi-discreet captions of GI's hooking up with local girls. The exhibit is always open, even to nonguests.

4. Japanese Pillboxes ★★

Baluarte Beach Resort, San Jose Street, Palo, 9 kilometers south of Tacloban City

On White Beach are two intact concrete pillboxes on the grounds of Baluarte Beach Resort. The smaller one is located just in front of the pool. The larger one is about thirty yards south. Nonguests are charged five pesos to enter the resort.

5. MacArthur Landing Memorial ★★★★

National Road, Red Beach, Palo, 10 kilometers south of Tacloban City

The *pièce de résistance* of Philippine war memorials, (cover photo) this 1.5-times-larger-than-life bronze statue features MacArthur, Philippine president Sergio Osmeña and five others wading through the surf in fulfillment of the General's "I shall return" vow. Heated debate continues among several coastal communities regarding the "real" site of the famed landfall, but this spot is generally regarded as accurate (but don't tell that to the locals down the coast in Dulag). Mac and company stand eternally in a manmade lagoon. The beach behind them has been blocked by a seawall—no man will ever walk up it again.

On the well-maintained grounds are indigenous "peace" stones donated by emissaries of twenty-three countries including Russian president Boris Yeltsin and Czech Republic president Vaclav Havel. MacArthur's footprints—bronzed during his 1961 "sentimental journey" to the Philippines—are preserved in a glass case. The full text of his "return" speech is engraved on a plaque. As bombastic and vainglorious as Mac's critics claim, it's nevertheless a powerful speech to read, particularly in the presence of Filipino tourists, who are as noisy as any other tourists, but who stand in reverential silence before this document. For the majority of Filipinos, who still revere the controversial general, this memorial is a national treasure worthy of a pilgrimage. A large museum and expanded park are currently under consideration for the site.

6. Hill 522 ★★

Barangay Guindapunan, Palo

Commonly called Guindapunan Hill, this high ground overlooking the first town liberated in Leyte (Palo) was the scene of intense fighting. Japanese foxholes still exist. Traveling south on the National Road, pass the MacArthur Landing Memorial and turn right just before the Caltex gas station. After about a kilometer the road T's at a small Virgin Mary shrine known as La Purisima. The trail up the hill begins just behind La Purisima, climbing 522 feet to the top. A large wooden cross stands about halfway up the hill. For locals, the hike to the summit bears religious significance, not a historical one, and visitors are requested to tread accordingly.

7. Bernard Reed Bridge ★

National Road, Palo

This small bridge is named for the first American casualty in the campaign to liberate Leyte.

8. Palo Metropolitan Cathedral ★★

Barangay Luntad, Palo

Built in 1596, this well-preserved church was used as a military hospital from October 1944 to March 1945. The massive wooden doors with Biblical carvings are Spanish originals.

9. Valerniano Abello Marker ★

Tolosa Beach, 23 kilometers south of Tacloban City.

From the National Road follow the roadside sign to the "Scout Valerniano Abello Marker." Where the road dead ends at the beach, the marker sits about seventy-five yards to the left (north) on the beach in front of a large blue-and-white house.

There's not much to see on this strip of barren beach, but an interesting event that took place here is described on a small marker. Just before Allied landings, local Boy Scout Valerniano Abello used semaphore flags to apprise American ships of the locations of Japanese defenders: "Don't bomb beaches. There are civilians. If possible let me direct the shellings." The reply from a ship soon came: "Come immediately—awaiting." Abello became a local hero. He died on Leyte in 1999.

10. Hill 120 ★★★

National Road, Dulag, 34 kilometers south of Tacloban City

Atop this hill the first American flag carried by liberation forces was raised on October 20, 1944. A five-minute walk leads to the top and a large, helmet-shaped monument to the 96th Infantry Division, which took the hill. Picnic tables dot the grounds. An observation tower affords commanding views of Leyte Gulf. At the bottom of the hill are figures of American soldiers climbing palm trees, as well as small Japanese monuments.

11. Dulag Liberation Marker ★★

About 300 yards toward the beach from the Dulag town plaza, a thirty-foot-high inverted V marker reads: "The exact spot where the first batch of the Allied Liberation Forces landed at Dulag at about 10 a.m. on 20 October 1944."

12. Japanese War Memorial Cemetery ★

Barangay San Diego, Barauen, 52 kilometers southwest of Tacloban City

These remnants of a Japanese airfield and fenced flower garden and cemetery are frequently visited by Japanese memorial tour groups.

13. Jaro Municipal Library ★

Real Street, Jaro, about 38 kilometers west of Tacloban City

An unexpected legacy of the war, this is one example of the many libraries found around the country donated by U.S. veterans organizations. Many Japanese organizations also contribute to education projects and scholarships on Leyte and in the Philippines.

14. Battle of Baluarte Marker ★★

Baluarte, Barangay Minuhang, Barugo, 52 kilometers northwest of Tacloban City

This site of a large battle between Japanese soldiers and Filipino guerrillas is marked by a monument with rifles, helmets and bayonets.

15. Breakneck Ridge ★★

National Road, Capoocan, just past kilometer marker 972, 59 kilometers northwest of Tacloban City

A roadside sign points up a short trail to a Japanese shrine commemorating the "site of one of the bloodiest battles in the liberation of the Philippines." From the shrine, a path leads to the top of the ridge and views of Carigara Bay, Biliran Island and the mountain approaches to this heavily defended position.

16. Buga-Buga Hills ★★

Villaba, 146 kilometers west of Tacloban City via city of Palompon

In this mountain stronghold, 10,000-15,000 Japanese and hundreds of Americans died in a series of pitched battles equal in ferocity to anything seen in the Far East. Large Japanese tour groups, bone-hunting expeditions and seekers of the mythic hidden treasure of General Tomoyuki Yamashita often visit the area. Small Japanese markers and memorials dot the hills.

The mountains are high and separated by several wide valleys. Especially in the afternoon, hiking is a muggy, miserable endeavor. Still, there are many trails in the area. The road leading into the hills from Barrio Abihao in the town of Villaba is well known. It follows the main Japanese retreat line. On the western side of the hills, about ten miles from Villaba as the crow flies, less-frequented trails lead into the hills from the small town of Matag-ob.

17. Philippine-Japan Peace Memorial ★

Carlota Hills, Ormoc City, 109 kilometers southwest of Tacloban City

On one of the picturesque hills overlooking Ormoc City is this impressive memorial erected by the relatives of Japanese veterans. Though Ormoc was an important Japanese port, little of interest remains in the town.

OTHER AREA ATTRACTIONS

Santo Niño Shrine and Heritage Museum

Real Street, Tacloban City
T: 53-321-9775
Daily, 8 a.m.-4:30 p.m.
(closed 11:30 a.m.-1 p.m.)
200 pesos for first five persons,
20 pesos per person after first five

Former First Lady Imelda Marcos (Leyte is her home province) had this lavish shrine and mansion built between 1979-81 as an opulent showcase to her family's legacy of wealth and, by all evidence here, gaudy taste. Personal collections on display range from Chinese porcelain

to solid silver chairs from Spain to African ivory. Photos of Imelda and Ferdinand (chumming it up with Jack Nicklaus, etc.) decorate nearly every room. Built of rich native hardwoods and bamboo, the enormous structure itself is worth stopping for. The Philippine government now operates the priceless palace, the opulence of which comes as a shock amid this island of comparative rural poverty. Imelda nevertheless remains popular in Leyte, her queenly self-image on excessive display here being more a point of pride than outrage.

RELATED SITES BEYOND LEYTE

Guiuan Operating Base ★

Guiuan, Eastern Samar

On Leyte's neighboring island of Samar (connected by bridge) is the site of a 1.5-mile runway constructed by World War II Seabees. No longer in use except as a picnic site, the airstrip was used

throughout the campaign to liberate the Philippines.

Navy 3149 Base ★

Ngolos, 23 kilometers from Guiuan
Markers and remnants remain of a large American base. The area offers good views of the Pacific Ocean.

GETTING TO/AROUND LEYTE

Philippine Airlines (800-435-9725) operates daily flights between Manila and Tacloban City. Flights take about one hour and generally cost less than $100 round trip. Once in Tacloban City, driving is easy and a rental car is essential. RE

Rent A Car (53-321-4682) and FMC Rent A Car (53-523-6718) are reputable. Ferries and bridges make it possible to drive or bus (about twenty-four hours) from Manila to Leyte.

ACCOMMODATIONS

MacArthur Park Beach Resort

Government Center, Candahug, Palo
T: 53-323-4095 F: 53-323-2877
58 rooms
$30-$50

Just a few minutes walk from the MacArthur Landing Memorial, this decent beachfront resort has a pool and the best location on the island. Photos of the General decorate the open-air restaurant, key chains are shaped like his famous pipe.

Balhuarte Beach Resort

San Jose Street, Palo
T: 53-323-2389 F: 53-523-6540
10 rooms
$20

For budget travelers, this once-nice-now-rundown beach hotel has a pool and is a ten-minute walk up the beach from the MacArthur Landing Memorial. Two Japanese pillboxes are on the property.

Leyte Park Resort

Magsaysay Boulevard, Tacloban City
T: 53-325-6000 F: 53-325-5587
100 rooms
$45-$100

At the north end of the capital city is the only hotel on Leyte that measures up to Western standards. The Veranda Cafe bar, pool and ocean view compensate for the out-of-the-way location.

16

Tinian

MARIANA ISLANDS

THE WAR YEARS

I t's been argued, with some justification, that the most decisive weapon of the Pacific War was the bulldozer. The ability of U.S. Navy "Seabee" construction battalions to transform scorched battlegrounds into operational airfields, sometimes within hours, was without doubt a critical and innovative part in the Allied arsenal, one that vexed the Japanese war effort across the Pacific. Part of the Marianas chain, Tinian Island was to become the ultimate proving ground of the bulldozer and Seabee engineering prowess—and, as a result, linked forever with the most fateful day of the twentieth century. Before that could happen, however, the raised volcanic plateau, just twelve miles long and five miles across at its widest point, had to be taken from its determined owners.

Part of the overall Operation Forager effort to capture the Marianas, the Allied assault on Tinian and its 9,000 Japanese defenders commenced on July 24, 1944, with a massive naval feint near Tinian Town, the spot the Japanese guessed would be chosen for the inevitable amphibious invasion. The fake landing was based on a formidable U.S. intelligence effort. From July 10 to 12, "underwater demolition teams crawled right up on the beaches and observed the Japanese at work (constructing defenses near the town)," wrote Marianas historian Don Farrell in *Tinian*. The Japanese took the bait, pummeling the decoy U.S.S. *Colorado* with twenty-two direct hits from shore batteries. Meanwhile, more than 15,000 of the ultimately 42,000 invaders were landing on two narrow beaches—designated White Beaches One and Two—on the island's northwestern shore. The feint was a tactical success—"The most brilliantly conceived and executed operation in World War II," wrote Admiral Raymond Spruance after the war.

U.S. Marines quickly captured critical Ushi Airfield, soon to be renamed North Field. Japanese resistance stiffened with the drive down the island but the battle was short-lived, culminating in mass civilian suicide jumps from Suicide Cliff, a repetition of tragic events that had taken place on Saipan earlier in the month. By August 1, the island had been secured at a cost of 389 American lives. All but 252 of the 9,000 Japanese defenders were killed. Living a "troglodyte existence," hundreds of individual holdouts hid in caves and vowed to take at least one American life before they died. By January 1, 1945, an additional 542 Japanese had been killed with 163 more Americans killed or wounded.

Nevertheless, the island's population quickly swelled with the arrival of 150,000 American personnel. The Seabees who had made the damaged runways at Ushi Field operational within two days now set to work laying fifty-five miles of road on tiny Tinian, and building what was to become the largest and busiest airport in the world. Six 8,500-foot runways were constructed, four at North Field, two more at West Field.

Under commanding officer General Curtis LeMay, new B-29 Superfortress bombers began round-the-clock "Empire runs" on the Japanese home islands, just 1,200 miles away. From the runways of Tinian, American pilots delivered incendiary payloads that soon set ablaze Tokyo and other major Japanese cities. To American strategists, this proximity to Japan was the payoff for the costly operation to seize the Mariana Islands.

By June 1945, Colonel Paul Tibbets of the elite and ultra-secret 509th Composite Group had arrived on Tinian and begun making incessant and mysterious practice takeoffs and landings on the runways at North Field. On July 26, the ill-fated cruiser U.S.S. *Indianapolis* delivered the materials needed to make the world's first atomic weapon operative (having delivered the bomb parts, the *Indianapolis* was sunk and most of her crew lost on July 29 en route to the Philippines).

On August 6, 1945, following a massive photo event staged for the U.S. media, Tibbets and the twelve-man crew of the *Enola Gay* (the plane had been renamed the day before for Tibbets' mother) took off from Runway Able at 2:45 a.m. At 8:15 a.m. over the city of Hiroshima, the plane's bomb-bay doors opened, and the first atomic bomb dropped free of it restraining hook. Forty-three seconds later, the world changed forever.

"In the first millisecond after 8:16 a.m., a pinprick of purplish-red light expanded to a glowing fireball hundreds of feet wide," wrote Gordon Thomas and Max Morgan Witts in *Enola Gay*, the comprehensive account of the crew who dropped the bomb. "The temperature at its core was 50 million degrees centigrade. The flash heat started fires a mile away, and burned skin two miles distant.... All uilities and transportation services were wrecked. Over 70,000 breaks occurred in the water mains. Only sixteen pieces of fire-fighting equipment survived to plug into the ruptured system."

Most of Hiroshima's buildings were made of wood and clustered together within a natural bowl of green hills—qualities that made the city a prime target for the new weapon. Of its estimated 90,000 buildings, about 62,000 were destroyed in the blast and subsequent firestorm. Between 70,000 and 140,000 would soon be dead. Tibbets and the *Enola Gay* returned to Tinian for an island-wide hero's-welcome celebration that included free beer, a softball game and jitterbug contest.

Three days later, on August 9, the B-29 *Bock's Car*, flown by Captain Charles W. Sweeney, took off from Tinian and dropped another atomic bomb, this one on Nagasaki. On the evening of August 14, in a message transmitted to the Japanese legation in Switzerland, the Empire of Japan announced its surrender. With its final act having commenced on the runways built by American Seabees on Tinian, World War II was over.

SOURCES & OTHER READING

Tinian, Farrell, Don A., Micronesian Productions, 1992

Tinian: The Final Chapter, Russell, Scott, CNMI Division of Historic Preservation, 1995

Enola Gay, Thomas and Witts, Stein and Day Publishers, 1977

The War in the Pacific: From Pearl Harbor to Tokyo Bay, Gailey, Harry A., Presidio, 1995

World War II Remnants: Guam, Northern Mariana Islands, Lotz, Dave, Arizona Memorial Museum Association, 1998

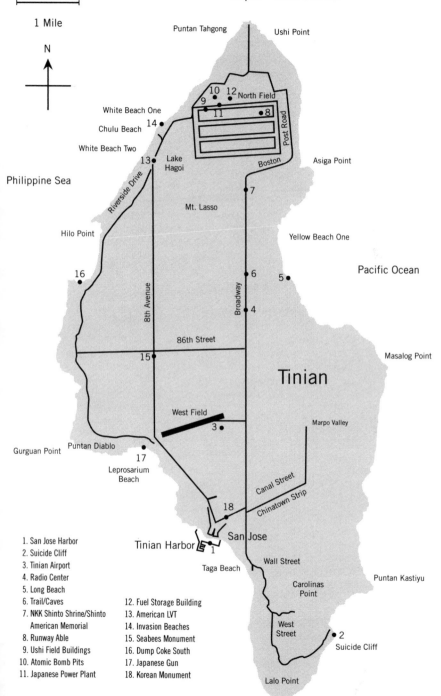

Saipan – Tinian Channel

Puntan Tahgong

Ushi Point

1 Mile

N

White Beach One
Chulu Beach 14
White Beach Two

13 Lake Hagoi

Philippine Sea

Hilo Point

16

Riverside Drive

8th Avenue

86th Street 15

West Field 3

Puntan Diablo 17
Gurguan Point
Leprosarium Beach

10 12
9 North Field
11 8

Post Road

Boston

Asiga Point

Mt. Lasso 7

Yellow Beach One

Pacific Ocean

6
5
4

Broadway

Masalog Point

Tinian

Marpo Valley

Canal Street

Chinatown Strip

18
San Jose

Tinian Harbor 1

Taga Beach

Wall Street

Carolinas Point

Puntan Kastiyu

West Street

Lalo Point

2
Suicide Cliff

1. San Jose Harbor
2. Suicide Cliff
3. Tinian Airport
4. Radio Center
5. Long Beach
6. Trail/Caves
7. NKK Shinto Shrine/Shinto
   American Memorial
8. Runway Able
9. Ushi Field Buildings
10. Atomic Bomb Pits
11. Japanese Power Plant
12. Fuel Storage Building
13. American LVT
14. Invasion Beaches
15. Seabees Monument
16. Dump Coke South
17. Japanese Gun
18. Korean Monument

TINIAN TODAY

Population: 2,000 • Country code: 670 • Currency: U.S. dollar

Few places in the Pacific have been as misrepresented as Tinian, part of the fourteen-island U.S.-affiliated Commonwealth of the Northern Mariana Islands (CNMI). Often described as dull, flat and featureless, the island, filled with numerous wartime sites and relics, answers in many ways to the enthusiastic description American atomic-mission flier Robert Lewis gave it in 1945: "It's wonderful! The jungle looks just like in the movies! And the water's the bluest I've ever seen!"

Tinian is not, however, the bustling place it was in 1945. About two-thirds of the island is still owned by the U.S. government and is occasionally used for military exercises. Its 2,000 residents are clustered mostly in the lethargic town of San Jose (site of former Tinian Town). Excluding a freakishly placed Chinese mega-casino, there are few services to entice the visitor for anything more than an overnight stay.

Still, Tinian is worth the trip. Just three miles from Saipan, the atmosphere is markedly different. Perhaps no American community anywhere displayed as many flags per capita after September 11, 2001, as Tinian, an island with streets laid out and named after Manhattan in 1944 by homesick American soldiers. Long and wide, Broadway still runs the length of the island as the main thoroughfare, flanked by Eighth Avenue. Brilliant blue-and-white kingfishers swoop over gorgeous cliff-side vistas and scenic spots such as picturesque Taga Beach. Undeniably slow-paced and rural, breezy and quiet Tinian nevertheless delivers one of the pleasant surprises of the Pacific.

Tinian's principle points of interest can be covered as a day trip from Saipan, though it's best done as a two-day, one-night excursion.

POINTS OF INTEREST

Sites are ordered in a loop beginning at the ferry terminal.

1. San Jose Harbor ★

At this facility built by the U.S. military, the U.S.S. *Indianapolis* dropped off the critical parts for arming the atomic bombs dropped on Hiroshima and Nagasaki. In front of the harbor is a damaged propeller and engine from what is likely a Japanese seaplane.

2. Suicide Cliff ★★★

Southeast coast between Carolinas and Kastiyu areas

At this beautiful spot, hundreds of Japanese and Okinawan civilians flung themselves (or were coerced by Japanese soldiers) to their deaths on the jagged rocks and pounding surf below, rather than be captured by American soldiers. The windy bluff is now a place of solemn grandeur, marked by simple Japanese, Okinawan and Buddhist monuments. The high cliffs above are pocked with Japanese caves.

3. Tinian Airport ★★

Off of Broadway, just north of San Jose

From this airfield—called West Field during wartime—American B-24s and B-29s carried the war to the Philippines, Iwo Jima, Okinawa and the Japanese mainland. In front of the airport is a small collection of weaponry, including the huge British-made naval cannon that scored hits on the U.S.S. *Colorado*.

4. Japanese Radio Communications Center ★★

On Broadway, 2.2 miles north of Point 3

The large concrete radio building with heavy iron blast shutters was used by the Japanese as a communications station, and later as a U.S. brig and post-war slaughterhouse.

5. Long Beach (Unai Dankulo) ★★

On a side road leading east off of Broadway, just north of Point 4

A Japanese machine-gun position is visible in the rocks on the south end of the beach. A small cave and similar fortification sit on the beach north about 150-200 yards. Americans captured the beach from the rear on July 24, 1944. Thereafter it was used mostly as a swimming and rest area for troops.

6. Japanese Defensive Trail/Caves ★★

Off of Broadway. At about 3 miles north of Point 3, follow signs 0.2 miles down rough jeep trail

Starting at a set of overgrown steps, a short (five minutes) trail leads to the first cave and bunker, partially concealed amid a huge bamboo grove. Similar fortifications exist around the base of the hill.

7. NKK Shinto Shrine/Shinto American Memorial ★★

Off of Broadway, about 4 miles north of Point 3

Built in 1941 by the NKK sugar company, the shrine and its two distinctive, large *torii* (gate) partially survived wartime bombing. North on Broadway a few hundred yards is Hinode Shrine, or Shinto American Memorial. Using rocks and shrine pieces from around the island, it was rebuilt by U.S. personnel in memory of all who died on Tinian.

North Field

A 1.1-mile loop trail includes all points listed in this box. With interpretive signs along the way, it can be picked up at any point, but with overgrowth and disuse it's often difficult to find and follow. In addition, all sites can be accessed by car. With all sites combined, North Field merits a ★★★★ rating.

8. Runway Able ★★★

Turn west off of Broadway onto a dirt road about 5.5 miles north of Point 3. The turnoff is directly across the road from the signed road to Blowhole. Follow the dirt road, turning right, then left, to reach Runway Able (aka Runway 1).

As long as military exercises aren't being conducted on this half of the island, it's possible to drive or walk the length of the abandoned but intact 8,500-foot runway used by the *Enola Gay* on its fateful

atomic bomb mission of August 6, 1945. One of the most massive construction projects of World War II, six gargantuan runways were constructed on Tinian (four at North Field, two at West Field), making this the largest and most active airfield in the world at the time.

9. Ushi Field Buildings ★★★

North along a short dirt path at west end of Runway Able

The concrete remnants of bullet-riddled air-raid shelters, a two-story Japanese Command Post and smaller Air Control Center for the Japanese Navy's First Air Fleet can be walked through. Torn open with obvious bomb holes, the large Command Post is particularly worthwhile. The kitchen, toilets and deep Japanese soaking tub remain, as does the concrete stairwell to the ruined second floor. The general area also includes numerous memorials erected by American military groups, including the 509th Composite Group, which from North Field flew the B-29 missions over Hiroshima and Nagasaki.

10. Atomic Bomb Pits ★★

From the Command Post, follow the dirt road north to the paved road and turn right at the sign. After about 100 yards, veer left at fork.

At 9,000 and 10,000 pounds respectively, the Hiroshima uranium-atomic bomb "Little Boy" and Nagasaki plutonium-atomic bomb "Fat Man" were too heavy for conventional loading. They were instead lowered into pits. The planes were then towed over the pits and the bombs winched into the bomb bays. Much ado is made of the bomb pits

today, but they've been filled in with dirt and are marked only by a sign and concrete outline. It's an historic location with little to see.

11. Japanese Power Plant ★★

Down a short jeep path just south of Point 10

The bomb-wrecked plant once supplied power to Ushi Field. The generators and heavy equipment are gone, but the basic concrete structures remain intact.

12. Japanese Fuel Storage Building ★★

A quarter-mile down an overgrown jeep path off the main road, just east of Point 10

Inside a large concrete building half-hidden in the jungle are hundreds of rusting fuel drums, the remains of a fuel dump from the old Ushi Field.

13. American LVT ★★

In the center of the Eighth Avenue traffic circle

Moved from its original resting place on the nearby Chulu Beach, the LVT (Landing Vehicle, Tracked) is badly rusted, but otherwise in one piece.

14. Invasion Beaches ★★

Head north from Eighth Avenue traffic circle and follow signs (veering left) to Chulu Beach. The beaches are less than a mile west of North Field as the crow flies.

At sunrise on July 24, 1944, U.S. troops swept ashore on two beaches—White Beaches One and Two—that had a combined coastline of just 220 yards, tiny for an assault force of 15,000. White Beach Two is now called Chulu Beach. White Beach One, now called Babui Beach, is 0.6 miles north of Chulu Beach along a primitive road. A Japanese blockhouse sits on Chulu Beach.

15. Seabees Monument ★

Eighth Avenue about 1.4 miles north of Point 3

On the site of the camp of the 107th U.S. Naval Construction Battalion, a small memorial is dedicated to all World War II Seabees. An engraved map shows Tinian as the Manhattan-minded Seabees built it in 1944-45, complete with Harlem and Central Park.

16. Dump Coke South ★★

From Point 15, head west off of Eighth Avenue on unmarked 86th Street. Where the pavement ends, turn right (north) and follow the grassy road (part of Riverside Avenue) 1.5 miles to its end. Turn left (west) and follow tracks downhill to the open plateau at the top of the cliff.

A few vehicle parts are visible in the shallow surf below the spot named by locals for the large amount of Coke bottles and heavy debris dumped into the sea by U.S. forces. It's the panoramic views of the dramatic coastline that bring people here now. On the opposite end of the bay is Dump Coke North.

17. Japanese Naval Gun ★★

On Turtle Cove at Peipeinigul Cliff, 1.8

miles north of San Jose on Riverside Avenue, then west 0.6 miles down rough road

In a cave at the end of the road sits a large Japanese naval gun still pointing toward the southern coastal approaches, the direction from which the Japanese expected the Allied assault to come.

18. Korean Monument ★★★

Eighth Avenue, less than half-a-mile north of San Jose

Upon this intense and perhaps least politically correct monument in the entire Pacific, the translated text in part reads: "Here lie five thousand nameless souls ... suffered by chains of reckless imperial Japanese army, by whom they were taken to (these) islands like innocent sheep, and then were fallen to this ground leaving behind them an eternal grudge." A small, brick Japanese crematory sits to the side of the monument. A chilling site.

OTHER AREA ATTRACTIONS

See Tinian Dynasty Hotel and Casino under Accommodations.

GETTING TO/AROUND TINIAN

By air, Tinian is reached via Saipan and Guam on flights operated by Northwest Airlines-partner Pacific Island Aviation (670-647-3603 in Saipan). Easier and cheaper, the Tinian Express modern high-speed ferry operates between Saipan and Tinian fives times daily each way. The first ferry departs Saipan at 9:30 a.m. Last boats depart Tinian at 11 p.m. and 2 a.m. The cost is $15 each way (free for children under four), plus a $2.95 passenger tax. The trip takes about an hour each way. The ferry is operated by Tinian Shipping and Transportation (670-323-2000 on Saipan; 433-0865 on Tinian). Ferries

operate from Saipan Commercial Port off Middle Road (just north of American Memorial Park) and the main port of San Jose on Tinian.

Rental cars are a necessity. Driving on Tinian's empty, country roads is easy. Islander Rent A Car (433-3025), Hertz (328-2233 ext. 2894; 800-654-3131 in U.S.) and Avis (433-2847; 800-331-1212 in U.S.) have local offices. Running through the center of the island, Broadway is always easy to identify. Otherwise roads are largely unmarked. As with other rural Pacific locales, asking for directions becomes inevitable.

ACCOMMODATIONS

Tinian Dynasty Hotel and Casino

One Broadway
T: 328-2233 F: 328-1133
412 rooms
From $110

The 75,000-square-foot, Hong Kong-based casino in a backwater like Tinian provides highly unexpected and incongruous comfort and distraction. In addition to the huge casino, there's a shopping arcade, good restaurants, swimming pool,

tennis courts, spa and karaoke lounge. Destined to fold, it's Tinian's only legit hotel ... while it lasts.

Meitetsu Fleming Hotel

San Jose, Tinian
T: 433-3232 F: 433-3022
13 rooms
$33

Several magnitudes below the Dynasty Hotel, this is nevertheless the island's best alternative. Simple but clean rooms.

17

Kanchanaburi

THAILAND

THE WAR YEARS

N o episode in the history of the Pacific War has had its public perception distorted by the movies so much as the events that took place during the building of the Burma-Siam Railway. By the time *The Bridge on the River Kwai* (based on a Peter Boulle novel of the same name) was released in 1957, the Western public knew well the saga of inhuman treatment Allied POWs received while building Japan's strategic railway through the jungles of Southeast Asia. But that didn't stop director David Lean's classic work from recasting the infamous "Death Railway" into a myth that inaccurately portrayed all sides of the story.

"Few of the prisoners who worked on the bridge would have recognized their commanding officer in Alec Guinness's Colonel Nicholson," wrote Britain's former Director of Army Education Clifford Kinvig in *River Kwai Railway*, by far the most authoritative and readable history of the event. "The bridge itself was destroyed not by commandos as the film would have us believe but, as many prisoners knew to their cost, by B-24 Liberators flying down from eastern India on long haul interdiction missions."

The matter of accuracy aside, it's the cinematic legacy that has to a large degree granted extended life to a story that might otherwise have been forgotten amid the war's litany of tragic episodes. Following its rapid conquest of the Far East in 1941-42, Tokyo's Imperial General Headquarters concluded that a rail link between Bangkok and Rangoon would provide a vital supply route to its forces now perched within striking distance of India. With 120,000 prisoners taken in Singapore, and whole countries now under its thumb, the Japanese command also concluded that it had an unlimited labor pool from which to draw the manpower needed to push its empire through some of the most inhospitable terrain on earth.

On September 16, 1942, at Thanbyuzayat, Burma, 3,000 Australian prisoners began construction of the Burma-Siam Railway. On the opposite end of the line, thousands of Allied prisoners—mostly Australian, British, Indian and Dutch—soon began pouring into the infamous base camp at Kanchanaburi, Thailand, about eighty miles west of Bangkok on the Kwai River (correctly known as the Kwae Yai and Kwae Noi rivers). From here they began work or were reassigned to camps working west to connect the two lines.

In addition, as many as 300,000 Javanese, Tamil, Malayan, Burmese and Chinese laborers were conscripted to help build the railway. Through malarial swamps, jungle-shrouded ravines and fast-racing streams and rivers, workers from more than 100 camps along the route laid track and constructed 688 bridges. Upon connection of the lines at Konkoita, about twenty-five miles from the Burma border, the track ran 257 miles—188 miles in Thailand, sixty-nine miles in Burma.

For POW and conscripted Asian workers, life became a daily appointment with torture, starvation and despair. Japanese overlords often forced sixteen-hour work shifts upon men who were barely fed and denied even primitive clothing and aid. "There were no medical supplies whatsoever," wrote American railway survivor Stanley Willner. "We were fed a handful of rice a day, a watery soup a couple times a week, and a pint of boiled water a day."

Worse were the dangers posed by the Southeast Asian jungle in which, according to author of the British medical history of the Burma campaign, "all the dread agents of fell disease and foul death lay in wait. There were very few other theatres on earth in which an army would encounter so many and such violent hazards." Where tropical ulcers had eaten through flesh until bone was exposed, amputations were performed by Allied doctors working with little more than old knives.

Among the approximately 61,000 Allied POWs taken to work on the Burma-Siam Railway, at least 12,399 died (the number is almost certainly higher). Most of these men were in their twenties or early thirties. Some were still teenagers. Of the more than 700 American POWs—most of whom worked on the Burma side—about 150 died. Estimates of Asian labor fatalities range from 60,000 to 150,000.

"The railway along the Kwai was built like the pyramids of old, with the labour and lives of a multitude," wrote Kinvig.

If the film version embellished the details, ignored the Asian labor pool and skipped much of the gore, it did capture the superhuman will of the men who not only survived, but, using mostly crude tools, forged a modern railway through the ruinous jungle. Bearing crossed Japanese flags, the first train chugged across the Burma-Siam Railway on October 25, 1943, signaling completion in about a year of a job that a pre-war survey had estimated would require five.

If the prisoners completed Japan's war work in remarkable time, they didn't have to worry about abetting the enemy cause. "Shipment over the Thailand-Burma railroad did not meet with any degree of success," wrote a Japanese logistics officer following the war. Bombing and strafing attacks by Allied B-24 Liberators wreaked havoc in the jungle, causing delays and necessitating repairs. Original projections called for the railway to carry 3,000 tons of cargo a day in each direction. Through the entire run of its operation, less than 500 tons per day crossed the tracks.

On August 28, 1945, the first groups of POWs were transported home from Bangkok via India. By November, 21,000 had returned to the UK and many others to Australia, Holland and other countries. Almost all rapidly regained weight and returned to health. Many would begin telling the stories and publishing the secretly kept diaries that have since turned the muddy, little River Kwai—in fact and fiction alike—into one of the most recognizable and mythic symbols of the war.

SOURCES & OTHER READING

River Kwai Railway, Kinvig, Clifford, Brassey's, 1992
The War Diaries of Weary Dunlop, Dunlop, Edward E., Nelson Publishers, 1986
Into the Smother, Parkin, Ray, Hogarth Press, 1963
The Railway Man, Lomax, Eric, W.W. Norton & Company, 1995
Speedo! Speedo!: To the Limits of Endurance, Spalding, Bill, Majic Ink, 2001
Tales by Japanese Soldiers, Tamayama and Nunnely, Cassell Military, 2000
The Bridge on the River Kwai, Boulle, Pierre, Vanguard Press, 1954

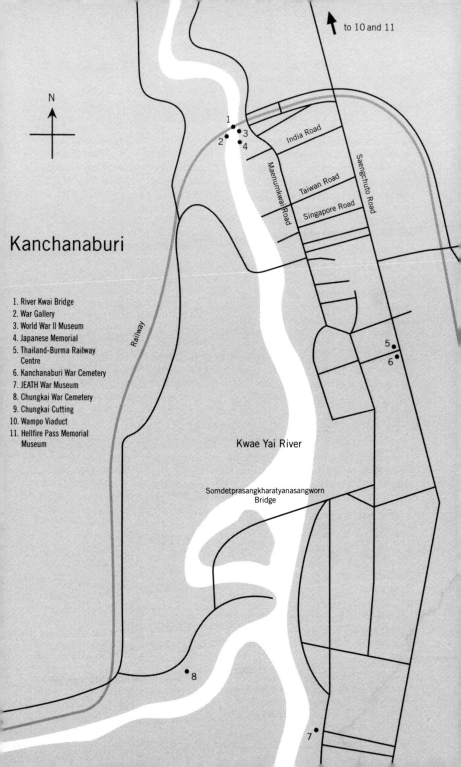

to 10 and 11

N

Kanchanaburi

India Road

Maenumkwai Road

Taiwan Road

Saengchuto Road

Singapore Road

1. River Kwai Bridge
2. War Gallery
3. World War II Museum
4. Japanese Memorial
5. Thailand-Burma Railway Centre
6. Kanchanaburi War Cemetery
7. JEATH War Museum
8. Chungkai War Cemetery
9. Chungkai Cutting
10. Wampo Viaduct
11. Hellfire Pass Memorial Museum

Railway

1
2 3
4

5
6

Kwae Yai River

Somdetprasangkharatyanasangworn Bridge

8

7

KANCHANABURI TODAY

Population: 400,000 • Thailand country code: 66 • $1 = 43 baht

Located about eighty miles west of Bangkok, Kanchanburi is a large Thai city set in the valley of the Mae Klong River. Downtown is noisy, congested and unremarkable. The city is the capital of the province of Kanchanaburi, Thailand's third-largest province, which borders Myanmar (formerly Burma) along its western edge.

According to a 1988 edition of Lonely Planet's Thailand guide, "not many Western visitors make it here." That changed in the 1990s as Thai and foreign traffic picked up around word of mouth and other River Kwai Bridge publicity. Tourism has helped make Kanchanaburi War Cemetery a major attraction and made feasible the new, state of the art Thailand-Burma Railway Centre.

Still, there remains one part of the Death Railway story that, due to local sensitivities, may never be told. Acting essentially as Japanese collaborators during the war, the Thai government and business community played an active role in the Death Railway, signing agreements and providing the Japanese Army with much-needed supplies. Those facts have been whitewashed here and are conveniently overlooked at every display, museum and memorial. It's worth noting that many Thai traders and civilians, at great personal risk, secretly supplied POWs with eggs, fruit and other survival essentials. It's also unlikely that many Thais, in government or otherwise, were aware of the horrors of the POW and Asian labor camps.

All Kanchanaburi sites can be visited in a single day. An additional day is recommended for the trip to Hellfire Pass.

POINTS OF INTEREST

Many addresses in Kanchanaburi are listed without numbers, only street names, and occasionally not even that. Most taxi drivers will know the way, regardless.

1. River Kwai Bridge ★★★

North end of Maenumkwai Road

Running about 1,000 feet over the Kwae Yai River, it's built of concrete supports and iron trestles, not giant timbers lashed together as depicted in the film. The bridge and languid, brown river beneath nevertheless possess a grim and captivating austerity. More vibrant are the bustling trinket and food hawkers on either side of the bridge.

As to the question of authenticity, this is the "real" bridge on the River Kwai erected by POWs. The bridge was heavily damaged and eventually knocked out of commission during bombing raids of 1944-45. The British, then the Japanese, repaired it shortly after the war. The curved spans and all but one of the concrete pilings are original. The two rectangular center spans are post-war replacements.

The River Kwai Bridge train station sits at the eastern end of the bridge. Trains bound for Nam Tok cross the bridge daily at about 6:15 a.m., 11 a.m. and 4:40 p.m. The two-hour, 17-baht train ride to Nam Tok roughly follows the Death Railway route. Contact the main Kanchanaburi station (34-511-285) for train information.

Every year between the last week of November and first week of December (dates depend on where the weekend falls) the Kanchanaburi Provincial Office

(34-511-778) sponsors the Voice of the Bridge Over the River Kwai light-and-sound presentation. For two weeks, fireworks and explosions light the sky above the bridge each night at 8 p.m. and at 7 and 9 p.m. on Saturdays. Seat tickets are 50, 100 and 200 baht.

2. War Gallery ★

Beneath western end of the bridge
Daily during market hours
10 baht

A thin attempt to cash in on the bridge trade, there's nothing remarkable inside this one-room, dirt-floor shack with sixty-two fuzzy black-and-white prints glued to dusty bamboo mats. What's striking given the events that transpired here is the pair of large Japanese flags heralding visitors out front.

3. World War II Museum ★★

395 Maenumkwai Rd., about 100-150 yards south of the bridge
Daily, 8 a.m.-6:30 p.m.
30 baht

This disorganized array of supplies, vehicles and weapons also features ghoulish, life-size painted, concrete figures of POWs at work, as well as figures of major Axis and Allied leaders. Perhaps nowhere else will you see Joseph Stalin and Douglas MacArthur resolutely standing next to one another, nor looking so strikingly similar. In an unscrupulous attempt to profit from publicity received by the original JEATH War Museum (see Point 7), a sign out front claims this is the "real" JEATH museum. It's not. The wooden remains of the "original" River Kwai Bridge inside are probably bogus as well.

4. Japanese Memorial ★

Maenumkwai Road, behind the World War II Museum

This monolith was erected by the Japanese, using POW labor, in February 1944, "in memory of the personnel of the Allied Forces together with other people who died during the construction of the Thailand-Burma Railway."

5. Thailand-Burma Railway Centre ★★★★★

73 Jaokannun Rd., adjacent to Kanchanaburi War Cemetery
T: 34-510-067
Daily, 9 a.m.-5 p.m.
Adult: 60 baht
Child (under 12): 30 baht

After years of relying on misinformed guides, visitors to Kanchanaburi finally have an authoritative center for information on nearly everything dealing with the Death Railway. The impressive Thailand-Burma Railway Centre was scheduled to open January 2003 in a new custom-designed two-story, 8,000-square-foot building. It's one of the best new attractions in the entire Pacific Theater. Exhibits include touch-screen computers, videos, relics and a large model of the entire railway. The center is also a research facility, with conference rooms and an extensive library, including out-of-print books published by POWs. The tour culminates in the second-floor gallery/coffee shop, which offers a stunning view overlooking the Kanchanaburi War Cemetery. The center is the brainchild of Australian curator Rod Beattie who has devoted the better part of the last decade (see also Hellfire Pass Memorial Museum) to delivering "the full story of the railway" amid the myths, errors and distortions generated by the well-known film and competing local efforts to capitalize on the famous bridge.

6. Kanchanaburi War Cemetery ★★★

Saengchuto Road
Daily, 7:30 a.m.-6 p.m.

This beautifully maintained cemetery contains the remains of 6,982 Allied servicemen, most of whom perished during the construction of the railway. An arched marble monument and enormous red flame tree dominate the magnificent southern corner.

7. JEATH War Museum ★★

At Wat Chaichumpon (Chaichumpon Temple)

Daily, 8:30 a.m.-4:30 p.m.
30 baht

Established in 1977 by Buddhist abbot Phra Theppanyasuthee, JEATH (an acronym for Japan, England, Australia-America, Thailand, Holland) displays photos and relics in a pair of narrow bamboo huts, replicas of the wretched POW quarters in use along the railway. Newer museums are beyond its league, but it's worth noting that long before the tourist explosion here, the humble JEATH was for many years the only organized local attempt to educate the public and keep alive the memory of the Asian and POW workers who died on the railway.

8. Chungkai War Cemetery ★★★

On the west bank of the Kwae Noi River, about 3 kilometers west of Kanchanaburi Bus Station
Daily, 7:30 a.m.-6:30 p.m.

Smaller but in a more serene location than the Kanchanaburi War Cemetery, Chungkai contains the remains of 1,740 Allied POWs who perished during construction of the Burma-Siam Railway. Maintained by the Commonwealth War Graves Commission, the cemetery sits on the southeastern corner of what was during the war a large POW camp.

9. Chungkai Cutting ★★

Follow the road to Chungkai War Cemetery and continue southwest about one kilometer past the cemetery. Where the road crosses the railway, turn left and walk about 500 yards.

The major cuttings through the rock at this spot mark the first major excavation of the railway.

10. Wampo Viaduct ★★

Highway 323, about forty kilometers north of Kanchanaburi. Turn left on the downhill road at signs to the district center of Sai Yok. Where the road crosses the railway, turn left and proceed about 3 kilometers.

The large timber viaduct still carries trains and exists largely as it did during the war.

The major modification is the addition of concrete bases for all the bridge piers.

11. Hellfire Pass Memorial Museum ★★★★

Highway 323, just past kilometer marker 66, about 80 kilometers north of Kanchanaburi
01-754-2098
Daily, 9 a.m.-4 p.m.

This beautiful Australian government-funded museum includes a seven-minute film with disturbing footage of skeletal POWs. Outside is a spectacular teak observation deck from which, on a clear day, Myanmar is visible less than twenty-five miles away. But the real attraction is the 4.4-mile hike along the actual railway route. Highlights include the small memorial at the excavation through the rock known as Hellfire Pass, and the Kwae Noi Valley lookout with its panoramic view of the 2.5-mile rail line that horse-shoed around the valley. Unlike much of Kanchanaburi, the terrain here remains undeveloped and thus more conducive to the kind of quiet reflection that perhaps makes it possible to edge closer in spirit to the events of the war—exotic insects, giant spiders and insufferable humidity included. Evidence of wartime construction work is visible along the trail, which was cleared in the 1990s with machete and chain saw by Rod Beattie (curator of the Thailand-Burma Railway Centre) and his wife. As the original line is impossible to follow—much of it lies beneath highways and farmland—this trail is especially valuable.

Buses for Hellfire Pass leave Kanchanaburi Bus Station every half-hour during the day and cost 25 baht. Motorbikes rentals cost 150-200 baht per day. The motorbike ride takes a little less than two hours. Local tour companies offer trips to Hellfire Pass, but usually as part of an all-day package that includes stops at several area waterfalls and swimming holes. Toi's Tour (45/3 Rongheepoil Rd.; 34-514-209; toistour@yahoo.com) is one of many local operators.

OTHER AREA ATTRACTIONS

Erawan Falls

Highway 3199, about 65 kilometers north of Kanchanaburi

Along with the famed bridge, most visitors come for the many waterfalls and swimming holes in the hills north of Kanchanaburi. The best and most well-known is

Erawan Waterfall within Erawan National Park, easily one of the most beautiful spots in Thailand. Many local companies offer day trips, including River Kwai Canoe (34-620-191) and Jumbo Travel Centre (3/13 Chao-Khun-New Rd., A. Muang; 34-512-280)

RELATED SITES BEYOND KANCHANBURI

Three Pagoda Pass ★

Many ads in Kanchanaburi for day trips to Three Pagoda Pass tout the area's Death Railway significance. There were

POW camps in the area, but there's nothing much left to see here. The three pagodas themselves are tiny, highly disappointing and not recommended.

GETTING TO/AROUND KANCHANBURI

Kanchanaburi is located on Highway 323. From Bangkok, the trip by car takes a little more than an hour once you're out of the city. Air-conditioned buses from Bangkok's Southern Bus Terminal depart every fifteen minutes during daylight hours, cost 70 baht and take about two hours. Slower but cheaper and vastly more interesting is the train from Bangkok's Thonburi station (no trains departing from Bangkok's main Hualumphong Railway Station travel to Kanchanaburi). The ride takes about three-and-a-half hours, but there's nothing quite like a Thai train, with its old wooden fittings and wide-open windows, chugging through the green countryside. Along Bangkok's Khao Sanh Road dozens of tour operators offer day and overnight package trips to Kanchanaburi.

Many attractions are within walking distance of the bridge. Motorcycle taxis are plentiful and cheap, usually charging about a dollar or two for rides just about anywhere. Motorbikes are available for rent at several shops along Maenumkwai Road for 150-200 baht per day.

ACCOMMODATIONS

Felix River Resort

91/1 Moo 3 Thamakham
T: 34-515-061
255 rooms
$60-$150

The Felix is the closest hotel to the bridge (a few minutes walk) and Kanchanaburi's only legit resort. With several good restaurants, bar, large pool, it's the best choice in town.

C & C River Kwai Guest House

265/2 Moo 1 Tanon, Maenumkwai Rd.
T: 34-624-547
Ten thatch huts
$5-$10

Several no-frills guest houses are located along the river on Maenumkwai Road, about a kilometer south of the bridge. Clean rooms, fans, private baths and a decent restaurant.

18

Chuuk (Truk)

FEDERATED STATES

OF MICRONESIA

THE WAR YEARS

During the early phases of the war, the mere mention of Truk (called Chuuk since 1979) curdled the blood of Allied war planners. With extensive fortifications and 40,000 to 50,000 defenders, Truk's gargantuan Japanese naval-air base was commonly referred to as the "Gibraltar of the Pacific." Used extensively in support of battles at Wake Island, Guam, Papua New Guinea, Guadalcanal and the Solomon Islands, its unchallenged power and strategic location made it the most important (and seemingly impregnable) forward anchorage for the Combined Fleet. It was at the time the largest Japanese naval installation outside the home islands.

As American forces began advancing westward across the Pacific—victories at Tarawa and the Marshall Islands moving them closer to Truk—plans to invade the island citadel became a point of increasing discussion and debate within the U.S. command. Unlike the massed Japanese troops stationed on other "leapfrogged" islands, Truk's mobile arsenal demanded direct confrontation. That finally came February 17-18, 1944, when waves of American Hellcat, Avenger and Dauntless aircraft were launched against Truk from the decks of fast carriers commanded by Rear-Admiral Raymond Spruance and Vice-Admiral Marc Mitscher.

The attack came as no surprise to the Japanese. Tipped off by American reconnaissance planes, Admiral Mineichi Koga had earlier ordered the island's big ships— including the super-battleships *Yamato* and *Musashi*—to disperse to safe harbors in the Philippines, Palau and Japan. Nevertheless, a large portion of Japan's supply and support vessels remained in the harbor.

Even with the escape of its capital assets, the American attack proved devastating for the Imperial Navy. Flying without current maps of the atoll, the first wave of seventy fighters—called the "Mitscher Shampoo"—destroyed or damaged two-thirds of Truk's 360 aircraft. American torpedo- and dive-bombers followed, turning the idyllic lagoon with its "Bali Hai" peaks into a smoking, blazing inferno, far surpassing the destruction wrought on Pearl Harbor. Throughout the assault, Japanese pilots tirelessly fought in the skies, returned to base, refueled, rearmed and rose to battle again. But they were outnumbered and usually outmaneuvered, particularly by the new and improved Grumman Hellcat fighters. Outside the atoll, Spruance, in his giant flagship *New Jersey,* along with other battleships and destroyers, "paraded around the reef sinking everything in sight," according to historian Robert Leckie.

In the two-day operation Japan lost two light cruisers, four destroyers, three subchasers, one torpedo boat, one merchant cruiser, thirty-one auxiliary ships and between 250 and 275 aircraft. Seventeen other ships were badly damaged. Seventy-five percent of the base's supplies lay in ruins. Estimates of American aircraft lost range between seventeen and twenty-four. No U.S. ships were lost though the carrier *Intrepid* lost eleven men and retired from action after being hit by a torpedo launched from a Kate torpedo-bomber. Nevertheless, with spectacular finality, the Truk operation proved the argument being increasingly voiced by fervid Navy airmen—aircraft carriers had indisputably replaced battleships as the capital ships of the fleet.

Admiral Koga was forced to move his headquarters to Koror in Palau. Though many of his warships had escaped the carnage of Truk—had they been caught there the Battle of Leyte Gulf might never have needed to be fought—Japanese shipping and auxiliary losses severely limited its ability to defend the vast ocean across which it had spread its might. Though the ultimate decision to cancel the invasion of Truk wasn't made until March 1944, the once-invincible naval-air base was no longer a significant power, from either the Japanese or American point of view. It would sit out the rest of the war as a broken, useless appendage.

"The outer perimeter of the Japanese Empire was pierced," wrote historian Louis L. Snyder. "With the neutralization of the master base at Truk the U.S. Navy could now roam at will through the Western Pacific."

The famously self-deluding Japanese command was rocked to realism by the calamity. With uncharacteristic candor, Radio Tokyo delivered news of the defeat to a stunned public. "The war situation has increased with unprecedented seriousness. The tempo of enemy operations indicates that the attacking force is already pressing upon our mainland."

Despite that increasing tempo, Truk remained in Japanese control throughout the war. As on so many isolated Pacific islands, its Japanese troops, imported labor and local Trukese existed increasingly on starvation rations until the end of the war. On September 2, 1945, in Truk Lagoon, aboard the cruiser U.S.S. *Portland*, the Japanese command surrendered roughly 38,300 Navy and Army troops still on duty throughout the atoll's many islands. U.S. occupation of Truk officially began in November 1945.

SOURCES & OTHER READING

World War II Wrecks of the Truk Lagoon, Bailey, Dan E., North Valley Diver Publications, 1992

The War in the Pacific: From Pearl Harbor to Tokyo Bay, Gailey, Harry A., Presidio Press, 1995

Delivered From Evil: The Saga of World War II, Leckie, Robert, Harper, 1987

The War: A Concise History, 1939-1945, Snyder, Louis L., Julian Messner, Inc., 1960

Dive guides

Diving Micronesia, Hanauer, Eric, Aqua Quest Publications, New York, 2001

Diving the Pacific, Volume 1: Micronesia and the Western Pacific Islands, Leonard, David, Periplus, 2001

Diving and Snorkeling Chuuk Lagoon, Pohnpei and Kosrae, Rock, Tim, Lonely Planet Publications, 2000

Truk Lagoon Wreck Divers Map, Bailey, Dan E., North Valley Diver Publications

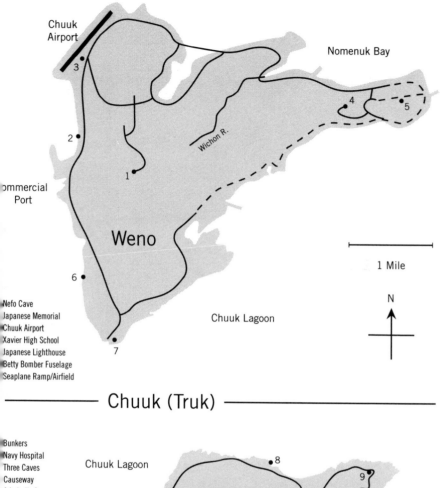

Chuuk Airport

Nomenuk Bay

Wichon R.

3

1

2

Commercial Port

Weno

6

Chuuk Lagoon

4

5

1 Mile

N

Nefo Cave
Japanese Memorial
Chuuk Airport
Xavier High School
Japanese Lighthouse
Betty Bomber Fuselage
Seaplane Ramp/Airfield

7

Chuuk (Truk)

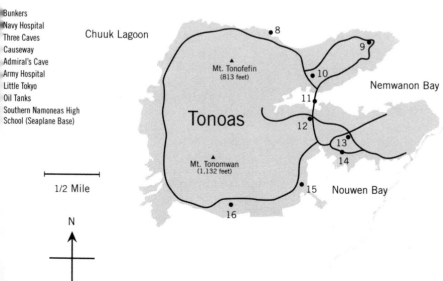

Bunkers
Navy Hospital
Three Caves
Causeway
Admiral's Cave
Army Hospital
Little Tokyo
Oil Tanks
Southern Namoneas High
School (Seaplane Base)

Chuuk Lagoon

8

9

Mt. Tonofefin
(813 feet)

10

Nemwanon Bay

11

Tonoas

12

13

14

Mt. Tonomwan
(1,132 feet)

15

Nouwen Bay

1/2 Mile

N

16

CHUUK TODAY

Population: 60,000 • Micronesia Country Code: 69 • Currency: U.S. dollar

One of the four Federated States of Micronesia (Pohnpei, Kosrae and Yap being the other three), Chuuk is, according to its license plates, a "diver's haven." The more than forty identified submerged Japanese wrecks within its forty-mile-wide lagoon have, more than anything, provided Chuuk with its outside identity. There are about 290 Chuukese islands in all, but most of the wrecks and population are found on the capital island of Weno (aka Moen Island) and nearby Tonoas Island (aka Dublon Island).

Stunning from the air and sea, Chuuk's rugged, jungle-covered mountains look straight out of a nineteenth-century South Seas adventure story. Up close, most of Weno, regrettably, looks straight out of a Peace Corps photo album. Ramshackle, tin-roofed houses, crumbling infrastructure and a laissez-faire approach to basics such as waste disposal often serve as the visitor's strong second impression. The abundance of alcohol (technically illegal) and a visible population of disenfranchised young men have given Chuuk a hard reputation among many travelers. Still, with English being an official language (with Chuukese), the exotic setting makes the place an interesting off-the-path retreat, and the concentrated wreck-diving is unmatched in the world.

Months could be spent exploring the wrecks of Chuuk Lagoon, but two or three days of diving more than covers the highlights. For land-based sites on Weno, a half-day is needed. Land-based sites in Tonoas require a full day—with no overnight accommodations, it's best visited as a day trip out of Weno. For a combined dive-land trip, four to six days in Chuuk are recommended. Chuuk's ranking on this list is based on the World War II interest of the casual diver. Nondivers should drop Chuuk toward the bottom of the list. Dedicated divers should move it to the top.

POINTS OF INTEREST

Weno Island (aka Moen Island)
1. Nefo Cave ★★★

End of unmarked Capitol Hill Road. Just beyond the governor's residence, the road dead ends at a large water reservoir. On the right side of the road is a trail leading uphill (fork right) about seventy-five yards to the cave.

The deep cave was blasted through the rock by forced laborers. Inside is a massive Japanese naval gun pointed out to the harbor. The gun was of little use against the American air attack. The entire hill is pocked with caves, but they're difficult to find through the brush—this prime example is the easiest to reach on the island.

2. Japanese Memorial ★

Main Road, just north of the Bank of Guam

Overlooking the harbor, the small memorial to Japanese and Micronesian war dead is comprised of a black orb on a polished black stone pedestal. The shipwreck in the background makes for a nice picture, but it's a civilian boat that ran aground after the war.

3. Chuuk Airport ★

Main Road, northwest end of the island

The old Japanese runway is still in use. The hills across the road are dotted with defense caves. Most entrances are overgrown or collapsed. A few anti-aircraft guns are scattered around the hills, but all are on private land, in dense jungle and difficult to access.

4. Xavier High School ★★★

At north end of the island, the pavement ends and the Main Road dead ends at a T. Turn right at the T, travel uphill about half a mile, turn right at another T and travel uphill a little less than half a mile to the collection of school buildings on the right (mountain) side of the road.

Surrounded by new buildings, the heavy concrete structure with thick iron blast shutters was the Japanese radio and communications center for the entire atoll. Heavily bombed, the building was repaired and now houses classrooms, a faculty center and auditorium. On the second floor are a student-painted mural recalling the war, and a small collection of relics taken from ships—sake bottle, gas mask, machine-gun rounds. To this day a defunct communications cable runs from the school undersea to the site of a former communications facility on Tonoas Island, which can be seen from the school's front lawn. The super-battleships *Yamato* and *Musashi* were usually anchored just beyond the small Yanagi Island, also visible from the lawn.

5. Japanese Lighthouse ★★

Small service road to northeast end of island, about 1.5 miles from Xavier High School

The large white lighthouse was built before the war, but the adjacent auxiliary building was constructed later to house munitions and supplies. U.S. planes bombed the whole structure. Sometimes blocked by the landowners, the jungle road leads to a set of steps leading to the lighthouse.

6. Betty Bomber Fuselage ★★

In the Tawaran neighborhood, about 0.5 miles north along the beach from Blue Lagoon Resort

The shiny aluminum front section of a Betty bomber sits on the beach. The wreckage is on private property and generally not open to public viewing. It's visible from the water as the only silver cylindrical object around.

7. Seaplane Ramp/Airfield ★

Main Road, southern tip of island

Behind the Blue Lagoon Dive Shop and Chuuk Coconut Processing Plant is the bombed-out remains of a Japanese seaplane ramp. The Blue Lagoon Resort and the road and flat area to the immediate east of the resort were the sites of a seaplane base and airstrip. Small holes in the hill along the road are collapsed personnel caves.

Tonoas Island (aka Dublon Island)

Getting to Tonoas requires a boat and likely a guide (see Getting to/around Chuuk). This section begins on a route assuming the normal northern approach from Weno Island and docking near Kuchua village on the northeastern fork of the island. Tonoas is circled by unmarked and mostly unnamed dirt roads. Distances are gauged by setting an odometer at zero at Point 9.

8. Bunkers ★★

Northwestern shore

On the boat ride from Weno, an array of coastal defense bunkers can be seen along the beach.

9. Navy Hospital ★★★

Kuchua village, northeastern corner of island

Around the area of the old, Spanish church (perched on a bluff overlooking the sea and still in use) is a collection of concrete remains of the Japanese's primary medical facility in Chuuk. The wooden buildings are gone. Left are concrete foundations, pilings and walkways. The church was used as a makeshift hospital ward after the American attack.

10. Three Caves ★★

From Point 9, down the road 0.7 miles along the road roughly following the north shore

On the mountain side of the road are entrances to three small caves. The area down the hill across the road was used for jungle-combat training.

11. Causeway ★

About 1 mile from Point 9 along the road roughly following the north shore

The small causeway crossing Tonoas' large Nemwanon Bay offers a good view of the island's two main peaks—Tonomwan (the taller peak on the left) and Tonofefin. In the jungle at about the notch between the two is a memorial to Pearl Harbor attack master Admiral Isoroku Yamamoto. The memorial is on private land and not accessible as of this writing. The commanding lookout from atop Tonofefin can be reached by difficult trail (see Point 13 for directions to the trailhead).

12. Admiral's Cave ★★

About 1.2 miles from Point 9, continuing south along road over causeway

The large accessible cave next to the road is about seventy-five yards deep. During wartime, the end of the cave contained a ladder leading to the atoll commander's quarters—that small passageway has been since filled in. A flashlight is helpful here.

13. Army Hospital ★★

1.6 miles from Point 9. From Point 12, follow the road south and fork left at the large sports field (built by the Japanese for baseball and other activities)

The large concrete building shortly after the left fork was a secondary hospital for locals, laborers, POWs and others of low status. If you fork right at the field and proceed about twenty to thirty yards, grassy trail leading uphill ascends Tonofefin mountain. The trail is overgrown and extremely difficult to follow.

14. Little Tokyo ★

About 2 miles from Point 9, on Nouwen Bay

Today, about 6,000 people live on Tonoas. During the war, more than 22,000 Japanese soldiers and workers could be found on the island at given times. This wide area just past the Catholic church (on the same road that passes Point 13) was once jammed with a thriving city of wooden buildings known as Little Tokyo. At least one small Japanese monument is visible from the road, but there's little else left to see.

15. Oil Tanks ★★

About 2.4 miles from Point 9, following the road past Point 14 to the road along the southern shore

Five gargantuan oil tanks, bombed and melted like plastic toys (the effects of explosions and subsequent fires), sit behind a growth of jungle about forty yards off the south side of the road. Pieces of the rusting hulks are visible through the trees. It's worth stomping through the jungle to get back to them.

16. Southern Namoneas High School (Seaplane Base) ★★

About 3 miles from Point 9, following road past Point 15

The open area along the southern shore—now a high school—was the site of a Japanese seaplane base. The wide concrete area served as the pad and hangar decks. The current school administration building is built directly atop an air-raid shelter next to the main ramp. Just down the road a remaining military office building with thick, concrete walls and massive blast shutters is being used as a residence.

OTHER AREA ATTRACTIONS

Dive and Snorkel Sites ◤

It's impossible here to cover all of Chuuk's shipwrecks and submerged aircraft (Zeros, Betty, Jills, Judy, Emily). Below are the can't-miss favorites. A selection of good dive guides to Chuuk can be found in this chapter's Sources and Other Reading section. A boat and guide are needed to access the following sites (see Truk Stop Hotel in Accommodations section).

Dive sites

Fujikawa Maru ★★★★★

South of Eten Island
Depth: 40 to 110 feet

Sunk upright, this 437-foot-long aircraft ferry is Chuuk's most popular dive. Among the many reasons are the broken Japanese Zero fighters in a hold and a well-preserved engine room. Easy penetration is possible into the superstructure.

Shinkoku Maru ★★★★★

Southwest coast of Weno Island
Depth: 40 to 120 feet

Extraordinary coral gardens and marine life are the hallmark of this 500-foot-long tanker. Penetration of the wheelhouse is possible. The sick bay includes operating table and surgical instruments. The galley has dishes. The port side torpedo hole that sunk her is visible.

Fumitsuki ★★★★★

Far west of Weno Island
Depth: 110 to 140 feet

Transports and freighters make up almost all of the lagoon's sunken fleet. The 320-foot-long Fumitsuki is a destroyer that, except for the collapsed bridge, still looks menacing compared with the other wrecks. Deck gun and torpedo tubes are visible.

Snorkel sites

Japanese Zero Fighter ★★★

Northwest tip of Eten Island
Depth: 15 feet

Even if you can't make it to the bottom, the intact though upside-down fighter is easily visible from the surface. One wheel and wing-mounted machine gun remain attached. This is a good swim to attach to any boat ride between Weno and Tonoas Islands.

Hino Maru No. 2 ★★★

West side of Uman Island
Depth: 5 to 40 feet

Upright on an incline, the badly damaged 998-ton cargo ship's forward gun sits just below the surface.

Patrol Boat No. 34 ★★★

West side of Tonoas Island
Depth: 10 to 40 feet

The armaments have been removed, but the coral covered bow is in shallow water. This 1,162-ton ship, upright on an angle, gives snorkelers a good idea of what the deeper wrecks look like.

RELATED SITES BEYOND CHUUK

Pohnpei and Kosrae ★★★

Part of the Federated States of Micronesia (FSM), the island states of Pohnpei and Kosrae were Japanese outposts during the war. Both were bombed by the United States but otherwise bypassed in the leapfrogging effort. Today, the picture-book islands are characterized by dramatic volcanic peaks and lush emerald jungle. Both have a smattering of leftover Japanese relics.

The FSM capital of Phonpei has a number of big guns, including an anti-aircraft gun on Sokehs Mountain, a wealth of Japanese tanks and a military dump. Four large naval guns can be found in the high jungle of Temwen Island. Off the eastern side of Pohnpei, Temwen is home to the Nan Madol ruins, a mysterious archaeological site of stone compounds and buildings with imposing walls as high as twenty-five feet. The sprawling complex was constructed between 1285 and 1485 and is among the most impressive attractions in the Central Pacific. The best place to stay is The Village Hotel (T: 691-320-2797; F: 691-320-3797). Rooms go for $80-$100.

For typical Micronesian beauty it's tough to choose between Pohnpei and Kosrae (as island destinations, both are superior to Chuuk), but Kosrae has more war artifacts and better beaches. The Mt. Oma hiking trail includes a honeycomb of Japanese caves. Lelu Hill includes air-raid shelters, trenches, foxholes and caves. The remains of a PBY flying boat and Japanese freighter can be dived in Lelu Harbor at thirty to seventy-five feet and seventy feet, respectively. In the town of Lelu, the Lelu Ruins are Kosrae's leading attraction. Similar in style, the stone fortress pre-dates Pohnpei's Nan Madol and is as impressive. In addition to being one of the few places on the island that sells beer and wine, the Kosrae Nautilus Resort (T: 691-370-3567; F: 691-370-3568) is clean, efficient and modern. Rooms are $75-$90. Pohnpei and Kosrae are reached via Continental Micronesia's island-hopper route (See Getting to/around Chuuk). Pillboxes and other coastal defense works can be found at Morsal, located near the southern village of Malem.

GETTING TO/AROUND CHUUK

Chuuk is reached via Continental Micronesia's (800-231-0856) island-hopper route that leaves Honolulu and services Majuro, Kwajalein, Kosrae, Pohnpei and Chuuk before finishing in Guam. The island-hopper flies in opposite directions on alternating days.

At seven square miles, Weno Island is essentially a one-road town with a few taxis and fewer places to go. Hotels listed below can arrange rides anywhere for a few dollars. Still, a car is essential for visiting points of interest. Rental agencies include Truk Stop Hotel (691-330-4232), Bernie's Car Rental

(691-330-2677) and Kurassa (691-330-4415).

Hotels can help arrange boat rides to Tonoas Island. No taxis and few private vehicles exist on the hilly, dirt road island. Everybody walks, but covering Tonoas' points of interest on foot makes for a very tough if not impossible day. The best way to visit the island is with Mason Fritz of M Tours (691-330-2065). A native of the island, Weno-based Fritz has a boat and a vehicle on Tonoas. Tours of Tonoas cost $50 and include snorkeling on the Japanese Zero listed above. Tours of Weno cost $20.

Accommodations

Truk Stop Hotel

Main Road, Weno Island
T: 691-330-4232 F: 691-330-2286
23 rooms
$95-$130

For a "diver's haven," Truk accommodations and dive shops can be surprisingly disorganized. Not at Truk Stop, a Western-standard operation on the lagoon that combines the island's most reliable dive shop with clean rooms, a good bar, restaurant and central location. Even for nonguests, this is the dive operation of choice. There's a small internet cafe next door.

Truk Blue Lagoon Resort

Main Road, southern end of Weno Island
T: 691-330-2727 or 800-367-5004
F: 691-330-2439
53 rooms
$105-$120

On beautiful secluded grounds, the Blue Lagoon is the best-looking hotel in Chuuk. It also has the best rooms and restaurant, but it's a little out of the way and the dive shop could use some improvements.

R.S. Plaza

Main Road, next to Chuuk International Airport
T: 691-330-2652 F: 691-330-2207
20 rooms
$50

In a five-story building that includes Chuuk's only elevator, the hotel has clean, comfortable rooms and a decent restaurant. With only a couple flights a day, airport noise isn't a concern. Internet service at Chuuk Telecom is next door.

19

Manila

PHILIPPINES

THE WAR YEARS

U nlike the war in Europe, waged often through towns and cities, Americans in the Pacific Theater mostly fought across desolate islands, barren hillsides and primal jungle. Manila was the exception. The only occasion on which American and Japanese forces fought in a major city, its ultimate ruin rivaled any other in the war. "No city suffered a more cruel fate. Not Cologne, nor Hamburg, nor London. Only Warsaw, perhaps," observed Filipino historian Alfonso Aluit.

Following the Japanese 14th Army invasion and advance across Luzon in December 1941, commander of American forces in the Philippines General Douglas MacArthur declared Manila an open city on December 26. Soldiers and guns were removed and American forces retreated to Bataan and Corregidor.

Japanese bombers nevertheless blasted Manila, destroying several prominent land-marks. About 8,000 American and British civilians were rounded up as POWs and herded into prisons at the suburban University of Santo Tomás campus and the national prison at Bilibid. Both were soon overflowing.

When General Masaharu Homma's army entered Manila on January 2, 1942, "it was accompanied by a large, well-trained propaganda corps: cultural warriors with a mis-sion to win the hearts and minds of the Filipinos," according to *The Battle For Manila* (Connaughton, Pimlott, Anderson), the most thorough account of the city in World War II. Japan planned to fold the Philippines into its Greater East Asia Co-Prosperity Sphere—the Asian world it envisioned free of European and American control. With motives ranging from nationalist zealotry to basic survival, some Filipinos collaborated with their new rulers.

But Japan had underestimated widespread Filipino loyalties to the United States and overextended its empire. Japan couldn't feed the massive population now beneath its military rule. As the Occupation wore on, guerrilla resistance gained strength. Deemed too lenient on the Filipinos, Homma was relieved from command and eventually replaced by General Tomoyuki Yamashita, the infamous Tiger of Malaya.

On October 20, 1944, 200,000 U.S. troops, led by MacArthur, began the invasion of the Philippines on Leyte Island. The drive through Luzon would be MacArthur's great triumph, the major land campaign of the Pacific War, second in size only to the U.S. push across Central Europe. Manila was the prize. On February 3, 1942, escorted by wildly cheering Filipinos, American tanks of the First Cavalry Division smashed through the gate at the University of Santo Tomás. Four-thousand skeletal prisoners were freed. MacArthur entered the city shortly after and pronounced its liberation imminent.

The battle for Manila, however, was only beginning. With Yamashita pulling back his army to the surrounding hillsides, Rear-Admiral Sanji Iwabuchi took over the defense of Manila with 20,000 troops. Unleashing a scorched-earth policy, Japanese troops burned docks, warehouses and other installations. Soon all of Manila was aflame, its 800,000 residents and doomed Japanese defenders thrown into chaos. Japanese troops embarked on a spree of killing, rape and mutilation "matched only by the pil-lage of Nanking in 1937," according to American historian Stanley Karnow. Babies were impaled on bayonets, women were raped, men were beheaded, bodies were mutilated.

"Once again the world was confronted by the now emblematic mark of the imperial bayonet," observed historian John Dower.

From street to street, hand-to-hand battle raged for a month. The final stand and most intense action took place at Intramuros, the Spanish-built fortress surrounded by a moat and twenty-foot-high stone-block walls. By March 4, the city was cleared of Japanese defenders, but the Pearl of the Orient had been reduced to rubble. One hundred thousand Manileños were counted dead. During World War II, the only larger city battles were fought in Berlin and Stalingrad.

Ironically, most Manileños lost their lives not to Japanese arms but to American artillery bombing. To preserve the city (or win laurels for the Army, according to critics), MacArthur prohibited air strikes on Manila. Nevertheless, American shelling destroyed most of the city's utilities, factories, residential areas and business district.

Indiscriminate and continuous bombardment killed tens of thousands and flattened residential areas that were hardly considered Japanese strongholds. In his activity report for the 37th Infantry Division, General Robert Beightler, among the chief architects of the wanton artillery attacks, wrote: "I have no apologies to make. ... So much for Manila. It is a ruined city—unhealthy, depressing, poverty stricken. Let us thank God our cities have been spared such a fate."

MacArthur reestablished his headquarters in Manila and from here arranged final surrender details with Japanese envoys in August 1945. Though officials from all major Allied powers were in attendance at Japan's formal surrender ceremony on September 2, 1945, aboard the U.S.S. *Missouri* in Tokyo Bay, no representative from the Philippines was invited to attend.

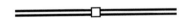

SOURCES & OTHER READING

The Battle For Manila, Connaughton, Pimlot, Anderson, Presidio Press, 1995

By Sword and Fire: The Destruction of Manila in World War II, 3 February-3 March 1945, Aluit, Alfonso, Bookmark, 1994

Retaking the Philippines: America's Return to Corregidor, Manila and Bataan, October 1944-March 1945, Breuer, William B., St. Martin's Press, 1986

The Philippines Under Japan: Occupation Policy and Reaction, Ikehata and José (editors), Ateneo de Manila University Press, 2000

In Our Image: America's Empire in the Philippines, Karnow, Stanley, Random House, 1989

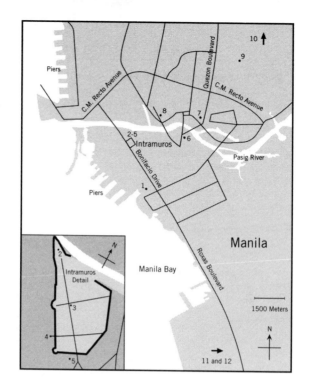

1. Manila Hotel
2. Ft. Santiago
3. Memorare Manila
4. Reducto de San Pedro
5. Revellin de Real de Bagumbayan
6. Manila Metropolitan Theater
7. Bilibid Prison
8. National Mapping Building
9. University of Santo Tomás
10. Chinese Cemetery
11. VFP Museum
12. Manila American Cemetery and Memorial

MANILA TODAY

Population: 11 million • Philippines country code: 63 • $1 = 50 pesos

Comprised of eleven separate cities, Metro Manila sprawls around the dirty Pasig River to the shores of Manila Bay. Heavy industry has reduced its status as one of the world's most beautiful harbors, though in the right light, the glory days can seem deceptively near.

Manila's extreme overcrowding and near-constant traffic jams are legendary. Heat, humidity and vehicle emissions render walking unpleasant. From cardboard shanties to children begging in the streets, reminders of the appalling poverty here are never far from sight.

Then there's the other Manila, the one of prestigious universities, world-class hotels, new shopping malls, crowded bars and restaurants and a civic leadership determined to restore the city to its former position of prestige. Millions have been spent in recent years on restoration and development projects, including the construction of modern mass-transit lines and near eradication of the city's infamous red-light districts.

A remnant of the Spanish legacy, the lost charm of public protocol is practiced throughout the Philippines. Service and courtesy are matched in Asia only in Japan. Along with this, the unflagging good humor and generosity of the people are the reasons why so many visitors, despite its endemic troubles, hold Manila and the Philippines in such high regard.

Most of the city's points of interest can be visited in a single, busy day.

POINTS OF INTEREST

1. Manila Hotel/MacArthur Suite ★★★

1 Rizal Park, Manila
2-527-0011

The hotel that was home to Douglas MacArthur from 1935-1941 (he was appointed hotel chairman and thus avoided paying rent) was the scene of room-to-room fighting in 1945. The hotel has been fully restored. MacArthur's top-floor penthouse, 10,000-volume library and personal collections were destroyed, but ten of his rooms have been rebuilt as the "MacArthur Suite," which rents for $2,000 a night (as president, Bill Clinton stayed here twice). When not in use, hotel guests can arrange tours of the suite through the guest services desk. Highlights include a spectacular view of Manila Bay, and MacArthur's original office and desk chair. Everything else inside is a replica.

Intramuros

The ancient walled city built by the Spanish beginning in 1589 was the site where Japanese forces made their final defensive stand in 1945. The walls stretch to more than four miles in length, enclosing an area of sixty-four hectares. About two hours are suggested to tour the area.

2. Ft. Santiago ★★★

2-527-3138 or 2-527-2961
Daily, 8 a.m.-9 p.m.
40 pesos

The pre-war headquarters of the U.S. military became the headquarters of the Japanese Imperial Army and Kempetai secret police. Hundreds of civilians and guerrillas were imprisoned, tortured or executed in the underground Spanish dungeon, which can still be viewed. Bullet holes and mortar damage are evident on walls throughout the fort—most of these came during the final eight-day siege in 1945 during which thousands died. Ft. Santiago was declared a Shrine of Freedom in 1950 and is now a national park. The Intramuros Visitors Center and adjacent gift shops occupy converted ammo dumps and storage areas.

3. Memorare Manila ★★

Plaza de Santa Isabel, corner of General Luna and Anda Streets

Depicting St. Isabel caring for the wounded, this large statue dedicated in 1995 commemorates the victims of the battle to liberate Manila.

4. Reducto de San Pedro ★★

1 Victoria St., Intramuros

This pentagonal structure built outside the Intramuros walls served as headquarters of the United States Armed Forces in the Far East (USAFFE). Directly behind it is "Number One Victoria," MacArthur's military headquarters, also known as Baluartillo de San Jose. From here you can walk along the top of the Intramuros wall—200-300 yards to the left (southeast) is Baluarte de San Diego, within which is the oldest fort in Manila. Outside is a deck gun from a Japanese cruiser.

5. Revellin de Real de Bagumbayan ★★

Corner of General Luna and Muralla Streets

The site of the final Japanese redoubt has been converted into a garden. Bullet and mortar damage is evident along the walls. The long red-and-cream colored building directly behind the wall along General Luna Street is the former barracks of the 37th Infantry, among others. It's now a school building.

6. Manila Metropolitan Theater ★

Corner of Padre Burgos and Basa Road, Manila

One of the few major buildings in Manila to survive the war, this formerly magnificent structure was once Manila's glitzy society center. It's now derelict and likely destined for demolition.

7. Bilibid Prison ★

Quezon Boulevard, Santa Cruz, Manila

The site of POW horrors remains a functioning city jail. Admission is generally not allowed, but small groups requesting visits through local tour companies (such as those mentioned in Getting to/around Manila) usually are accommodated. A former American POW visiting the facility in the 1990s remarked that conditions inside were better when the Japanese were running it.

8. National Mapping and Resource Information Authority Building ★

421 Barracca St., Binondo, Manila

Now the site of government offices, the building was used as a comfort-women brothel during the Japanese occupation.

9. University of Santo Tomás, Main Building ★★

Calle España, Manila
2-731-3101
Daily, 8 a.m.-9 p.m. during school year

The first area of Manila liberated in 1945 was this campus of the oldest university in Asia, where thousands had been imprisoned since 1942. The Main Building in the center of campus, where most prisoners were kept, now functions as an administration building. Prisoners lived in the classrooms such as those on the third floor and were allowed to exercise in the inner courtyards. Visitors are welcome to wander through the building. The gate the First Cavalry Division charged through on February 3, 1945, is directly in front of the Main Building on Calle España.

10. Chinese Cemetery ★★

South Gate on Aurora Avenue, Caloocan City
7:30 a.m.-7 p.m.

A section of the gaudy cemetery (a tourist destination in its own right) is reserved for the often-overlooked Chinese-Filipinos and immigrant Chinese who joined guerrilla groups or otherwise opposed the Japanese occupation. A large memorial stone stands in their honor.

11. VFP Museum ★★★

Veterans Road, Tuguig
2-838-5312
Monday-Friday, 7 a.m.-Noon, 1-4 p.m.
50 pesos

With life-sized, hand-carved wooden tableaus, the Veterans Federation of the Philippines (VFP) Museum brings to life the major "ambuscades" of the Filipino guerrilla movement. Unfettered by the restraints of political correctness, many models depict scenes of gore and violence. The result is a fascinating insight into the Filipino veteran's view of the war. Also displayed are weapons, uniforms and a bust of "Tomboy" Trinidad Diaz, a cement-factory accountant who led an ambush at Binangonan, Rizal.

12. Manila American Cemetery and Memorial ★★★★★

Fort Bonifacio at junction of Nichols Field and Fort Bonifacio roads
2-88-0212
Daily, 6:30 a.m.-5 p.m.

In terms of area and number of graves, this is the largest of all cemeteries built and administered by the American Battle Monuments Commission. The grounds cover 152 acres and include the graves of 17,206 military personnel who lost their lives throughout the Pacific. Seemingly endless Italian marble headstones are arranged in concentric circles around the massive and stunning memorial, which contains a chapel, twenty-five enormous mosaic maps chronicling major Pacific War campaigns and twenty-four marble hemicycles inscribed with the names of 36,279 missing soldiers. The serene setting amid Manila's chaos feels otherworldly. Located within Fort

Bonifacio (formerly Fort William McKinley), the cemetery was dedicated on December 8, 1960. Particularly for Americans, this is among the most moving sites in the entire Pacific.

RELATED SITES BEYOND MANILA

MacArthur Highway, Pampanga and Tarlac provinces

Two or three hours north of Manila, on the drive north toward the Lingayen Gulf invasion beaches, an approximately fourteen-mile-stretch of MacArthur Highway includes several interesting sites.

Kamikaze East Airfield ★★

MacArthur Highway, 2 kilometers north of the turnoff to the Clark Economic Zone, Mabalacat, Pampanga

Just south of the large, arched Mabalacat-Bambam Bridge stands a rising-sun roadside sign and large Japanese gate commemorating the original kamikaze pilots. Volunteers of the Imperial Nippon Air Force trained in this flatland. On October 25, 1944, the first kamikaze group took off from this field, sinking the U.S.S. *St. Lô* in the Battle of Leyte Gulf. Credited with the kill, Lieutenant Yukio Seki is hailed here as "the world's first official human bomb!"

Japanese Cave ★★

MacArthur Highway, 2.2 kilometers north of Kamikaze East Airfield, Bambam, Tarlac

To defend their airfields from the Allied advance of 1944-45, 30,000 Japanese troops entrenched themselves in caves, tunnels and bunkers throughout this area. Among the easiest to find is this unmarked cave on a hillside grotto featuring a statue of the Virgin Mary. Traveling north, just past the large Mabalacat-Bambam Bridge, the hill and grotto are visible to the left. About 140

steps lead to the top of the hill. Climb ninety-six steps to the small landing. Turn left and follow the dirt path about fifty yards to the cave entrance. The cave once accommodated many troops and went through the entire hill. It's since been blocked at about the halfway point, but it's still deep enough to make a flashlight useful.

Japanese Naval Aviators Shrine/Bunker ★★

MacArthur Highway, 5.4 kilometers north of Kamikaze East Airfield

Traveling north, on the right side of the highway is a small sign pointing to the "Japanese Naval Air Group Memorial Peace Shrine." Follow the narrow road about 2.5 kilometers. After it turns into a dirt road, the small stone shrine is located in a field about forty yards directly behind the fifth house on the right. The shrine honors "the brave spirits of Japanese pilots" as well as those of Americans and Filipinos. Each October 25, a Shinto priest and group from Japan come here to commemorate the first kamikaze mission during the Battle of Leyte Gulf. To the immediate left of the shrine is a large depression and concrete rubble, the ruins of a Japanese bunker complex. A fully intact Japanese bunker lies 300-400 yards to the left of the shrine. Built to accommodate twenty or thirty men, it sits mostly underground and is nearly impossible to find without help. The land belongs to the Arellano family, who live in several of the houses in front of the shrine. Someone is usually willing to lead visitors to the bunker if asked for permission to enter the field.

Related to the Bataan Death March,

Capas National Shrine, Capas Railway Station, Capas Death March Monument and Cabanatuan Memorial are all nearby. See Bataan chapter.

Lingayen Gulf

Used as the major troop-landing area in both the Japanese (1941) and Allied (1945) campaigns to capture Luzon, the Lingayen Gulf area is about 230 kilometers (a four-to-five-hour drive) north of Manila. The main Japanese landing beaches were on the eastern side of the gulf at Agoo, Caba, Santiago and Bauang. The main American landings were just south at Lingayen City, Bonuan, San Fabian and Damortis.

Lingayen Beach/Capitol Compound ★★★

Capitol Compound, Kalantiao Road, Lingayen City

Directly behind the Pangasinan provincial capitol building is a wide plaza with some of Luzon's few remaining large Pacific War relics. The intact shell of a plane is said by locals to be a Japanese Zero, but it's actually a Nakajima Kate torpedo bomber with parts attached from several other planes. Two American tanks, anti-aircraft guns and a covered photo display of the 1945 landings (203,608 Americans came ashore here) are also on the site. The actual landing beach is about 100 yards behind the plaza. It's wide and sandy and used by locals for recreation and fishing.

Bonuan Blue Beach ★★

National Road, Dagupan City, about 26 kilometers north of Lingayen Beach.

To find the beach, travel through Dagupan City on the National Road. Turn at the sign for Blue Beach, just after the Bonuan High School and University of

Pangasinan campus. This dirt road dead ends at the Ivory Coast Classic Homes subdivision. The plaque is in front of the gate. To the right is a dirt path leading directly to the MacArthur statue and beach.

A plaque here reads: "On this shore … the first combat troops of the Sixth Army of the United States of America under the command of General Douglas MacArthur landed 9 January 1945 to liberate the island of Luzon, thus fulfilling his promise to the Filipino people: 'I shall return!'" About 200-300 yards directly behind this plaque is a concrete statue of MacArthur. In contrast to the Leyte Landing Memorial, this MacArthur looks gaunt and rundown (perhaps the humiliation of yet more Navy assistance was by this time taking its toll on the General).

White Beach/San Fabian
PTA Beach Resort ★★

National Road to Barangay Bolasi, San Fabian, Pangasinan, about 45 kilometers north of Lingayen City
75-523-6502

On the beach just behind the pool at the PTA Resort a large plaque was dedicated in 1995 to "this sacred and historical site" where both the U.S. Liberation Task Force 78 (1945) and General Masaharu Homma and Japanese Imperial Army forces (1941) came ashore. The plaque has since been stolen but the empty stone housing remains. The resort itself was once the opulent private getaway of

Ferdinand Marcos. The Philippine Tourism Authority (PTA) now operates the property. With rich bamboo and tropical hardwood construction, it's the nicest place to stay or swim on any of the landing beaches. Rooms go for $15 to $30, not counting the Marcos Presidential Suite, priced at $120.

Northern Luzon ★★★ (for scenery)

When the Allied landings came in 1945, General Tomoyuki Yamashita pulled back the majority of his forces into defensive positions in the rugged mountains of northern Luzon. Areas around the towns of Kiangan (which includes a War Memorial Shrine in the shape of a large native dwelling) and Hungduan (which reportedly includes the house Yamashita used before surrendering) are popular with Japanese memorial tour groups. The area is also canvassed by Filipino, Japanese, American and other treasure seekers convinced that Yamashita's legendary gold treasure is buried somewhere in the surrounding mountains.

From Lingayen, it's another four-to-five-hour drive, though worth it for the incredible, 2,000-year-old Banaue rice terraces, a sprawling maze of landscaping genius that deserves its title of "Eighth Wonder of the World." This is by far the premier attraction in the entire country and well worth the long trip. Banaue information, as well as reservations for the Banaue Hotel and Banaue Youth Hostel, can be obtained from the Philippine Tourism Authority (2-812-1984 in Manila; 73-386-4087 in Banaue).

GETTING TO/AROUND MANILA

From the United States, Philippine Airlines (800-435-9725) offers daily flights to Manila from San Francisco and Los Angeles.

Because of Manila's chaotic traffic, rental cars for visitors are highly discouraged. Taxis are cheap and plentiful—usually a few dollars to anywhere in the city.

Several tour companies specialize in historical tours, including Rajah Tours Philippines (3/F Physicians' Tower, 533 United Nations Ave., Ermita, Metro Manila; 2-522-0541). Tony Estrada of Guides, Inc. (2-912-2719) is a superb, accredited Manila-based guide.

ACCOMMODATIONS

Manila Hotel

1 Rizal Park, Manila
T: 2-527-0011 F: 2-527-0022
500 rooms
$200-$400

For the combination of history, location and luxury, this former MacArthur residence is the clear choice. Still Manila's official hotel for visits by foreign dignitaries. A modern tower has been added to the original five-story hotel, so guests wanting to stay in the original building should request it when making reservations. The restored pub-style Tap Room bar was once ruined by furious fighting. War-era guests included Glenn Miller.

Makati Shangri-La Manila

Corner of Ayala and Makati Avenues, Makati City
T: 2-813-8888 F: 2-813-5499
698 rooms
$155-$330

Chosen as the Most Preferred Hotel for Business Travel in Manila by the *Asian*

Wall Street Journal, the Shangri-La has emerged as Manila's lavish hotel of choice. From high-speed internet access to toadying staff, no amenity is overlooked. For a five-star hotel, the prices aren't bad. The lobby alone is worth a look.

Bayview Park Hotel

1118 Roxas Blvd., Manila
T: 2-526-1555 F: 2-521-1285
275 rooms
$95-$130

A short walk from the Manila Hotel, this one offers a less opulent option on Manila Bay. The building is one of the few in Manila that survived the war. Good internet rates are usually available.

Manila Midtown Hotel

Corner of Pedro Gil and Adriatico Streets, Ermita
T: 2-526-7001 F: 2-522-2629
528 rooms
From $125

First-rate amenities adjacent to popular Robinson's Mall, putting dozens of restaurants within walking distance.

Heritage Hotel Manila

EDSA corner of Roxas Boulevard, Pasay City

T: 2-854-8888 F: 2-854-8833
453 rooms
$125-$250

This first-rate hotel often advertises discounted rates. There's nowhere good to walk from here, but the cab ride to the business and entertainment district of Makati makes it convenient.

Pan-Pacific Hotel

M. Adriatico Street, Malate
T: 2-536-0788 F: 2-536-6220
236 rooms
$125-$350

Another superb hotel that often offers internet specials well below the official rates listed above. Several good restaurants are located within the hotel.

Hotel Kimberly

770 Pedro Gil St., Malate
T: 2-521-1888 F: 2-526-7270
58 rooms
$35-$60

This reliable budget hotel is located in the Malate tourist belt. The deluxe rooms tend to be far better than the standard rooms and not much more expensive.

20

Guam

U.S. TERRITORY

THE WAR YEARS

When the U.S. Navy asked Congress in 1939 for $5 million to improve the Apra Harbor facility in Guam, Admiral Robert "Fighting Bob" Evans criticized the idea. "Anyone who wants it can take it in an hour," the Admiral noted blandly. He wasn't far wrong.

On December 8, 1941 (Guam time), moments after the first torpedoes began tearing holes in the American Pacific Fleet at Pearl Harbor, Japanese aircraft sank the ancient patrol craft U.S.S. *Penguin* in Apra Harbor and began a systematic bombardment of the farflung American territory. Two days later, 5,000 Japanese troops swept ashore at Asan Beach near the capital city of Agana and quickly overwhelmed the garrison of 550 U.S. Navy personnel and poorly armed All-Chamorro Guam Insular Defense Force. On the afternoon of December 10, naval governor George McMillan surrendered Guam, the most critical American port and airfield between Hawaii and the Philippines.

The thirty-one months of Japanese occupation that followed produced a succession of atrocities brutal even by the standards set in other Asian and European theaters of war. "The Chamorro people suffered more cruelly at the hands of the Japanese than any other indigenous people," wrote Pacific historian Arthur Dudden Powell in *The American Pacific.*

Guam historian Don Farrell called the occupation "two-and-a-half years of indignity, terror and death." Beheadings, torture, rape and forced labor terrorized the population. Several locals were executed for harboring radio operator George Tweed, the only American serviceman to survive the Japanese occupation without surrendering. Tweed hid in the jungle for two-and-a-half years before being rescued by the Allied invasion force of 1944.

The liberation of Guam was the final major act in the sweeping Operation Forager that took control of the entire chain of Mariana Islands. Following two weeks of naval and air bombardment, the first of 39,000 American attackers waded ashore at Asan and Agat beaches on July 21, 1944.

Guam-based Japanese aircraft had been destroyed in the June 19-20 Marianas Turkey Shoot, during which Japan lost 476 airplanes and 445 aviators. As a result, Japanese commanders lectured ground forces to perform with extraordinary valor. The 18,000 defenders of the Empire didn't disappoint them, fighting with a grim and often sake-filled intensity. Battles were savage, typified by the experience of the 2nd Battalion of the 9th Marine Regiment: forty percent casualties in the first twenty-four hours.

Japanese counter offenses were occasionally successful, but the better-equipped invaders slowly and painfully overwhelmed their entrenched positions. A final three-pronged banzai charge commenced at about midnight on July 25. In darkness and pelting rain, human bombs broke through American lines, waking groggy, wet Marines into a night of unforgettable carnage.

"Japanese orange signal flares and American white illumination shells lit up the night like the Fourth of July, silhouetting the running forms of the enemy," wrote Marine combat correspondent Sergeant Alvin M. Josephy, Jr. "The night was hideous with explosions, lights, screaming enemy and the odor of sake."

To their surprise and delight, the Americans would later discover that Guam had been Japan's major storage port for the sake, beer and alcohol reserves that fueled similar suicide charges across the Central Pacific. The July 25 battle, however, would last until early morning. With its final major charge exhausted, the Japanese army began to collapse.

The ruined city of Agana was captured on July 31. Soon after, at Yona, about 2,000 cheering and weeping Chamorros were freed from a prison camp. Organized resistance on Guam ended August 11, when the Mataguac command post fell after its commander General Hideoyoshi Obata committed ritual suicide. Total U.S. casualties for the twenty days of intense jungle fighting were about 1,400 killed, 5,600 wounded. Nearly all 18,000 Japanese soldiers were killed.

The capture of Guam, along with Saipan and Tinian, put Japanese cities just 1,200 miles away, within range of the new land-based B-29 Superfortresses, the huge bombers that from high above would drop fire and ruin on enemy cities. As the Allies inched closer to the Japanese home islands, Admiral Chester Nimitz moved his headquarters from Hawaii to Guam, where, in the closing months of the war, he helped orchestrate the final destruction of the Empire.

A bizarre postscript to the Guam battle story was added in 1972 when Japanese straggler Sergeant Shoichi Yokoi, after being discovered by hunters, emerged from the jungles at age fifty-eight following twenty-eight years of hiding. A tailor's apprentice before being drafted in 1941, Yokoi lived for nearly three decades in a tiny underground burrow, made clothes from the fibers of hibiscus bark and survived on coconuts, breadfruit, papayas, snails, eels and rats. Yokoi became an instant if not dumbfounded celebrity in Japan. His heroic effort was lauded by many, but ridiculed by a new generation of Japanese who viewed Yokoi's fanaticism as the type of dangerous anachronism that had lead to the country's disastrous war.

Sources & Other Reading

The Pictorial History of Guam: Liberation-1944, Farrell, Don A., Micronesian Productions, 1984

The Liberation of Guam: 21 July-10 August 1944, Gailey, Harry, Presidio Press, 1988

A Complete History of Guam, Carano, Paul Sanchez, Charles E. Tuttle Co., 1964

The Recapture of Guam, Lodge, O.R., Government Printing Office, G-3 Division, U.S. Marine Corps, 1954

The American Heritage Picture Dictionary of World War II, Sulzberger, C.L. American Heritage Publishing Co., 1966

Last Japanese Soldier: Corporal Yokoi's 28 Incredible Years in the Guam Jungle, Sankei Shimbun Fuji, Tom Stacey, 1972

World War II Remnants: Guam, Northern Mariana Islands, Lotz, Dave, Arizona Memorial Museum Association, 1998

1. Andersen Air Force Base
2. South Pacific Peace Park
3. Gun Beach
4. Hilton Gun
5. Skinners Plaza/Plaza de España
6. Latte Stone Park
7. Guam Museum
8. War in the Pacific National Historical Park
9. Piti Guns
10. Veterans Cemetery
11. Asan Bay Overlook
12. Yona Tank Farm
13. U.S. Naval Station
14. Ga'an Point
15. Umatac Bay
16. Japanese Fortifications
17. *Aratama Maru*
18. Yokoi's Cave

Philippine Sea

Guam

Two Lovers Point

Yigo

Tumon Bay

Agana Bay

Asan

pra Harbor

Pacific Ocean

Yona

Talofofo Bay

Talofofo Falls

atac Bay

Cocos Island

3 Miles

N

GUAM TODAY

Population: 150,000 • Area Code: 671 • Currency: U.S. dollar

With its mile-and-a-half crescent of white sand and bustling tourist parade, it's easy to pass off Guam as simply an island vacation retreat for Japanese travelers. The central Tumon Bay area has been called Waikiki West, and it is in fact lined with high-rise hotels, ramen shops, karaoke bars and overpriced souvenir stores where English is rarely spoken. But on the rugged thirty-mile-long by nine-mile-wide island—the largest in Micronesia—Japanese tourism plays only a part.

As an unincorporated U.S. territory, Guam remains home to several key U.S. military installations, notably the sprawling Andersen Air Force Base. The local population—about forty percent indigenous Chamorros along with a large community of Filipinos, and other Asians and Micronesians—are spread throughout the lush mountainous island. The pleasant capital city of Agana (also called Hagatna) is located on the western coast.

Though much more developed than other Micronesian islands, most of Guam still runs on "island time" and, away from the busy roads, retains many of the fabled charms of the region.

Even so, the most striking impression for the visitor—particularly one arriving from more rustic Asian and Pacific locations—is one of a tropical American town, complete with fast food, well-maintained roads, hip hop and classic rock on the radio and a high level of eating, drinking, shopping, entertainment, medical and other services. A rare privilege in Micronesia, visitors can confidently drink the tap water. For ease of travel, Guam is tough to beat for a mid-Pacific beach destination.

More than 200 World War II sites have been identified on Guam. Two to three days are recommended to cover the highlights listed below.

POINTS OF INTEREST

1. Andersen Air Force Base ★★★★

Route 1, northern end of island. Access restricted. Visitors pass must be obtained from Visitors Center.
T: 671-366-5651 (Andersen Visitors Center)
T: 671-339-6156 (NCTAMS Protocol Office)

Used as a base for B-29s flying missions against Japan, Andersen houses the remains of B-29s, Japanese fortifications and war memorabilia in Heritage Hall. The adjacent Naval Computer and Telecommunications Area Master Station (NCTAMS) includes the remains of a Japanese Jill torpedo-bomber, the site where Japanese war criminals were exe-

cuted and the cave used by fugitive radioman George Tweed. For access to NCTAMS contact the Protocol Office.

2. South Pacific Memorial Peace Park ★★★

End of Milalek Drive, off Route 1 (traveling north on Route 1, turn left just before the Mormon church) in Yigo
Daily, 8 a.m.-5 p.m.

The park sits on the site of the fierce, end-game battle for Guam on August 11, 1944. Japanese commander General Hideoyoshi Obata killed himself here alongside many of his soldiers. Down a short path from the small chapel are his caves and hara-kiri site, registered as a Historic Place by the Government of

Japan. A flashlight is needed to enter the caves. Other areas of interest include grave markers often decorated with fresh incense, sake bottles, beer cans and cigarettes. Stairs lead to a tranquil bamboo grove and spring with trickling water. In tone and design, perhaps no spot in the Central Pacific matches this one for traditional Japanese ambience.

3. Gun Beach ★★

Northern terminus of Route 14, about 100 yards down a dirt road near Hotel Nikko Guam

The rusted hulk of a 20cm Japanese naval gun and accompanying cement fortifications are tucked against the cliff at the northern end of the beach. The small quiet beach with easy public access is a good find on touristy Tumon Bay.

4. Hilton Gun ★

At Hilton Guam Resort and Spa, Tumon Bay
T: 671-646-1835

Several Tumon Bay hotels display war relics. On the grounds of the Hilton— next to the outdoor Tree Bar—is a relocated 20cm Japanese naval gun.

5. Skinners Plaza/Plaza de España ★★

Bordered by Martyr Street and O'Brien Drive, center of Agana

The adjacent plazas cover several pedestrian-only blocks. Skinners Plaza contains a bust of Douglas MacArthur, Guam Heroes Monument and a monument to Wake Island defenders from Guam. Once the seat of Spanish power, there's little left at Plaza de España, though the site where the U.S. surrendered to Japan in December 1941 is marked. Guam was the first American soil lost in the war. One block west of Plaza de España, two Japanese anti-tank guns sit in front of the Guam Police Department. A few blocks west along West O'Brien Drive are overgrown entrances to Japanese caves.

6. Latte Stone Park/Air-raid Shelter ★★

Corner of West O'Brien Drive and Chalan Obiso, directly behind Plaza de España

The principle attraction here are eight mysterious "latte" stone pillars, probably the foundation of a structure from a vanished Micronesian civilization. Also on the site is a series of interlocking caves used by the Japanese for storage and air-raid shelters. Visitors can enter the deep caves (the entrances are closed after dark), among the most well-preserved and accessible on Guam. Flashlight recommended.

7. Guam Museum ★★

Back of Richard J. Bordallo Governor's Complex (on hill overlooking the ocean), at intersection of Routes 1 and 6
T: 671-475-4228

Closed for some time as of this writing, the museum has in the past included a fascinating collection of war relics, and an exhibit with personal items recounting the dramatic story of Japanese straggler Shoichi Yokoi.

8. War in the Pacific National Historical Park ★★★★

Off Route 1 at Asan Beach
T: 671-472-7240
Visitors Center/Museum hours:
Monday-Friday, 9 a.m.-4:30 p.m.
Saturday, Sunday, federal holidays,
10 a.m.-noon, 1-4:30 p.m.
Closed Thanksgiving, Christmas and New Year's Day
Asan Beach Unit park hours:
Daily, 7 a.m.-6 p.m.

Part of the U.S. National Park System, the park encompasses seven separate units around Guam (a map is available at the Visitors Center). The primary units are the Visitors Center/Museum and adjacent Asan Beach Unit. The small museum features a thirty-minute film on the 1944 recapture of Guam and houses numerous artifacts including uniforms, weapons, photos and models of American and Japanese tanks, planes and warships.

Several hundred yards down the beach

interpretive signage tells the story of the American amphibious assault and bloody battle that occurred along this long stretch of beach. Within the park are pillbox ruins, an American submarine torpedo and Asan Cave, a Japanese fortification that runs deep inside a small hill (flashlight needed). Behind Asan Cave, the Asan Ridge Trail, which takes about twenty minutes to complete, travels past Japanese fortifications and two gun emplacements (sans guns).

9. Piti Guns ★★★

Trailhead next to Our Lady of Assumption Church in Piti. Follow Route 1 two miles west of Point 8, turn left on J.M. Tuncap Street, right on Assumption Drive and left on Fr. Mel Street. Parking and trailhead are 100 yards ahead on right.

At the top of a quarter-mile trail—it's mostly uphill stairs—three large, Japanese coastal guns remain near their original positions overlooking the Asan landing beaches. The third gun is in particularly good shape. The area is part of the War in the Pacific National Historical Park.

10. Guam Veterans Cemetery ★

Junction Route 1 and Route 6
T: 671-447-4013
Daily, 8 a.m.-6 p.m. Walk-in gate open 24 hours

A large dual naval gun assembly is at the entrance, but the eighteen acres are otherwise sadly unkempt.

11. Asan Bay Overlook ★★★

On Route 6, about two miles from junction with Route 1 at Guam Veterans Cemetery

Part of the War in the Pacific National Historical Park, this roadside pullout offers commanding views of Asan Bay, Orote Peninsula and the American land advance. As recorded on interpretive signs, from this hillside Japanese forces launched their massive banzai attack on July 25, 1944. The Route 6 loop here is known as the Historic Route. It includes

Nimitz Hill (site of the Admiral's headquarters at the end of the war), War Crimes Trial Site (now a high school parking lot) and locations of a Japanese command post, hospital and other sites.

12. Yona Tank Farm ★★

Central mountains of Yona

From Route 1 turn onto Route 6 at Point 10. After two miles turn right on Larson Road (unmarked), drive 0.1 miles, turn right on Turner Road (unmarked) and continue two miles to the top of the hill (Mt. Tenjo area). Just past the turnoff to the service road leading to three large radio towers, the road peters out into very rough jeep trails. Walk on jeep road until several even rougher jeep tracks (all interconnected and leading in the same direction) begin bearing east through the red clay. Walk the red-clay jeep roads about two miles to tanks, staying on the high ridges and not dropping into the canyons. There are no signs or trail markers—you have to keep an eye out for the tanks.

Including the words "farm" or "graveyard" in the name over-promises this site by several degrees. Five tanks are scattered in the area—they were disabled by the Japanese to keep them from falling into American hands—but only three are readily visible. Two of these are badly mangled and sunk into the ground and brush, but the third, a U.S. Sherman, sits above ground and is reasonably intact. There's no cannon, but its rusted engine is visible. As much as the tanks, the attraction is the hike through Guam's rugged interior. The four-mile round trip takes a tough two-to-three hours. There's no water on the trail.

The tanks actually sit about 700-800 yards from the rear boundary of the new, upscale Leo Palace Resort Country Club (671-471-0001). From the eighth floor balcony of condo building E, the large Sherman is visible. Access from the resort is officially blocked, but taking off from a road behind the resort will get you to the tanks in about fifteen mostly level minutes. For all that, the tanks remain tricky to find and are recommended only for dedicated boony stompers.

13. U.S. Naval Station (aka ComNavMarianas) ★★★★

Intersection of Route 1 and Route 2A, Orote Peninsula.
Access restricted. Visitors Pass must be obtained from the Protocol Office.
T: 671-339-6156 (ComNavMarianas Protocol Office)
T: 671-339-3319 (Marianas Military Museum)

On the large naval installation are many points of interest including Japanese anchors, a World War II memorial with a pair of 40mm guns, Japanese caves, Marianas Military Museum (many large guns), Japanese coastal fortifications at Gab Gab Beach, Orote airfield (built by the Japanese), bunkers, gun emplacements and a Japanese midget submarine. The War Dogs Memorial and Cemetery is one of the more interesting memorials in the Pacific—the 3rd Marine Division's K-9 Corps served as scouts, messengers, mine detectors and sentries. Twenty-five of the "Devil Dogs" were killed while in service on Guam. The names of all twenty-five—Pepper, Koko, Duke, Hobo, etc.—are engraved on the memorial with a bronze Doberman Pinscher sitting alertly on top.

14. Ga'an Point ★★★

Route 2, a little less than half a mile south of the junction of Route 12
Part of the War in the Pacific National Historical Park, Ga'an Point was the geographic center of the long Agat Beachhead and a firing base for Japanese coastal defense guns. Following the July 21, 1944, U.S. landings, viscious fighting took place here. Overwhelming heat and driving rain added to the misery on both sides. A Japanese dual-purpose cannon (used against both airplanes and ships) and 20cm short-barrel naval gun sit beneath flags of the United States, Guam and

Japan. A largely buried Japanese block-house includes the Japanese inscription, "Lt. Takagi, 2nd Group." Along Route 2 (0.4 miles north of Ga'an Point), the site of the command post used during the July 1944 invasion by Marine Brigadier-General L.G. Shepherd is marked by a red-and-yellow roadsign.

15. Umatac Bay ★★

Route 2 at Umatac Bay Park, southern end of island

Tides and storms have carried away all traces of the Japanese midget submarine that once sat on the beach at Umatac. All that's left are very broken remains of Japanese fortifications in the rocks along the south side of the bay. Regardless, Umatac Bay (and the drive to it) is included for being one of the most scenic places on Guam. Rimmed by impressive cliffs, the small beach has picnic tables near a large spire marking Ferdinand Magellan's landing here in 1521.

16. Japanese Coastal Fortifications ★★

Jeff's Pirates Cove, on Route 4 in Ipan, a few miles north of the junction with Route 4A
T: 671-789-1582
Daily, 8 a.m.-6 p.m.

Many Japanese fortifications remain along the eastern coast. One of the easiest to find is a pillbox on the beach about 100 yards north of Jeff's Pirates Cove, a good beach bar, restaurant and trinket shop once used as a rehabilitation camp for American pilots.

17. *Aratama Maru* ★ ◼

Junction of Route 4 and Route 4A, Talofofo Bay
A roadside sign marks the location and tells the story of the *Aratama Maru*, a 6,800-ton Japanese munitions ship sunk by the submarine U.S.S. *Seahorse* on April 8, 1944, in Talofofo Bay. The ship is broken apart at a depth of fifty feet. The waters here are murky, so it's not a great dive.

18. Yokoi's Cave ★

Talofofo Falls Park, about 3 miles south of Inarajan on Route 4. Follow signs to resort.

Daily, 9 a.m.-5:30 p.m.

T: 671-828-1150

$10

The original cave of the war's most famous straggler—Shoichi Yokoi hid out on Guam until 1972—is overgrown and essentially inaccessible. This replica (tacitly advertised as the real thing) pretty much consists of a narrow hole in the ground, barely big enough to crawl through. The burrow does as good a job as any random hole in the ground for illustrating Yokoi's hardships, but other exhibits are sparse at this tourist trap. The park is run by Koreans and visited primarily by Japanese tourists, so one might at least see a small amount of irony at work. A short cable-car ride takes visitors to the falls, which are one of the island's more scenic attractions. It's a nice place to visit, but not for the cave.

OTHER AREA ATTRACTIONS

Dive site ★ ★ ★ ◤

Tokai Maru

Apra Harbor

Scuba Dive Micronesia

T: 671-646-7440

Inclined on its port side and resting against the *Cormoran* (a Russian-built German World War I mail ship), the *Tokai Maru* is a 440-foot-long freighter sunk by a U.S. submarine in 1943. It rests at a depth of forty to 125 feet. Machine parts and the wheelhouse are highlights.

RELATED SITES BEYOND GUAM

Rota ★ ★

Between Guam and Saipan is the small (32.8 square miles) volcanic island of Rota, part of the U.S. Commonwealth of Northern Mariana Islands (CNMI). A Japanese base during the war, Rota was bombed but never invaded. As a result, it's retained a number of wartime sites including various fortifications, heavy guns, buildings, aircraft debris, caves and tunnels. Hotels in the main village of Song Song include Rota Coconut Village (about $100; 670-532-3448) and Bay View Hotel (about $60; 670-532-3414). Budget Rent A Car (670-532-3535) and Islander Rent A Car (670-532-0901) operate on the island. Daily flights from Guam are operated by Pacific Island Aviation (671-647-3600) and take about twenty-five minutes.

GETTING TO/AROUND GUAM

Guam is served daily with direct flights from Honolulu by Continental Airlines (800-523-3273; 671-647-6453 in Guam) and Northwest Airlines (800-225-2525; 671-649-8380 in Guam). Japan Airlines (800-525-3663) and other Japanese carriers operate many daily direct flights to Guam from Tokyo/Narita, Osaka and other cities across Japan. Philippine Airlines (800-435-9725; 02-879-5601 in Manila) operates nonstop flights from Manila.

Taxis and buses are plentiful, but a car is essential on Guam. Most major car rental companies are here including Hertz (800-654-3131; 671-646-5875 in Guam) and Nissan Rent A Car (671-647-7300).

Accommodations

Outrigger Guam Resort

1255 Pale San Vitores Rd.
T: 671-649-9000 or 800-688-7444
F: 671-647-9068
600 rooms
From $200

Upper-floor ocean views are spectacular at this five-star resort, which also has superb restaurants and lounges. Its beach and central location are among the best on the Tumon Bay strip.

Hilton Guam Resort and Spa

Tamuning (south end of Tumon Bay)
T: 671-646-1835 or 800-445-8667
F: 671-646-6038
691 rooms
From $185

On the southern end of the main tourist strip, the sprawling and impeccable Hilton is one of Guam's landmark, full-service resorts. Great ambience, popular spa, good outdoor bar.

OHANA Bayview Guam

1475 Pale San Vitores Rd.
T: 671-646-2300 F: 671-646-8738
148 rooms
From $149

A block off the busy Tumon Bay strip, the OHANA is a good hotel that offers a slightly discounted option in the main tourist area. Many rooms have balconies overlooking the gorgeous bay.

Airport Hotel Mai' Ana

253 Chalan Pasaheru St., Tamuning
T: 671-646-6961 F: 671-649-3230
48 rooms
$60-$85

With twenty-four-hour complimentary airport pickup and free shuttle service to restaurants and shopping centers around town, this clean, family-run hotel near the airport is a great find for transit passengers or anyone looking for a bargain. All rooms have kitchenettes.

21

Nanjing

C H I N A

THE WAR YEARS

For Americans, the beginning and end of World War II are easy to pinpoint: the December 7, 1941, attack on Pearl Harbor, and Japan's official surrender on September 2, 1945. For the Chinese, however, all-out war with Japan began in the summer of 1937 when the Japanese army, occupying Manchuria since 1931, launched determined offensives against China's most important cities. When Shanghai fell in November 1937 after stubborn resistance, Japan's Kwantung Army, led by the famously sadistic General Iwane Matsui, marched on the Nationalist government capital of Nanjing (also Nanking).

The result was the Rape of Nanjing, an orgy of murder, rape, torture and destruction that began almost as soon as Japanese troops smashed through the walls of the city in the predawn hours of December 13. "If one event can be held up as an example of the unmitigated evil lying just below the surface of unbridled military adventurism, that moment is the Rape of Nanking," wrote Iris Chang in her definitive *The Rape of Nanking.*

"The city's gutters literally ran red with the blood of its own people," reported historian Robert Leckie. "Chinese were machine-gunned en masse, 20,000 of them in a single day. Others were used for bayonet practice. ... The Yangzte River (became) a human logjam, thick with bobbing and bloated corpses."

The terror spree continued into the spring of 1938. Even conservative estimates of the carnage are difficult to fathom. Killing contests were organized among Japanese soldiers. Random beatings and beheadings were commonplace. More than 20,000 rape cases of women of all ages were reported. The actual number may be closer to 80,000, and this not accounting for those conscripted into Japanese military brothels, or "comfort stations." The death toll is generally placed around 300,000, though some sources claim the number more likely is about 400,000.

A small number of Western observers in Nanjing risked their lives to help the Chinese by setting up an international safety zone within the city and attempting to get news of the atrocities to the outside world. "These outsiders were, for one moment at least in Chinese history, heroes," wrote Chang.

Despite all of this, many Japanese remain unconvinced that the atrocities at Nanjing ever took place, saying the event was fabricated or at least wildly exaggerated for Chinese propaganda purposes. The dispute is based partly on the claim that stories about the massacre weren't widely circulated until after the war and that photographs of atrocities were staged. In 1996, a few years before his death, in an interview with American Scott Hards that was posted on a military website, famed Japanese fighter ace Saburo Sakai repeated the "staged photos" argument and summed up the contrarian view. "There's no question that Japanese soldiers probably killed a few thousand people there, but stories of 100,000 to 300,000 dead are complete fiction," said Sakai. "There weren't even 300,000 people in Nanjing at the time. Most of the city's population had fled when they heard the Japanese were coming. Most of the 'civilians' that got killed were probably Chinese soldiers masquerading as noncombatants by not wearing their uniforms." The legacy of skepticism continues to be a sore point in diplomatic relations between China and Japan.

The first Americans to face the Japanese in battle were not at Nanjing in 1937, nor Pearl Harbor in 1941. This distinction belongs to an unlikely group of pilots and ground support who would eventually be lionized as heroes in China and around the world. When Japanese troops took control of the legendary Burma Road, cutting off China from a critical overland supply route, American pilots (as well as pilots of other nationalities) employed by the China National Aviation Corporation pioneered flights over "The Hump," the terrifying flight route from India and Burma over the Himalayas. During the war, CNAC crews flew more than 38,000 trips over the Hump, braving violent blizzards and 125 mph crosswinds to deliver supplies to besieged China.

Separately, on April 15, 1941, President Franklin Roosevelt signed an executive order authorizing the formation of a top-secret organization of American fliers—the American Volunteer Group—to fight a Japanese air force that had already decimated China's paltry air defenses. Holding out the promise of a $500 bonus for each Japanese aircraft shot down, AVG recruiters initially signed up 100 pilots along with 200 mechanics, radio operators, meteorologists and assorted ground personnel. With its shark-toothed grin painted on the sides of its P-40 Curtiss Tomahawks (Walt Disney studios created the logo as part of a media campaign), the AVG became known as the Flying Tigers, one of the most colorful and successful outfits in the history of the war.

"The one undisputed force in Burma were the unforgettable heroes of the Flying Tigers," wrote *Life* magazine in March 1942. "They were a new type of fighting man."

Led by General Claire Chennault and counting among its ranks aces such as Gregory "Pappy" Boyington, the Flying Tigers amassed one of the greatest kill/loss ratios in the history of aerial combat, destroying a confirmed 296 Japanese aircraft, while losing only twelve of its own in combat. After only seven months in operation, the AVG was disbanded on July 4, 1942. Most of its pilots and aircraft were incorporated into the U.S. Army Air Force. Only on July 4, 1991, at a ceremony honoring the heroic airmen, did the U.S. government finally admit the truth—that the Flying Tigers had been secretly organized to fight against Japan more than half a year before the attack on Pearl Harbor.

SOURCES & OTHER READING

The Rape of Nanking: The Forgotten Holocaust of World War II, Chang, Iris, BasicBooks, 1997

Nanjing Massacre, 1937, Zhigeng, Xu, Panda Books, 1995

American Goddess at the Rape of Nanking, Hua-ling, Hu, Southern Illinois University Press, 2000

When Tigers Fight: The Story of the Sino-Japanese War, 1937-1945, Wilson, Dick, Viking Press, 1982

The Comfort Women: Japan's Brutal Regime of Enforced Prostitution in the Second World War, Hicks, George, W.W. Norton & Company, 1994

The Hump: The Great Military Airlift of World War II, Thorne, Bliss K., Lippincott, 1965

Way of a Fighter, Chennault, Claire, James Thorvardson & Sons, 1949

Baa Baa Black Sheep, Boyington, Gregory "Pappy," Bantam, 1958

Nanjing

Zhongshan Scenic Area

Xuanwu Lake

Yangtze River

Qinhuai River

Mochou Lake

Ningzhu Highway

Zhongyang Road

Bejing Road

Hanzhong Road

Jiangdong Road

East Zhongshan Road

Xin Jie Kou

To Yuhuatai

Hucheng River

N

1 Kilometer

1. Nanjing Massacre Memorial
2. Aviators Martyrs Monument
3. Zhongshan Wharf

NANJING TODAY

Population: 6.2 million • China country code: 86 • $1 = 8.26 yuan

On the southern bank of the Yangtze River, about 185 miles northwest of Shanghai, Nanjing was important in China long before the Japanese invaded. Starting in the 1920s, it served for a time as capital of Chiang Kai-shek's China, and was also capital of the country during the early Ming Dynasty (1368-1644). Along with a number of tree-lined streets and preserved woodlands, most of the city's attractions recall its days of Ming glory.

The capital of the Jiangsu Province, Nanjing is an important industrial center—electric, petroleum processing, chemicals, transportation, machinery—a beneficiary of the explosive economic prosperity of nearby Shanghai. Most of the city is in some stage of the noisy destroy-it-to-rebuild-it phase engulfing much of rapidly developing China. A new subway is being dug (target opening 2005). Working men and women hustle along the sidewalks throughout the days, especially around the busy city circle known as Xin Jie Kou. As in most major Chinese cities, life most often grinds along beneath a bank of gray pollution. Nanjing is not scenic, but it is appealing, a place where bicycles still battle cars for street space, and the odd revolutionary blue cap and jacket occasionally appears amid the pack of business suits and Western casual wear.

Whether for social, political or economic motives, the communist government has steadily plowed under many links to its past—immediate physical remnants of the Sino-Japanese/World War II era are few. All of Nanjing's wartime attractions can be visited in a single, easy afternoon.

POINTS OF INTEREST

1. Nanjing Massacre Memorial ★★★★★

418 Shuiximen, in the southwestern corner of Nanjing known as Jiangdongmen
25-661-2230
Daily, 8 a.m.-5 p.m.
10 yuan

Built in 1985 and officially called The Memorial Hall of Victims of the Nanjing Massacre by Japanese Invaders, this striking black-and-white granite memorial is comprised of large, open courtyards and several indoor exhibition chambers dedicated to the approximately 300,000 Chinese slaughtered in 1937-38. It's built on the site of a mass burial ground and the exhibit of victims' bones—housed in a large structure built to resemble a coffin—offers chilling and sometimes gory documentation of "Asia's forgotten holocaust." Arrows indicate bullet and bayonet wounds in excavated bones (human remains were still being uncovered by construction workers around Nanjing into the late 1990s). Skulls are displayed with thick iron nails driven into them—a favored torture method—along with the skeleton of a six-year-old child with bayonet scars.

The main museum lies half beneath the ground "like a colossal tomb." Inside the museum are graphic photos of executions—bayonet practice being held on a prisoner tied to a post being just one example—most reportedly taken by Japanese soldiers. One section describes similar horrors committed in other

Chinese cities. Another pays tribute to the International Safety Zone maintained in Nanjing's foreign community. With the contrast of lush pines and large bronze sculptures (a severed head, a grieving mother), the outdoor courtyards are at once beautiful and appalling. Interpretive signage is in Chinese, English and Japanese.

Located in one of Nanjing's least attractive suburbs, the memorial is nonetheless well maintained. Much of it is shocking— "Such things are rarely seen in this world," reads one sign—but it's ultimately a place of solemn grandeur. Like all memorials, this one carries a political message, good for some perspective on China's current drive at modernization and military empowerment. "The history of the Nanjing Massacre shows that slowly developing and backward countries can easily come under attack and be humiliated," reads concluding signage. "Therefore, we must do our best to build China into a stable, united, prosperous, powerful Socialist country and at the same time, do everything possible to maintain world peace."

2. Aviators Martyrs Monument (Kong Ri Zhan Zheng Hang Kong Lei Shi Gong Mu) ★★★

Ban San Road, at north tip of Zhongshan Scenic Area

Perhaps the least-known major monument to Pacific War veterans, this is also one of the most intriguing. It honors aviators from three countries—China, the United States and the Soviet Union— which for one brief, strange moment in history shared a common purpose, or at least a common enemy. This is a rare monument in China, recognizing foreign heroes, and one of particular interest given the history (and probably future) of ideological and political discord among the three powers jointly honored.

Surrounded by large pines, high shrubs and three Chinese pavilions, the focus of this monument is a fifty-foot-high, two-sided granite obelisk that rises like a pair of wings from a quiet courtyard at the top of 167 stairs. Flanked by two massive sculptures depicting triumphant fighter pilots, the obelisk is surrounded by stark, black marble tablets reminiscent of those found at the Vietnam Veterans Memorial in Washington, D.C. Inscribed on the tablets are the names of Chinese, American and Russian pilots and crew killed in the War of Resistance Against Japan. The majority of the names are American—about 2,000—reserved for the stones in the center of the courtyard. Most lost their lives over China in 1943-44.

The monument is large, but easy to miss. From the road, the entrance is marked by what looks like another Chinese gate of no major significance. With the Chinese name (Kong Ri Zhan Zheng Hang Kong Lei Shi Gong Mu) any cab driver will know the way. Because this extraordinary monument is listed in almost no English-language guides, a trip carries the added bonus of putting visitors in an interesting neighborhood that's rarely visited by travelers.

3. Zhongshan Wharf ★

Western terminus of Zhongshan Road, on the bank of the Yangtze River

Aside from busy port traffic, dirty Yangtze River and the blight of heavy industry, there's really nothing here to see. It's included simply for being, of the many areas around the city where mass killings took place, one of the easier to find. According to local sources, between December 16-18, 1937, about 9,000 Chinese were rounded up throughout the city on suspicion of "having served as soldiers." After being marched to the wharf and machine-gunned, their bodies were dumped in the river here along with about 900 area residents similarly killed.

OTHER AREA ATTRACTIONS

Yuhuatai (Rain Flower Platform)

East Yuhua Road
Monday-Saturday, 8 a.m.-6 p.m.,
Sunday, 8 a.m.-5:30 p.m.
15 yuan

This sprawling park of gardens, forest and a massive pagoda covers 1,537 hectares, but it's notable as a national center for Chinese Communist Party education and patriotism. An enormous granite sculpture of communist martyrs stands at the entrance of the park. Behind are the sort of gray, monolithic self-tributes for which communist governments are so renowned—an imposing monument, mausoleum and museum dedicated to the revolution. With Chinese and English signage, the museum documents the rise of the CCP and its bloody fight against Chiang Kai-shek's nationalist government. More than two million visitors a year—almost exclusively Chinese—arrive at this fascinating park. According to the Chinese, it's one of the top attractions in the country.

Zhongshan Scenic Area

This heavily wooded district on the northeastern side of the city includes the gorgeous white-marble-and-blue-tiled Sun Yat-sen Mausoleum. The nearby Lingu Pagoda is also nationally famous. Lingyuan Road runs past both the aforementioned, as well as several other sites of Ming-era relevance.

RELATED SITES BEYOND NANJING

Song-hu Museum ★★

Yuyi Road at Lijian Park, Boashan, Shanghai
Daily, 9 a.m.-4 p.m.
10 yuan

Located near the Yangtze River where Japanese troops first landed on August 13, 1937, the elegant museum commemorates the relentless, three-month battle fought for control of Shanghai. The unexpected struggle so enraged the Japanese Imperial Army it's said to have provided the catalyst for the eventual slaughter of soldiers and civilians in Nanjing.

Officially called the Shanghai Song-hu Campaign Memorial Hall and Museum, the story here is told mainly in photographs (signage is in Chinese only, but the message is easy to follow) augmented by relics, paintings and sculpture. The museum occupies three floors of an outstanding pagoda (one of the more interesting venues of a World War II museum) and is part of the small but pleasant Linjiang Park in the Boashan area on the outskirts of Shanghai.

Getting To/Around Nanjing

The best point of entry into Nanjing is Shanghai (which has an airport served by many major airlines). Many trains run between the two cities from very early morning (from Shanghai starting at 2 a.m.) to evening. Express trains take about two-and-a-half hours and cost 47 yuan. At the main Shanghai train station, English is spoken at the Foreigners Ticket queue at window number forty-nine. From here it's also possible to book forward or return passage from Nanjing—a good way to avoid the bedlam of Nanjing's train station where lines are long and English assistance is scarce. For those who don't speak Chinese, rental cars are generally more difficult than they're worth. Taxis are plentiful and cheap, from downtown no more than a few dollars to any point listed above.

Accommodations

Points of interest in this chapter are located on the fringes of Nanjing, with no worthwhile accommodations in the immediate area. Far better to stay in the city and cab to war-related sites.

Jinling Hotel

Xin Jie Kou Square
T: 25-471-1888 F: 25-471-1666
600 rooms
$175 and up

The standard bearer of luxury hotels in Nanjing is located in the busy city circle of Xin Jie Kou. Not counting historic points of interest, everything in the city is nearby. The hotel has every possible amenity, including good bars and restaurants.

Crowne Plaza Hotel

89 Han Zhong Rd.
T: 25-471-8888 F: 25-471-9999
300 rooms
$108-$350

Just off Xin Jie Kou, this reliable luxury/business hotel includes a department store on its lower floor.

Ramada Plaza Nanjing

45 N. Zhongshan Rd.
T: 25-330-8888 F: 25-330-9999
270 rooms
From $89

In the Drum Tower district about a ten-minute walk from Xin Jie Kou. Decent location, cheap internet rates at times.

22

Bataan

PHILIPPINES

DEATH MARCH

KM
00

THE WAR YEARS

Now synonymous with one of the greatest atrocities of the twentieth century—the Bataan Death March—the Philippines' twenty-mile-wide, twenty-five-mile-long Bataan Peninsula was in 1941 simply the obscure hinge upon which swung the American military's longstanding plan for the defense of the Philippines. In case of attack, War Plan Orange called for Filipino and American (Fil-Am) defense forces to fall back to the mountainous peninsula and await naval reinforcements. Unfortunately for the Fil-Am defenders, by the time General Masaharu Homma landed with an invasion force at Lingayen Gulf on December 10, 1941, most of the U.S. fleet was resting at the bottom of Pearl Harbor.

The Japanese command was intimately familiar with War Plan Orange—throughout the 1930s, Japanese exchange officers had studied it at West Point—but their invasion hardly went off on the fifty-day timetable they'd planned for the conquest of Luzon, the Philippines' largest island. The Battle of Bataan began at the Hermosa-Dinalupihan line on January 6, 1942. The Japanese infantry seemed almost superhuman—attackers threw themselves on barbed-wire entanglements, allowing comrades to cross over their writhing bodies. For three months, the battle became a seesaw of attacks and counterattacks between two armies at the point of collapse from lack of food, rest and medical supplies. As on Corregidor, Philippine Army regulars and regiments of the Philippine Scouts (part of the U.S. Army in the Philippines) distinguished themselves with spectacular bravery, strengthening bonds in the Fil-Am ranks.

With rations cut and tropical diseases ravaging its camps, 13,000 Japanese soldiers were forced into makeshift hospital beds. The isolated Fil-Am garrison had it worse. With rations halved in January, and halved again in March, the self-proclaimed "Battling Bastards of Bataan" were eventually subsisting on fifteen ounces of gummy rice per day. Nearly all had malaria, most had dysentery. Men and women foraged for any sustenance: dogs, mules, monkeys, iguanas, snakes, edible roots.

"With the possible exception of Stalingrad, no battle that year was fought under worse conditions," wrote historian William Manchester.

On March 12, General Douglas MacArthur, commander of all American forces in the Philippines, left the island of Corregidor under orders from President Franklin Roosevelt. MacArthur turned up in Australia, but there was to be no miracle escape for the men on Bataan. Boosted by reinforcements from the home islands and enjoying total air superiority, the Japanese opened their final assault on April 3. The Fil-Am fighters were too weak to mount a counter-attack. On April 9, U.S. Major-General Edward King surrendered 78,000 troops to Colonel Moto Nakayama. It remains the largest capitulation of American forces in history.

A gruesome sequel awaited the survivors. In blazing heat, Japanese soldiers forced their prisoners to walk fifty-five miles from Mariveles, Bataan, to San Fernando, Pampanga. Here they were crammed into rail cars—many died standing, with no room to fall—and transported twenty-four miles to Capas, Tarlac. They were then marched another six miles to Camp O'Donnell, the American facility hastily turned into a POW camp. This was the route of the infamous Bataan Death March.

Along the march, weakened men were denied food or water. Beatings, bayonetings and beheadings raged on in full view of the terrified prisoners. Stragglers were shot, as were those who attempted to help them. Men crazed with thirst were punished for falling out of line to drink from muddy potholes. Threatened with death, men were forced to bury their comrades alive. As if to reinforce the random nature of the brutality, many marchers were well treated. Some rode in trucks.

Of the 75,000 men—and 100 female nurses—who started the march, 54,000 completed it. About 10,000 died on the way, the rest escaped into the jungle. Camp O'Donnell brought no relief. Over the next three months, nearly 2,000 Americans and as many as 25,000 Filipinos died of disease, hunger or maltreatment. On June 6, most of the POWs were transferred to a new camp at Cabanatuan, where they were united with the defenders of since-fallen Corregidor.

The American campaign to retake Bataan met with little resistance. On January 25, 1945, troops landed unopposed on the Zambales coast of Northwest Bataan. The critical port of Olongapo on Subic Bay was taken without a single man lost. After an intense battle at Zigzag Pass near Olongapo, Fil-Am troops quickly dispatched the mere 1,400 Japanese defenders remaining on Bataan.

An interesting sidelight to the battle is the infamy it earned for the leading generals on both sides. MacArthur named his airplane *Bataan* and famously wrote about the servicemen of Bataan: "They were filthy, and they were lousy, and they stank. And I loved them." Yet while men starved, he'd ordered their food supply transferred to the island fortress of Corregidor. And despite the fact that Bataan was just a five-minute boat ride away, during his seventy-seven days on Corregidor he made only one visit to the peninsula. For these failings the embattled men of Bataan anointed him "Dugout Doug," an epithet that shadows MacArthur's legend to this day.

Serving with a British battalion in World War I, General Homma earned a Military Cross, but he was often out of favor with his superiors. For taking too long to bring the sprawling Philippine Islands to heel, he was recalled to Japan and spent the rest of the war as a reservist. Though post-war prosecutors believed Homma was not responsible for the Death March—insubordinate junior officers and overwhelming logistical problems are now popularly blamed for the atrocities—the "Butcher of Bataan" was sentenced to death at the Tokyo War Crimes Tribunal. Rather than being hanged, Homma was allowed a "soldier's death" by firing squad.

SOURCES & OTHER READING

Bataan: Our Last Ditch, Whitman, John W., Hippocrene, 1990
Horyo: Memoirs of an American POW, Gordon, Richard M., Paragon House, 1999
Death March: The Survivors of Bataan, Knox, Donald, Harcourt Brace Jovanovich, 1981
The Death March, Falk, Stanley L., W.W. Norton, 1962
Surrender and Survival: The Experience of American POWs in the Pacific 1941-1945, Kerr, E. Bartlett, William Morrow and Company, 1985

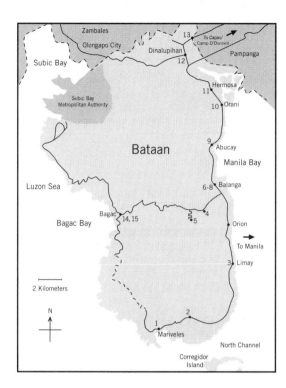

1. Zero Kilometer Marker
2. Wainwright Surrender Site
3. King Surrender Site
4. Final Battle Site
5. Mt. Samat National Shrine
6. Balanga Elementary School Surrender Site
7. St. Joseph's Church
8. Fall of Bataan Marker
9. Main Battle Position
10. Death March Sculpture
11. Commemorative Marker
12. First Line of Defense Statue
13. Democracy Marker
14. Zero Kilometer Marker
15. Philippines-Japan Friendship Tower

BATAAN TODAY

Population: 500,000 • Philippines Country Code: 63 • $1 = 50 pesos

Benefiting from industrial development and partial holding of the Subic Bay Metropolitan Authority economic zone (the former Subic Bay U.S. military installation), the small province of Bataan enjoys one of the highest employment rates in the Philippines. The province remains largely rural, rugged and unpopulated, but the spirit-crushing poverty of other parts of the Philippines is largely absent. Or at least not as visible.

Bataan has only twelve municipalities. Most of its cities and sites are located along the National Road, which runs along the eastern coast. The capital of Balanga City (population 71,000) is unremarkable.

The Battle of Bataan and subsequent Death March weren't onerous for the Allies simply because of the Japanese Imperial Army. Bataan's hills are steep. Much of its land is dry. The sun beats down mercilessly on bleak flatlands.

Filipinos are not great historical preservationists. Anything that can be salvaged for materials generally is—this includes wartime relics, commemorative plaques and markers. As a result, the best of what one gets in Bataan is an appreciation for the hostile, unyielding terrain of the battle and march.

All of Bataan's sites can be toured in a single, busy day. An additional day is recommended for those interested in walking part of the Death March route or visiting the end of the March at the Capas National Shrine in the province of Tarlac.

Walking the Death March Route

It's no longer possible to precisely retrace the steps of the Death March, large portions of which now lie beneath commercial, residential and other developments. Many sections, however, are marked and can be easily followed.

In the 1960s, the National Historical Institute (NHI) erected metal road signs marking all 112 kilometer points along the route. Over time, these signs—featuring two soldiers aiding a fallen comrade—have been stolen, vandalized or lost to the elements. Only a few remain. The March's sixtieth-anniversary year of 2002, however, saw a renewed commitment to historical preservation. The NHI began replacing the old signs with stone markers, about two-and-a-half-feet high, emblazoned with the original graphic of the three soldiers. These are easily spotted at various points along the National Road, which follows the approximate route of the March.

From the Zero Kilometer Marker in Mariveles to the 7km sign, the National Road follows the precise route of the March up a treacherous slope (National Road is also called Zigzag Road as it winds uphill here). Walkers wanting a feel for the original conditions should get plenty of authenticity at this location.

California-based Valor Tours (800-842-4504 or 415-332-7850) leads trips each April that walk the Death March route in four stages.

1. Zero Kilometer Marker ★★

Poblacion Road, Mariveles

Philippine and U.S. flags fly in this small park, which includes the first of the new Death March kilometer markers erected in 2002. From here, the National Road heads north along the original Death March route.

2. Wainwright Surrender Site ★

About 12 kilometers from Zero Kilometer Marker, Barangay Town Site, Mariveles

At a fork in the road, a small plaque marks the site where General Jonathan Wainwright formally surrendered Allied forces on Corregidor. The plaque is written only in Tagalog. The surrender took place in a house that no longer exists.

3. King Surrender Site ★

M. Roque Street, Lamao Plaza, Limay

Philippine and U.S. flags fly where Major-General Edward King surrendered the "Battling Bastards of Bataan."

According to the plaque, "faced with the slaughter of over 75,000 men, King showed great courage by his decision to end the bloodbath fearing a possible court-martial for his actions."

4. Final Battle Site ★

Governor Linao Highway, about 6.5 kilometers west of the junction with the Roman Superhighway

Marked by a plaque, the vital North-South Trail 4 sat astride this point. Japanese forces broke Fil-Am lines here on April 3, 1942. Bataan was surrendered on April 9.

5. Mt. Samat National Shrine ★★★★

Diwa, Pilar, at the end of a well-marked road off Governor Linao Highway, 7.7 kilometers west of the junction with the Roman Superhighway
Daily, 8 a.m.-9 p.m. Elevator closed noon-1 p.m.
30 pesos, 10 additional pesos for the elevator

At just over 300-feet high, this massive cross atop Mt. Samat in the center of Bataan is visible from miles away, particularly at night when brightly lit. Reached by elevator, the viewing gallery at the top provides sweeping views of Bataan, Corregidor, Manila Bay, South China Sea and, on clear days, Metro Manila.

As impressive is the adjacent colonnade, a marble-capped open-air memorial with a marble altar, stained-glass mural and nineteen marble relief carvings depicting major Battle of Bataan actions. The path between the colonnade and cross includes "bloodstones" from Corregidor (the reddish tint in the stones is due to iron oxides, not blood). The shrine is without question the primary attraction in Bataan.

6. Balanga Elementary School Surrender Site ★

Basa Street, Talisay, Balanga City

Major-General King's surrender of Bataan forces almost certainly occurred in Limay (Point 4). Nevertheless, in a small courtyard toward the rear of this school complex are a marker and paintings on an outdoor wall depicting King's surrender to Colonel Nakayama. Since King's Limay surrender was not documented by photographers, this is likely the spot where King was later brought for propaganda purposes. The school buildings were in use as Homma's command post at the time of King's capitulation.

7. St. Joseph's Church ★

Balanga City Center

The belfry was used as a site for the Japanese artillery bombardment of Mt. Samat, where Fil-Am forces made their final stand in April 1942.

8. Fall of Bataan Marker ★

Capitol Compound, Balanga City

Dedicated on April 9, 1952, this is one of the oldest memorials to Bataan veterans.

9. Main Battle Position ★

St. Antonine of Florence Church, National Road, Mabatang, Abucay

A marker on the church notes the Abucay-Morong Line. The line was assaulted by Japanese forces on January 9, 1942, and abandoned January 25 after terrible fighting.

10. Death March Sculpture ★

National Road at Silahis, Orani

Depicting two soldiers helping a fallen comrade, this roadside folk-art sculpture from 1973 is better than most march markers.

11. Commemorative Marker ★

Main Plaza, Hermosa

A marble plaque in front of the Catholic church honors the daring efforts of the people of Hermosa in providing food and water to Filipino and American soldiers during the March.

12. First Line of Defense Statue ★★

Layac Junction, Dinalupihan

At the junction of National Road and the San Ramon Highway to Olongapo City stand seven larger-than-life concrete Filipino soldiers, machine-gunning an invisible enemy and hoisting a Filipino flag.

13. Democracy Marker ★

National Road, border of Bataan and Pampanga provinces at Balsik, Hermosa

The text of this faded monument reads: "The little mountainous peninsula of Bataan saved democracy and the whole world from the evil hands of the devil. (From the radio broadcast of President Franklin Delano Roosevelt, January 5, 1945)."

14. Zero Kilometer Marker ★

Bagumbayan, Bagac

From this site on Bataan's western coast, a smaller number of soldiers began the Death March, walking east along the main road to link with the rest of the March. The small park includes a statue of a rifle thrust in the ground.

15. Philippines-Japan Friendship Tower ★

Bagac

This large tower symbolizes peace between the Philippines and Japan. Bagac is the area of the Battle of Toul Pocket. In February 1942, Japanese attackers were enveloped or "pocketed" in the nearby Gogo-Cotar river valley. The Japanese force was destroyed, marking a signal victory for Fil-Am forces.

OTHER AREA ATTRACTIONS

Montemar Beach Club
In Bagac, just off Layac-Balanga Highway
T: 2-892-6497 F: 2-811-5235
70 rooms
Under $100

Beyond World War II sites, the major attraction in Bataan is the beach. The best one is at Montemar, just south of Bagac on the province's western coast. On the white-sand shores of the South China Sea, the Montemar Beach Club has a nice pool and several restaurants. Day visitors are charged a small fee to use the facility.

RELATED SITES BEYOND BATAAN

The road to Capas National Shrine via the MacArthur Highway passes several points of interest. See Manila chapter for details.

Capas National Shrine/Camp O'Donnell ★★★

O'Donnell Highway and terminus of Capas Bataan Heroes Road, Barangay Aranguren, Capas, Tarlac
Daily, 8 a.m.-5 p.m.

On fifty-four hectares of parkland is part of the original site of Camp O'Donnell, the end of the Bataan Death March. About 25,000 Filipinos and 2,500 Americans died in this hot, exposed field. In place are a large walkway/mall, marble memorials marking mass gravesites and full-size replica of a thatch guard house and watch towers. (Constructed for fiftieth anniversary ceremonies in 2002, it remains to be seen whether these will stand up to the elements.) Representing each of the lives lost here, about 30,000 new plantings of mahogany, duhat and mango trees should someday make a beautiful grove. The focal point is a massive rocketlike obelisk reaching into the sky. Its three sections symbolize friendship between the Philippines, United States and Japan. Other than the Mt. Samat National Shrine, this is the primary Death March memorial.

Capas Death March Monument ★

National Road, Barangay Capas, Tarlac, about 8.5 kilometers south of Capas National Shrine

Set off the National Road is a large inverted V with relief carvings depicting scenes of Death March violence. The monument has fallen into disrepair. Graffiti, broken concrete and debris of all kinds are strewn about the grounds. In the shadow of Capas National Shrine, it seems destined to oblivion.

Capas Railway Station ★★

Eastern terminus of Capas Bataan Heroes Road, about 8 kilometers east of Capas National Shrine, Capas, Tarlac

The small railway station marked the beginning of the final leg of the Death March. After being subjected to cattle-car conditions, POWs were unloaded here and forced to march to Camp O'Donnell, about eight kilometers down what is now Capas Bataan Heroes Road. The station has been converted into a one-room museum featuring photos, small weapons and artifacts.

Cabanatuan Memorial ★★★

Cabanatuan, Nueva Ecija province

About twenty-five kilometers east of Capas National Shrine and 137 kilometers north of Manila, this large memorial marks the site of the Cabanatuan POW camp where about 20,000 American servicemen and civilians were imprisoned between 1942-1945. Upon the Wall of Honor are inscribed the names of about 3,000 Americans who died here. The American Battle Monuments Commission administers this well-maintained shrine.

Zigzag Pass ★★

National Road/San Ramon Highway, 7.7 kilometers east of Olongapo City, Zambales

In the center of the road stands a large white dove dedicated by a Japanese veteran whose brother died during the Battle of Zigzag Pass, fought in this area between February 1-May 27, 1945.

Wreck dives ★★★ N

Subic Bay at Olongapo City, Zambales

The infamous Japanese "hell ship" *Oryoko Maru* sunk by U.S. warplanes with 1,600 POWs on board rests at a maximum depth of sixty-five feet.

Several nearby World War I and II ships can also be dived, including the U.S.S. *New York* battleship. Magellan's Point (Lot 14, Arganaut Highway, S.B.M.A., Olongapo; 47-252-5987) is a dive shop that runs wreck dives.

GETTING TO/AROUND BATAAN

Mt. Samat Ferry Express high-speed ferries leave six times a day in both directions between Manila's CCP Bay Terminal on Roxas Boulevard and Orion, Bataan, about thirty-three kilometers north of Mariveles. Cost is 200 pesos each way, and the trip takes just under an hour. Mt. Samat Ferry Express is in Manila (2-551-5290) and Bataan (919-282-6952).

Rental cars in Orion are available with Ghileen's Rent A Car (47-244-4237), Penafrancia Rent A Car (47-244-5418) and W E R Rent A Car (47-244-4911). The drive from Manila (where rental cars are plentiful) takes about two hours. Tony Estrada of Guides, Inc. (2-912-2719) is an excellent, accredited Manila-based guide who can help arrange transportation. Bus lines from Manila to various points in Bataan include Panther Express (47-237-3950) and Genesis Bus Company (47-237-6170). By bus, the trip from Manila to Balanga City takes about three hours and costs 109 pesos. Because Bataan sites are spread along miles of baking highway, arriving with pre-arranged transportation is essential.

ACCOMMODATIONS

Subic International Hotel

Santa Rita Road, S.B.M.A., Olongapo City, Zambales
T: 47-252-2222 F: 47-894-5579
300 rooms
$75-$150

In the neighboring province of Zambales, and on site of a former U.S. Navy base, the hotel is clean and has basic amenities.

Piazza Hotel

BASECO Compound BEZ, Mariveles
T: 47-935-6170
Under $40

Located near the start of the Death March, this budget hotel is as good as it gets in Mariveles.

Hillside Garden Mansions

Roman Highway, Balanga City
T: 47-237-1771
24 rooms
Under $75

The best hotel in the provincial capital has suites with Jacuzzis.

23

Emiej Island

MARSHALL ISLANDS

THE WAR YEARS

Never invaded by the Allies, the Japanese stronghold on Jaluit Atoll—with primary garrisons on Emiej and Jaluit Islands—was nevertheless subjected to a devastating twenty-month campaign of aerial bombardment following the American victory at the Marshall Island of Kwajalein and occupation of nearby Majuro in early 1944. Choosing to avoid direct confrontation with 2,200 well-entrenched defenders, American forces neutralized Emiej and Jaluit by bombing them into submission. The same strategy was employed across the region, so that by mid-1944 Japanese troops throughout the Marshall Islands were hopelessly disconnected from the outside world.

In destroying air defenses at the major seaplane base on Emiej, the United States kept the island's Japanese garrison from having an impact on the war. But, as the buildings and fortifications remaining on Emiej attest, aerial bombardment wasn't yet a realistic way to destroy an enemy. In less than two years, the United States dropped 6.2 million pounds of explosives on the atoll. Of the 837 Japanese deaths on Jaluit only 381 were caused by bombing and strafing—most of the others were attributed to starvation and disease.

The money and effort expended for such small returns amounted to something of a Japanese victory. But it also pointed to a disparity that was to become increasingly disheartening (and evident) to Japanese troops throughout the Pacific as the war dragged on. In 1944, a Japanese officer in the Philippines summed up his country's grim plight after watching a single soldier on the beach being shot at by American naval guns aimed directly at him: "Machine guns, even mortars, yes, but naval guns against a single enemy straggler? Incredible! The enemy must have equipment and ammunition to throw away!"

The isolated men on Emiej could certainly have identified with the supposition, but the campaign on the sister island of Jaluit was even more lopsided. There, Marine pilot and future astronaut John Glenn took part in one of the first-ever systematic aerial napalm attacks, over the capital city Jabor in late 1944. The napalm attacks "had a horrible beauty," according to Glenn's 1999 autobiography. "The bright, reddish orange of the flames and billowing clouds of black smoke against the green of the trees, the light green of the ocean water on the reefs, and the dark blue deep water made one of the most eerie, awesome, and sobering sights I had ever seen. ... The destruction was total. Later, when we flew over Jabortown, there was nothing left."

As with neighboring islands, Emiej and Jaluit became target practice for gung-ho American pilots—often taking off from Kwajalein and Majuro where Glenn was stationed—who routinely bombarded the islands until the end of the war. The islands were so well known to pilots that "strikes were hatched during a poker game or over a cup of coffee," according to Alan Carey, historian and son of a Navy airman stationed in the Marshall Islands.

What looked like a shooting arcade to the young Americans appeared entirely different to the Japanese command in Tokyo. "Combined with the negation of Rabaul and the destruction wrought on Truk, the Marshalls campaign cracked the Japanese outer defense ring," wrote historian Harry Gailey. "These losses were a visible sign of Japan's growing weakness and caused a major shake-up in the highest levels of command." Navy and Army chiefs Admiral Osami Nagano and General Hajime Sugiyama were removed from their posts following the defeats.

Unlike isolated troops on other Marshall islands, many of whom starved to death in 1944 and 1945, the men on Emiej and Jaluit managed to fish, cultivate gardens and raise animals. Along with approximately 2,000 Japanese, more than 100 pigs were captured by the Allies on Emiej and Jaluit at the time of surrender. Thanks in part to a comparatively strong diet, morale among Japanese troops had remained relatively high and, for all the hardships, the tropical isles continued to enchant the soldiers stationed there. In September 1945, on behalf of his men, the atoll's Japanese commander Rear-Admiral Nisuke Masuda asked local chiefs to allow his men to remain on the island after the war. The request was immediately denied, and the men were shipped home as part of the 147,000 East Asians repatriated from the tropical Pacific at war's end.

Masuda never did leave. Declaring Jaluit "the place most fitted for my death," he killed himself on September 5, 1945, a few minutes before he was scheduled to make a confession regarding his order to execute American POWs (see Point 12). Declaring himself "King of Jaluit," Masuda's suicide note revealed the truth and sealed his fate: "After I have been called in connection with the treatment of the (American) prisoners of war, my return home could scarcely be expected ... I am ready to present them (U.S. Army) with reports all of which frankly confess the truth." Unlike Masuda, twenty-eight Japanese officers and men around the Marshalls stood trial for war crimes following the cessation of hostilities—of these, four received death sentences.

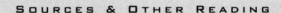

Sources & Other Reading

The Archaeology of World War II in the Marshall Islands, Volume III: Jalwoj, Christiansen, Henrik, RMI Historic Preservation Office, 1994

Breaking the Outer Ring: Marine Landings in the Marshall Islands, Marine Corps Historical Center, 1994

The Pineapple Air Force: Pearl Harbor to Tokyo, Lambert, John W., Phalanx Publishing, 1990

John Glenn: A Memoir, Glenn, John w/ Nick Taylor, Bantam Books, 1999

The Reluctant Raiders: The Story of the United States Navy Bombing Squadron VB/VPB-109 in World War II, Carey, Alan C., Schiffer Publishing Company, 1999

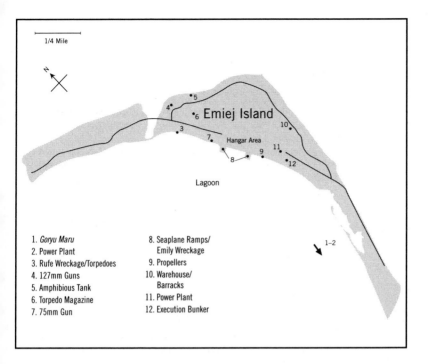

N

- 5
- 4
- 6 Emiej Island
- 10
- 3
- 7
- Hangar Area
- 11
- 9
- 8
- 12

Lagoon

1. *Goryu Maru*
2. Power Plant
3. Rufe Wreckage/Torpedoes
4. 127mm Guns
5. Amphibious Tank
6. Torpedo Magazine
7. 75mm Gun
8. Seaplane Ramps/ Emily Wreckage
9. Propellers
10. Warehouse/ Barracks
11. Power Plant
12. Execution Bunker

1–2

EMIEJ ISLAND TODAY

Population: About 150 (Emiej Island), 1,500 (Jaluit Atoll) • Country Code: 692 • Currency: U.S. dollar

Filled with dense jungle and numerous structures left from the Marshall Islands' Japanese period (1914-1945), Emiej is one of the more remote, atmospheric and unspoiled destinations in this book. Since 1945, time has gone backward here—no electricity, plumbing or services of any kind. The retrogression to pre-colonial primitiveness makes the reminders of a war of mass industrialization all the more poignant.

The incessant bombing raids that characterized the war here seem to belong to another eon. Today, locals in small houses scattered about the island lead subsistence lifestyles—coconuts, fish, pork and chicken are dietary staples. English is spoken, so getting around isn't a problem (see Marshall Islands chapter for more on the country).

A small flat island within the larger Jaluit Atoll, Emiej possesses a rugged tropical beauty. Surrounded by pristine blue water, its sea-torn coral beaches ring a palm-stuffed jungle that's easy to walk in most places. The settled area—including all but Points 1 and 2—covers an area a little less than a mile long and anywhere from 200 to 650 yards wide. Nevertheless, a full day on Emiej is recommended. The island is typically reached via thirty-minute boat ride from the atoll's capital city of Jabor on Jaluit Island.

The old German capital, Jabor has a large dock, a few streets, vehicles and stores, but little else of note. It's dull, but not a bad place to spend a day or so—a necessity for anyone visiting Emiej without a private boat or plane. Jabor's limited war sites can be seen in less than an hour.

POINTS OF INTEREST

There are no roads or motorized vehicles on Emiej. Trails through the jungle appear and disappear. Locations and distances in this chapter are close approximations. The area described is fairly compact—less than a mile long and anywhere from 200 to 650 yards wide—and the jungle is easy to pick a path through in most areas. After Points 1 and 2— both on the thirty-minute boat ride from Jaluit—it's best to start on Emiej at an easily identifiable landmark (Point 3 in this case). The crisscross pattern suggested below seems a little illogical but it eliminates excessive backtracking. Any walk through the small island, however, leads to numerous relics at nearly every turn, many, by necessity of space limitations, not listed here.

1. Goryu Maru ★★★

Lagoon side of Aineman Island

Near the reef at Aineman Island (the island is actually connected to the southeastern edge of Emiej), this large Japanese freighter struck a mine and ran aground, probably in late 1943. It was bombed repeatedly by U.S. pilots throughout the war, many of whom, new to the area, believed they were scoring significant hits on a distressed vessel. Partly in the water, mostly out, the monument-style hulk remains rusty though intact, stem to stern, including the gun platform on the bow.

2. Japanese Power Plant ★★★

Lagoon side of Aineman Island, about 800 yards up the beach (toward Emiej) from Point 1

About forty or so yards behind the beach but barely visible from the shore, this very large power plant can be tricky to find. It requires brief jungle stomping— start at a point directly behind the tallest stand of palm trees in the area—but the payoff is a huge camouflage-painted concrete structure that, like many buildings

here, rises from the primordial jungle like a Mayan ruin. Inside are two, fifteen-foot-long Yanmar generator engines, large coral-plaster support columns, kitchen-stove pits, toilet stalls and a deep Japanese soaking tub. Among other details, marble faces remain on the second floor switch-panel. Extensive bomb and strafing damage are obvious, but, like so many of the sturdy concrete structures built by the Japanese, the building remains essentially together. A separate warehouse sits behind the main structure. Various-sized copies of this construction plan exist across the Pacific, but this is the most well preserved of the lot.

3. Mitsubishi Rufe Wreckage/Torpedoes ★★★

Directly in front of Protestant church on Emiej, just north of seaplane ramps

As indicated by the two seaplane ramps on the beach just south (actually southeast, toward Aineman Island) of this wreckage, Emiej was the location of a major Japanese seaplane base. Scattered on the beach on the northern (away from Aineman Island) end of the lagoon side of Emiej are the rusted remains of several Rufe seaplanes. The site is identifiable by the single propeller blade sticking straight up out of the sand along the beach. Next to the church is a torpedo storage area with rusted torpedo racks, dual air-compressor engines and a large bunker with six torpedoes (nosecones removed) stacked on top. Naval bronze and stainless steel pieces have kept the visible torpedo motors well preserved. Up the beach (roughly north) about 200 yards, next to the channel connecting the ocean and lagoon, sits the wreckage of large pedestals upon which were mounted large dual-purpose guns, used for shooting at both air and naval targets. The guns are no longer there.

4. 127mm Guns ★★★

From the large pedestals described in Point 3 walk approximately east along the oceanside beach. The guns are in the jungle directly behind a bunker on the beach.

In a concentrated area are three large Japanese dual-purpose guns as well as dilapidated observation and command structures. Matt Holly, the leading authority on World War II relics in the Marshall Islands, calls this site one of the best finds in the country. The thick jungle and stark relics evoke a ghostly sense of the desperate activity that once took place here. One gun remains in rusted though otherwise perfect condition on its mount. All three guns are larger than typical 75mm Japanese dual-purpose guns found throughout the Pacific.

5. Amphibious Tank ★

About 200 yards roughly east of Point 4, just behind the oceanside beach

The badly decomposed shell of a small Japanese tank sits half-buried and all rusted amid a grove of palms, one of which is growing through it. The track wheels are visible, but the main cannon is gone. The tank is almost as tough to find as it is to identify.

6. Torpedo Magazine ★★★

From Point 5, walk about halfway across the island toward the lagoon to a large concrete structure—almost directly in line with the upright propeller from Point 3.

This large concrete building was used mostly to house torpedoes and other armaments. It's notable for the faded camouflage, which includes carefully painted palm fronds on the exterior walls.

7. 75mm Dual-purpose Gun ★★

From Point 6 continue across island and return to upright propeller from Point 3. Continue down the lagoon-side beach (roughly southwest) about 40 yards.

Another well-rusted dual-purpose gun remains on its mount at this location.

8. Seaplane Ramps/Emily Wreckage ★★

Continue up beach from Point 7 to visible ramps

The salient point of the former Japanese base, this pair of massive ramps was built to accommodate Mitsubishi Rufes and Kawanishi H8K Emily flying boats, only 167 of which were built during the war (including thirty-six "Seiku" transport variants). The ramps were built exceedingly wide to accommodate the Emily's 124-foot wing span. (For more on the Emily see Tokyo chapter Point 5.) Directly in front of the ramps offshore about 250 and 500 yards are the submerged wrecks of Emilys at sixty and 100 feet respectively. The deeper of the two is in much better shape. Directly behind the north ramp (the ramp on the right as you face the lagoon from the beach) about 150-200 yards into the jungle is the twisted wreckage of two hangars and skeletal structure of a completely destroyed Emily in the trees.

9. Seaplane Propellers ★★

In the shallow water just south of Point 8

In a few feet of water at the shore just in front of the elementary school are a dozen or so complete propeller units and other discarded or wrecked airplane parts.

10. Warehouse/Barracks Complex ★★★

Fifty to 100 yards down (approximately south) the lagoon beach from Point 8 is a collection of houses. Behind these houses, palm logs surround the large white gravestone of Neiherare Jorburg Ben. To the left (north) of this grave is a trail leading into the jungle. Follow trail several hundred yards to buildings.

Along the trail, massive concrete ruins rise from the dark jungle in dramatic fashion. Judging from the heavily reinforced construction—which did a remarkable job of withstanding a year and a half of continuous bombardment—the Japanese clearly intended to remain on Emiej for many years. That the buildings survived at all is a testament to the designers as well as the Japanese soldiers and forced Marshallese and Korean laborers who built them. In the general area are two warehouses, an electrical shop, ammo magazine and various bombed-out structures.

11. Power Plant ★★

In the jungle, about 250 yards roughly southwest of Point 10

The remains of this small bombed-out auxiliary power plant are less impressive than most in the area, but the plant's mere existence reinforces the size and complexity of the Japanese operation here. The same applies to the sparse remains of narrow-gauge railroad tracks—used to move supplies and heavy equipment—found here and there on the island.

12. Execution Bunker ★★

About 75 yards roughly southwest from Point 11, about 100 yards behind the lagoon beach

Within view of Point 11 is another building complex. On the north side of this complex is an oval-topped bunker, half-underground and usually filled with water. According to local accounts, three American fliers shot down in 1943 were brought to Emiej, interrogated and imprisoned in this gloomy bunker. When the American invasion of Kwajalein began in February 1944, Rear-Admiral Nisuke Masuda, commander of Japanese forces on Jaluit Atoll, ordered all three men executed. After the surrender of Jaluit in September 1945, Masuda confessed to the crime in writing then committed suicide, believing that the Americans would execute him for his actions. Other wrecked structures in the area include an air-control building near the lagoon beach. A local family is using part of the building as a residence. The vacant section includes identifiable kitchen, bathroom and Japanese soaking tub. Visible in the lagoon behind it is the wrecked hull of a fifty-foot Japanese work boat.

OTHER AREA ATTRACTIONS

Diving ◥

For diving on the Emily flying boats or other area wrecks, Marshall Islands Aquatics (692-625-3669; aquamar@ntamar.com) operated by dive instructor Matt Holly is the best option. At around $200 a day, it's also the priciest. Holly also leads land-based trips to Emiej. Marshalls Dive Adventures (692-625-3483; marshall@ntamar.com) is another good resource.

Fishing

With only 1,800 tourist visits per year, the tropical RMI is one of the least exploited water-sports destinations in the world. The country counts more than 1,000 species of fish, 800 reef systems and a typical water visibility of 100-plus feet. Abundant trophy fish include yellowfin tuna, wahoo, bonefish and Pacific blue marlin. Wind and sea conditions are pleasant all year, but the most favorable fishing season is May-October. Numerous charter fishing vessels of all sizes are available. Call MIVA (Marshall Islands Visitors Authority, 692-625-6482) for booking information.

RELATED SITES BEYOND EMIEJ ISLAND

Jabor, Jaluit ★★

With no overnight accommodations on Emiej, visitors stay in the small town of Jabor on nearby Jaluit Island. The island has a few sites of interest. The first large structure in town—0.8 miles from the airport terminal along the main road just before the Mobil station—is a bombed-out, two-story Japanese weather station. About 150-200 yards down the road, just past the Mobil station, is a large unidentified concrete building built by the Japanese and now in use as a local residence. In the opposite direction along the main road, 1.7 miles heading away from Jabor from the airport terminal, a turnoff down a small dirt road leads to the Jaluit Public Works camp. About 100 yards down this road on the left is an intact Japanese bunker built low to the ground. The unusually rough and irregular construction suggests it was hastily built during the war, probably after American air attacks began.

GETTING TO/AROUND EMIEJ ISLAND AND JALUIT ATOLL

Most trips to the Marshall Islands begin with a flight into the capital of Majuro. See Marshall Islands chapter for details. Emiej Island is accessed through the small town of Jabor on Jaluit Atoll. Air Marshall Islands (692-625-3733) flies from Majuro to Jabor twice a week (Monday and Saturday as of this writing). Flying into Jabor on Saturday and out on Monday—reserving all day Sunday for Emiej—is the best plan for most visitors. The entire one-road town of Jabor can be walked in about twenty minutes.

The boat trip from Jabor to Emiej takes about thirty minutes. Basic transportation, guides or dive trips can be arranged through Wildfire Charters (T: 692-247-7112; F: 692-247-7111), Marshall Islands Aquatics (625-3669; aquamar@ntamar.com), or MIVA (Marshall Islands Visitors Authority, 692-625-6482), all based in Majuro. For independent travelers, there are plenty of private boats around—arranging impromptu rides to Emiej with locals in Jabor isn't difficult. A rough amount to expect to pay is $50-$100 for the round trip. With no roads on Emiej, all travel is by foot. Visitors must carry in all supplies, including food and water.

ACCOMMODATIONS

Small stores in Jabor carry items such as ramen, chips, bottled water, Spam, bread and candy. Otherwise, visitors should bring their own food. Because Jabor is so small, formal addresses are neither used nor necessary.

Jawoj Hotel
Jabor, Jaluit Atoll

T: 692-625-3829 F: 692-625-3397
4 rooms
$50, no credit cards

The small rooms have private bathrooms and air-conditioning. Otherwise, it's a metal bed, four walls and a tile floor. A communal kitchen is available, and the owners are friendly.

JACA Guest Houses
Ionene community, Jaluit Atoll

T: 692-625-3035 (Biodiversity Conservation Office) or 692-625-5581 (MIVA)
F: 692-625-5202 (BCO)
5 thatch huts
$50

These palm-thatch houses were built in 2002 as a community development project under the auspices of JACA (Jaluit Atoll Conservation Area). On a small beach, they're picturesque and extremely remote. The houses are crude—mattresses, freshwater, cooking utensils. No electricity or running water. No wartime relics or commercial services are nearby. Worth considering for those needing complete disassociation from the civilized world.

24

Papua New Guinea

THE WAR YEARS

O ne of the war's most overlooked campaigns (at least in the United States), the fight for the area known today as Papua New Guinea was nevertheless so important that for a year and a half after the June 1942 Battle of Midway, Pacific fighting was limited almost exclusively to this (and adjacent Solomon Islands) area. Neutralizing the massive Japanese supply base at Rabaul on the island of New Britain was vital to the Allied victory at Guadalcanal and push northward to Japan. Conversely, Japan saw Port Moresby as an attractive location from which to continue its southward advance across the Pacific.

In March 1942, Japanese troops arrived on New Guinea and within weeks had control of most of the northern part of the mainland and islands of New Ireland, the Admiralties and New Britain. To the south, the Papua area was controlled by a small force of Australians, mostly stationed in and around the capital of Port Moresby. Japan sent three carriers and a troop convoy to the area in early May. The U.S. Navy deployed a large battle group to thwart the offensive. The ensuing Battle of the Coral Sea became history's first naval engagement fought exclusively between aircraft carriers. Despite heavier overall losses, the Allies won an important strategic victory—as a result of battle damage, the Japanese carriers *Shokaku* and *Zaikaku* were unavailable for the crucial Battle of Midway.

The Japanese assault on Port Moresby began on July 21, 1942, when Imperial forces landed at Gona and Buna, coastal villages roughly 100 miles north of Port Moresby. In between was the hellish Owen Stanley Range. Japan planned to storm Port Moresby by sending troops south across the Kokoda Trail, a switchback footpath over some of world's most inhospitable mountain terrain. The result was one of the finest hours in Australian military history. All along the trail "a handful of eighteen-year-old militia troops who had never fired a shot in anger," according to Australian journalist Patrick Lindsay, waged a fighting retreat against hardened, undefeated Japanese professionals. Action at Isurava was typical. Outnumbered five and six to one, the Australians held off the Japanese for four critical days.

Japanese troops eventually pushed to Imita Ridge, some twenty-five miles from Port Moresby. Here several hundred Aussies, with the help of the Fuzzy Wuzzy Angels—the nickname for the dauntless Papua New Guineans who assisted the Allies in the Kokoda effort—kept as many as 10,000 Japanese troops from breaking their lines. By October, the Japanese were in retreat, fearful of an American attack on their almost defenseless base at Buna. It was the closest the Imperial Army would ever get to the Australian mainland.

Simultaneously, on the southwest tip of the main island, a 1,500-strong Japanese fighting force arrived at Milne Bay in mid-August, also intent on a Port Moresby attack. After a week of desperate battle, they were forced to withdraw, allowing the Australians to claim the war's first Allied ground triumph against Japan.

With Japanese control of New Guinea slipping, General Douglas MacArthur's Buna-Gona offensive escalated into what has been called "one of the most horrendous campaigns of the Pacific War." No jungle fighting in the Pacific War was as brutal. The fetid, steaming jungles of PNG were home to a variety of poisonous plants and tropical diseases. Logistical nightmares, equipment failures and exhaustion plagued both sides. The campaign generated one of the highest disease-related casualty rates in a modern American war.

The Australian seizure of Gona on December 9 enraged MacArthur, who felt humiliated that Commonwealth troops appeared to be outperforming the Americans. In reality, U.S. forces were woefully under-supplied and made up mostly of National Guardsmen from Michigan and Wisconsin, who fought valiantly, but who had trouble acclimating to the jungle climate. Buna fell to the Americans on January 2, 1943, but not before MacArthur had replaced his field commander. Japan lost about 13,000 men, the Allies close to 8,500.

The intense fighting had taken its toll on both sides. Six months would pass before the next ground battle. On June 30, Allied forces began the push up the PNG coast with a series of hard, forgotten victories at places such as the Bismarck Sea, Lae, Salamaua, Wewak and Saidor. A combination of Australian amphibious forces and American paratroopers forced a hasty Japanese retreat from the coastal town of Finschafen through a rugged mountainous route. Mostly due to starvation, 2,000 of the 8,000 Japanese troops who began the gruesome trip never finished it.

Lacking the drama of Marine amphibious landings, set-piece naval movements or attendant press coverage, the Army-dominated campaign dragged on in anonymity. With the redemption of the 1942 horrors at Bataan and Corregidor now within reach, the American public's attention was drawn to the more romantic liberation of the Philippines.

"In the eyes of the American public, New Guinea soon became dreary," according to historians James Dunnigan and Albert Nofi. "That attitude carried on in the public's memory after the war."

The campaign also lacked a single crowning glory. The invasion of Rabaul never happened. With the seizure of several surrounding islands in early 1944, the Allied command agreed to bypass Rabaul, isolating its 100,000 men until the end of the war. Manus, the largest of the Admiralties, would become the staging ground for the invasion of the Philippines. By the summer of 1944, the Japanese were mostly out of PNG. The country had shifted from being a pivotal theater of operations to a battle-scarred paradise populated with recovering wounded and troops on leave.

SOURCES & OTHER READING

Touched with Fire: The Land War in the South Pacific, Bergerud, Eric, Viking, 1996
Fire in the Sky: The Air War in the South Pacific, Bergerud, Eric, Westview Press, 2000
MacArthur's Jungle War, Taaffe, Stephen R., University Press of Kansas, 1998
The Spirit of Kokoda: Then and Now, Lindsay, Patrick, Hardie Grant Books, 2002
The Pacific War Encyclopedia, Dunnigan and Nofi, Checkmark Books, 1998
Bushwalking in Papua New Guinea, Perusse, Yvon, Lonely Planet, 1993

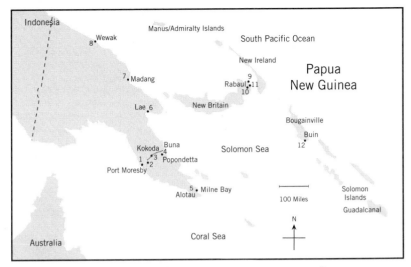

1. National Museum
   and Art Gallery
2. Bomana War
   Cemetery and Memorial
3. Kokoda Trail
4. Popondetta Memorial
5. Battle of Milne
   Bay War Memorial

6. Lae War Cemetery
7. Coastwatchers Memorial
8. Wewak/Cape Wom
   War Memorial
9. Japanese War Memorial
10. Kokopo War Museum
11. Bita Paka War Cemetery
12. Yamamoto Crash Site

PAPUA NEW GUINEA TODAY

Population: 5 million • Country code: 675 • $1 = 3.91 kina

Sprawling with endless tracts of unspoiled wilderness, dramatic trails, unique wildlife and little-known cultures, Papua New Guinea represents one of the last of the great expedition territories on earth. Littering regional newspapers with reports of inter-tribal violence and rampant crime, it represents the regrettable vision of a diseased paradise. The dichotomy makes PNG the most difficult country to visit in this book.

The Independent State of Papua New Guinea, which gained independence from Australia in 1975, comprises the eastern section of the island of New Guinea and about 600 other islands, including New Britain, New Ireland and Bougainville. English is the official language, but Tok Pisin, a Melanesian Creole English, is widely spoken. Eighty percent of the population lives in rural areas, many of which still have had relatively little contact with the Western world. The dreadful capital and entry point of Port Moresby has a population of 250,000.

PNG hosts the epitome of that animal that now goes by the name "adventure travel"—usually meaning rough going amid substandard facilities, impoverished locals and groups of Western backpackers. No location in the Pacific is as promising for undiscovered wartime relics.

Due to poor infrastructure, it could take weeks to cover all the sites listed below. For those without the luxury of unlimited time, a better strategy might be to focus on two or three sites over the course of a week.

POINTS OF INTEREST

Many addresses in Papua New Guinea are listed without numbers, only street names or general locations. Regardless, drivers and locals will know the way.

1. National Museum and Art Gallery ★★★

Independence Hill, just north of the flying-buttressed Parliament Building in Boroko, Port Moresby
Daily, 9 a.m.-5 p.m.

No fighting occurred in the capital, but the National Museum's modern history department houses the country's largest collection of war relics. Attractions include an American Stuart tank used in the Buna-Gona campaign and the fuselage door of the Betty bomber that was transporting Admiral Isoroku Yamamoto when he was shot down over Buin.

It's an impressive collection of basics—American and Japanese guns, mortars, helmets, mess tins. If it was used in PNG during the war, there's probably an example of it here (or at least a piece). The outdoor area houses the aforementioned Stuart tank, a Japanese Tony fighter (Ki-61 JAAF) and P-38 Lightning. These are only a few of the museum's many aircraft and large vehicles.

2. Bomana War Cemetery and Memorial ★★★

Off Sogeri Road, about 15 km from Port Moresby. From Sir Hubert Murray Highway, turn right onto Sogeri Road, then left at the sign for the cemetery. Cabs or PMVs run from Mary and Musgrave Streets.

Soon after the turnoff to the town of Sogeri is the pristine and large cemetery that houses some 4,500 fallen soldiers, both Australian and Papua New Guinean, most of whom died in the battle for the Kokoda Trail. The rows of white headstones commemorating the dead are an eerie sight amid the peaceful setting. On a rise is the Memorial to the Missing, a round structure with columns dedicated to unknown soldiers who perished in battle. Bomana is one of three Commonwealth war cemeteries in PNG—the others are in Lae and outside the Rabaul/Kokopo area—maintained by the Office of Australian War Graves (OAWG).

3. Kokoda Trail ★★★★

Central Province

The infamous Kokoda Trail (Kokoda Track to Australians) begins at Ower's Corner, about eighty kilometers northwest of Port Moresby, and officially ends at the large government station of Kokoda. (It's possible, and some say easier, to do the trek in the opposite direction.) In between, hikers on the roughly ninety-six-kilometer-long trail must contend with steep ridges, muddy gullies, multiple river crossings, capricious weather and constant up and down elevation changes. The entire trip—a tremendous physical challenge that runs through indescribably beautiful countryside and areas of monumental historical significance—takes four to ten days to complete. Because parts of the trail are owned by local tribes, many hikers go with a guide-led group (see South Pacific Tours below).

Tablets along the trail commemorate individual battles. The roughest fighting was at Isurava, where a new memorial was installed in August 2002, about ninety kilometers from the Ower's Corner trailhead. The memorial's history panels outline the brutal Kokoda campaign. Upon four granite plinths are inscribed the words courage, endurance, mateship and sacrifice. For the 39th Battalion that held off thousands of Japanese on the trail, it has been a point of contention that the infamous WWI battle at Gallipoli has historically received the lion's share of Australian press coverage. For Kokoda veterans, this memorial represents a long-awaited step toward vindication. The Kokoda Museum, located in Kokoda Station at the northern end of the trail, houses a few weapons, but mostly just photos and literature on the battle. It's worth a look from those hiking the trail.

Several landing strips along the trail allow the flexibility to fly in and/or out at various stages. Airlines of Papua New Guinea (675-325-7655) flies to airstrips along the Kokoda Trail. Hiking in the rainy season can be a slog, not to mention dangerous. Most of the rivers are bridged, but in a few cases they need to be forded. The best time to hike is the dry season between June and September. August and September are prime. Anyone considering the trail should pick up a copy of the indispensable 2002 book *The Spirit of Kokoda* by Australian Patrick Lindsay (Hardie Grant Books; www.hardiegrant.com.au). The book recounts Kokoda's wartime saga as well as Lindsay's nine-day trek along the route, complete with maps and vivid histories of each section of the trail.

Trail permits are required and cost K100. South Pacific Tours (675-323-5245 in Port Moresby; 61-740-392-251 in Cairns, Australia) can do everything from getting permits to handling all arrangements including guide, food and accommodations. Most villages along the trail have a guesthouse—prices run between K6-K30—but sudden storms make tents essential.

Once reaching the Kokoda terminus, two logical steps would be either to fly back to Port Moresby or take a two to three hour PMV ride from Kokoda Station to Popondetta, just south of Gona. For those not inclined to walk the entire trail, a plinth with a commemorative plaque sits at the Kokoda turnoff from Sogeri Road (outside Port Moresby), which was designed and built in 1943 by the 7th Australian Infantry brigade.

4. Popondetta Memorial (No rating)

Popondetta, Oro Province, about 20 km southwest of Buna. PMVs to Buna run from the Papua New Guinea Banking Corporation, just down the street from Popondo Supermarket.

The Popondetta Memorial at the centrally located park of the same name consists of a plinth with signs detailing the Buna-Gona campaign. The existing memorial is in poor shape and being rebuilt as part of an Australian government effort to repair or replace memorials here, at Milne Bay and on the Kokoda Trail. The memorial was scheduled to be completed by the beginning of 2003.

5. Battle of Milne Bay War Memorial
(yet to be built)
Alotau, Milne Bay Province

Isolated on the eastern tip of the mainland, Milne Bay Province is acquiring a reputation as the place to visit in PNG. The idyllic province offers unique flora, some of the best diving in the world (several pristine wrecks) and a scenic, fairly leisurely trek along the coast from Wedau to Alotau (the capital of Milne Bay Province), which takes about four days to complete. The peaceful residents have been compared to other South Pacific islanders in terms of their friendliness and openness to strangers.

Though there were no significant war memorials in place at the time of this writing, there are plans to build one on the bay side of Alotau leading down to the water. Donated by Australia, the memorial was scheduled to be completed in late 2002 and will include a central commemorative pillar and panels outlining the story of the Battle for Milne Bay.

6. Lae War Cemetery ★★★

Lae, Morobe Province
Center of town, adjacent to the Botanical Garden

Situated on the Huon Gulf in Morobe Province, the lush port town of Lae is laid out around the city's well-kept botanical garden. Adjacent is the war cemetery, where almost 3,000 Commonwealth soldiers are buried. A memorial cairn at the entrance pays homage to the soldiers who lost their lives in the battles around Salamaua. Names of the war dead are engraved in bronze on the main building. The cemetery is maintained by the OAWG and is as pristine as the one at Bomana, though not as large.

7. Coastwatchers Memorial ★★

Coastwatchers Road, Madang, Madang Province
PMVs run along palm-fringed Coastwatchers Road up to the memorial.

At the end of the Madang peninsula sits this ninety-eight-foot-tall memorial dedicated to those under the Royal Australian Navy's civilian coastwatching organization whose members helped spot and report Japanese military activity in the area. For much of the war Madang was at the center of Japan's New Guinea territory, so the Madang coastwatchers were in a particularly vulnerable position. To escape detection, they sometimes wore boots with a foot outline attached to the soles so the tracks they left would be interpreted by the Japanese as the bare feet of ostensibly harmless locals. The memorial is somewhat bare, but the views of Astrolabe Bay are fantastic.

8. Wewak/Cape Wom War Memorial ★★

Wewak, East Sepik Province
PMVs travel to Cape Wom from Wewak's Dagua Market

Though Wewak was the site of the Japanese Army headquarters for the bulk of the war, Allied air raids neutralized its large military presence by isolating the city from re-supply. Just down the street from the wharf, the Japan-PNG Peace Park has serene grounds that include a memorial and pond. On a hill six miles outside the city is a Japanese memorial at the site of a former mass grave, the bodies in which were later returned to Japan. There are great views of the Wewak area from here. The memorial is in Boys Town, in the hills south of town. Involving turns on unmarked, unpaved roads, the route is confusing, but the Wirui Road leads more or less south out of town.

The pyramidal cairn in Cape Wom Memorial Park is located about fifteen kilometers up the coast from Wewak, at the site where on September 13, 1945, Japanese Lieutenant-General Hatazo Adachi signed surrender papers and handed his sword to Australian Major-General Sir Horace Robertson. Artifacts in the park include small field weapons up to impressive 75mm guns. BBQ shelters, picnic tables and toilet facilities make it a habitable place to spend the day. Behind the memorial, several Japanese tunnels connect different parts of the cape. Some openings have caved in, but it's possible to crawl around others. Flashlight necessary.

9. Japanese War Memorial ★★

Rabaul, East New Britain Province
8 a.m.-4 p.m.

In May 1994 the eruption of two volcanoes —Tuvurvur and Vulcan—buried most of the New Britain Island town of Rabaul under ash. Most of the 20,000 residents moved to nearby Kokopo, which became the provincial capital. Rabaul natives hope someday to rebuild their town. A war memorial funded by the Japanese government is located above the town on Namanula Hill, which visitors must walk up since the road remains in a state of disrepair. The focal point of the memorial is an altar, behind which is a huge map of the Pacific detailing Japanese conquests in World War II. At the time of construction, controversy surrounded the memorial, which was seen to glorify the Japanese occupation. A pair of stylized bunkers didn't help. The memorial is striking, though not as interesting as the views of ash-covered Rabaul and Simpson Harbor (site of more than 100 war wrecks).

10. Kokopo War Museum ★★★

Kokopo, East New Britain Province
T: 675-982-8453
Daily, 8 a.m.-4 p.m.

This branch of the National Museum in Port Moresby contains a wide array of photos, munitions and other Japanese war relics. Because Japan occupied Rabaul and Kokopo for almost the entire war there are few Allied relics here. The exceptions are the engine of a P-38 Lightning and an entire B-17 Flying Fortress ("Naughty but Nice") in good condition. Both are located in the museum's yard along with Japanese war planes, anti-aircraft batteries and unexploded ordnance. Displays are accompanied by interpretive signage. The museum also houses a collection of East New Britain traditional masks, a bird aviary and crocodile pen.

11. Bita Paka War Cemetery ★★★

Kokopo, East New Britain Province
About 5 km southwest of Kokopo off Kabakaul Road (which leads out of town toward Bita Paka). PMVs run to the cemetery from the Kokopo and Rabaul markets.

This cemetery is home to more than 1,000 Allied war dead, including Indian POWs shipped from Singapore to help the Japanese effort. The well-kept cemetery, set amid beautiful gardens, is the smallest of the three cemeteries maintained by the OAWG. Graves are marked with bronze plaques atop low concrete pedestals. An avenue of stone pylons with bronze panels lists 1,224 names of those who died in the war but have no grave.

12. Yamamoto Crash Site ★★

Buin, Bougainville Island

Admiral Isoroku Yamamoto, the architect of the Pearl Harbor attack, was flying from Rabaul to Bougainville Island's Ballale Airfield in Buin on April 18, 1943, when two American P-38 pilots (Thomas Laphier and Rex Barber) shot down the admiral's Betty bomber. Yamamoto died in the crash. The question of who deserves credit for the kill remains in dispute. The attack on the bomber was made possible by cryptoanalysts who intercepted a flurry of messages between Rabaul and Buin outlining the details of Yamamoto's flight.

The bomber, intact except for a wing, sits in the jungle near Aku, a few hours drive outside the town of Buin. Bougainville Island, now coming out of a ten-year civil war, is plagued by poor infrastructure. As a result, visiting the crash site is extremely involved—a flight to Buka, a charter flight or one- to two-day four-wheel journey to Buin at the other end of the island, a three-hour jeep ride to the trailhead, then a two-mile hike over flat land. All with a couple nights in Buka, a couple nights in Buin and, if traveling by four-wheel drive instead of charter flight, probably a night in Arawa village (halfway between Buin and Buka). Obviously, this one is more about the journey than the destination.

The site is better visited through a tour/charter operator, which still isn't a sure bet. Nonetheless, Cairns, Australia-based South Pacific Tours (675-323-5245 in Port Moresby; 61-740-392-251 in Cairns) coordinates such trips and can let visitors know ahead of time if it will be possible to visit the site while in PNG.

OTHER AREA ATTRACTIONS

Diving ★★★★ N

In Madang
Niugini Diving Adventures
675-852-2766 (at Madang Resort Hotel)

In Rabaul
Kaivuna Resort
675-982-1766

With superb visibility and reef activity, it's hard not find a body of water around

PNG that isn't great for diving. Wrecks littering the coastline include Japanese and Allied planes and ships. With the exception of Port Moresby, just about every place appealing to visitors has at least a few wrecks, be they Japanese Zeros, sunken transports or barges abandoned and left to rust in the water. Most have been picked over, but in many cases the shell of the wreck remains.

PNGs's most famous wreck—some call it the best aircraft wreck dive in the world—is the B-17 bomber "Blackjack"

located near Tufi on the northeast coast of PNG, almost due east from Port Moresby. Unfortunately, it's at a difficult-to-reach depth of about 160 feet. At Madang, a B-25 is in good shape—with eleven machine guns—at about sixty-five feet deep. A memorable Rabaul dive is along the steep wall at Cape Tawui that the Japanese used as a wharf for submarines. There's a lot of sea life here, and the wall/wharf is usually done as a shore dive (no boat necessary).

GETTING TO/AROUND PAPUA NEW GUINEA

Air Niugini (949-752-5440 in Newport Beach, California) is the national airline that owns a virtual monopoly on air service in and around the country. Flights to Port Moresby (the only international airport) depart from Tokyo, Singapore, Manila and several Australian cities including Sydney, Brisbane and Cairns.

Air travel is the best way to get around PNG. Most cities have unpaved roads extending into their particular region. For instance, on the eastern coast of the mainland it's possible to drive from Lae to Madang, but not from Lae across to Port Moresby on the western coast.

World War II brought the addition of many airfields, many of which remain in use. Air Niugini's hub is Port Moresby. Most domestic flights start or end there. Flying around the country is fairly expensive. However, visitors flying to Port Moresby on Air Niugini are eligible for an air pass that costs $300 and allows four "free" legs of a flight. For example, a round-trip flight from Port Moresby to Rabaul normally costs upwards of $300, but the Air Pass allows passengers to fly there and back twice for the same amount of money. The Air Pass must be purchased in the United States and additional legs ($75 each) can be added only at the time of original purchase. Two or three flights a day depart Port Moresby

for Madang, Lae and Rabaul. There's one flight a day from Port Moresby to Wewak.

Ships run between several cities/islands in the north section of the country. The largest line, Lutheran Shipping (675-472-2066), operates a route from Lae to Madang and on to Wewak. Rabaul is reached via Lae. Schedules change often. The Shipping Notes section of the *Post Courier*, an English-language newspaper available throughout the country, publishes current schedules. The best accommodation on most ships is a bunk in a large dorm-style room. Cockroaches can be a problem, even though ships in PNG generally don't serve food.

Though the PNG road system isn't good, cars can be rented in most decent-sized cities, including a few on the outlying islands. Hertz (800-654-3131) and Avis (800-331-1212) are two of the major companies operating in PNG.

The often-cramped Public Motor Vehicles (PMVs) are a cheap and indispensable form of transportation and run the gamut from Japanese mini-buses to trucks with wooden benches. In urban centers, pick-up spots are marked with a yellow pole. PMVs making trips to outlying areas usually leave from city markets, and drivers tend not to depart until the PMV is uncomfortably full.

Accommodations

Port Moresby

Crowne Plaza Port Moresby

Corner of Douglas and Hunter Streets
T: 675-309-3000 F: 675-309-3333
157 rooms
$60-$90

Located in the business district of Boroko, the nine-floor building has sweeping views of the Coral Sea, two restaurants, pool and internet service. It's about five kilometers from the National Museum.

Popondetta

Oro Guesthouse

Kongho Avenue
T: 675-329-7127 F: 675-329-7246
20 rooms
$10-$25

The very simple guesthouse is a few minutes walk from Popondetta Memorial Park.

Lae

Lae International Hotel

Fourth Street
T: 675-472-2000 F: 675-472-2534
100-plus rooms
$65-$85

Colonial-style hotel has tropical gardens and a zoo and is located near the town center. Also on the grounds are tennis courts and a large outdoor pool.

Madang

Madang Resort Hotel

Madang Harbor
T: 675-852-2655 F: 675-852-3543
109 rooms
$102-$216

A lush resort with superb grounds (orchids, exotic birds) and great views of island-rich Madang harbor. Located at the end of the Madang peninsula, just down the street from the Coastwatchers Memorial. Pool, restaurant, TV.

Wewak

Paradise New Hotel

Beachfront, Wewak
T: 675-856-2155
22 rooms
From $50

This beach resort has a dive operator, laundry, restaurants, good bar and internet access.

Rabaul

Kaivuna Resort Hotel

Sulphur Creek Road
T: 675-982-1766 F: 675-982-1767
32 rooms
$34-$46

The hotel offers great views of the now-deserted city. It's a twenty- to thirty-minute walk from the Japanese War Memorial.

Kokopo

Kokopo Village Resort
Between Kokopo city center and Kokopo High School
T: 675-982-9096 F: 675-982-8360
23 rooms
$35-$47

New villa-style building on the western end of town is a five-minute walk from the Kokopo War Museum. As of this writing, a new hotel, Rapopo Plantation Resort, is being built near the center of town. Double rooms will cost about $45.

Milne Bay

Masurina Lodge, Alotau

Ealeba Street
T: 675-641-1212 F: 675-641-1406
30 rooms
$46-$57

This comfortable, convenient lodge is in the center of town, a couple minutes walk from the Alotau market—TV, kitchenette, complimentary airport transfers.

25

North America

NORTH AMERICA SITES

From nightly blackouts to production lines operating at unprecedented levels, World War II brought conflict to North American civilians, and for the first time in history transformed home fronts across the globe into battle zones. American industrialism's race to keep pace with a two-front war left literally thousands of World War II sites scattered across the continent. Though in need of updating, one of the best resources for information on American home front sites is Richard E. Osborne's *World War II Sites in the United States: A Tour Guide and Directory*. The exhaustive and indispensable paperback guide provides a state by state (some states missing) listing of seemingly everything from abandoned military bases to existing factories that once played a role in the war effort. Dealing largely with White House politics and the enormous social metamorphosis that occurred between 1941 and 1945, Doris Kearns Goodwin's *No Ordinary Time: Franklin and Eleanor Roosevelt: The Home Front in World War II* is one of many worthwhile home front histories.

With a notable exception—The National Museum of the Pacific War in Fredericksburg, Texas—historical exhibits dealing specifically with the Pacific War are usually a sub-section of a larger museum or facility concerning all of World War II or general military or social history. These exhibits and museums nevertheless provide fascinating reviews and tributes to everything from the Herculean work of the U.S. Navy "Seabee" construction battalions across the Pacific to the largely forgotten Canadian participation in the almost as largely forgotten Aleutians campaign. Various installations around the country also house an impressive array of mint-condition military aircraft, which contrast with the rusted, damaged hulks found in most Pacific sites. Below are twenty-five North American museums and sites that include some of the more fascinating displays dedicated to Pacific War history.

POINTS OF INTEREST

1. Columbia River Maritime Museum

1792 Marine Dr.
Astoria, Oregon
503-325-2323
www.crmm.org
Daily, 9:30 a.m.-5 p.m.
Closed Thanksgiving and Christmas
$5

Oregon's "official" maritime museum houses the Northwest's most comprehensive collection of maritime artifacts. More than 7,000 items include several interesting bits and pieces from World War II—submarine periscopes and torpedoes,

an LST propeller, anti-aircraft guns and a salvaged bridge from the destroyer U.S.S. *Knapp*. The lightship U.S.S. *Columbia*, the last of its kind on the West Coast and a National Historic Landmark, is moored next to the building.

Up the coast a few hours in Seattle, Boeing's Museum of Flight (9404 E. Marginal Way S., 206-764-5720. www.museumofflight.org) isn't dedicated to the war, but among its fifty-four magnificent aircraft are a B-29, Corsair and British Spitfire, which saw extensive action over Burma.

2. Tillamook Air Museum

6030 Hangar Rd.
Tillamook, Oregon
503-842-1130
www.tillamookair.com
Daily, 10 a.m.-5 p.m.
Closed Thanksgiving and Christmas
$9.50

Vulnerable coastlines along Oregon and Washington led to the rapid construction of several K-class blimp hangars in 1942, including two at this former Tillamook naval station. Hangar B (Hangar A was destroyed in a fire) now houses one of the country's top private aircraft collections under its seven-acre, fifteen-story-high barrel-roof. At any given time the collection includes around twenty-five World War II aircraft. Museum exhibits also include blimp engines, cabs, propellers, instruments, photos and other memorabilia that tell the story of this World War II patrol base. The chance to gape at the size of this building is worth the trip.

3. Civil Engineer Corps/Seabee Museum

Naval Construction Battalion Center
1000 23rd Ave., Building 99
Port Hueneme, California
805-982-5165
www.ncbc.navfac.navy.mil/cecmuseum
Monday-Saturday, 9 a.m.-4 p.m., Sunday, 12:30 p.m.-4:30 p.m.
Closed federal holidays, Easter and week between Christmas and New Year's Day

Navy construction battalions (aka Seabees) and the Civil Engineering Corps (CEC) are commemorated at this historic facility housed in a pair of World War II Quonset huts at the Ventura County Naval Base. The museum's collection of equipment, weapons, uniforms and other artifacts stretches back to the nineteenth century, with special emphasis on the history and development of the Naval Construction Force from World War II to the present day. Dioramas complemented by a historical timeline portray some of the Seabees' more important construction projects. Handicrafts, models and inventions by Seabee and CEC officers are also on display. Due to increased base security in the wake of events of September 11, 2001, the public is not permitted on the base without appropriate identification. Appropriate identification includes civilian Department of Defense ID and active and retired military ID.

4. Japanese American National Museum

369 E. First St.
Los Angeles
213-625-0414
www.janm.org
Tuesday-Sunday, 10 a.m.-5 p.m., Thursday, 10 a.m.-8 p.m.
Closed Monday, Thanksgiving, Christmas and New Year's Day
$6

Displays and artifacts that chronicle the history of Japanese Americans in the United States are featured in this new building (moved from the original Buddhist Temple next door) in the heart of Los Angeles' Japantown. World War II-era exhibits revolve mainly around forced Japanese relocation from the West Coast.

5. The Air Museum Planes of Fame

7000 Merrill Ave.
Chino, California
909-597-3722
www.planesoffame.org
Daily, 9 a.m.-5 p.m.
Closed Thanksgiving and Christmas
$8.95

The first permanent plane archive west of the Rockies, this seminal air museum and restoration facility still carries one of the best collections of World War II aircraft anywhere. Among many rarities here are the last functioning Boeing P-26A Peashooter and the only genuine, flyable Mitsubishi A6M5 Zero. The main exhibit is located on the museum grounds at Chino airport, with the balance held at a satellite location in La Valle, Arizona, near the Grand Canyon.

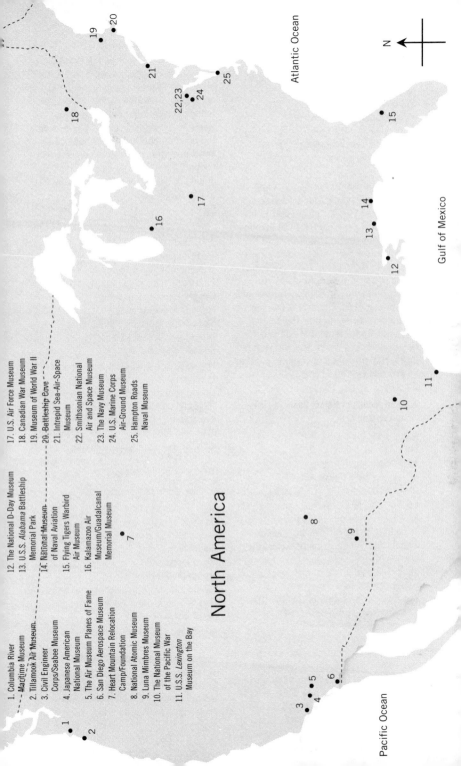

North America

Pacific Ocean

Atlantic Ocean

Gulf of Mexico

N

1. Columbia River
   Maritime Museum
2. Tillamook Air Museum
3. Civil Engineer
   Corps/Seabee Museum
4. Japanese American
   National Museum
5. The Air Museum Planes of Fame
6. San Diego Aerospace Museum
7. Heart Mountain Relocation
   Camp/Foundation
8. National Atomic Museum
9. Luna Mimbres Museum
10. The National Museum
    of the Pacific War
11. U.S.S. *Lexington*
    Museum on the Bay

12. The National D-Day Museum
13. U.S.S. *Alabama* Battleship
    Memorial Park
14. National Museum
    of Naval Aviation
15. Flying Tigers Warbird
    Air Museum
16. Kalamazoo Air
    Museum/Guadalcanal
    Memorial Museum

17. U.S. Air Force Museum
18. Canadian War Museum
19. Museum of World War II
20. Battleship Cove
21. Intrepid Sea-Air-Space
    Museum
22. Smithsonian National
    Air and Space Museum
23. The Navy Museum
24. U.S. Marine Corps
    Air-Ground Museum
25. Hampton Roads
    Naval Museum

6. San Diego Aerospace Museum

2001 Pan American Plaza, Balboa Park
San Diego
619-234-8291
www.aerospacemuseum.org
Daily, 10 a.m.-4:30 p.m.
Closed Thanksgiving, Christmas
and New Year's Day
$8

San Diego's tribute to flight is about as ambitious in its scope as an aerospace museum can get, with the world's only International Aerospace Hall of Fame and chronological exhibits that predate the Wright Brothers by more than 100 years and run to the most modern achievements. Close to seventy aircraft are housed in this large Balboa Park facility. The extensive World War II section includes a Grumman F6F Hellcat and a painstakingly restored Mitsubishi Zero fighter. Among aviation legends featured in the Hall of Fame are Jimmy Doolittle, Chuck Yeager, Carl Spaatz and Donald Douglas.

7. Heart Mountain Relocation Camp/Foundation

Nine miles southwest of Powell,
Wyoming on U.S. 14 Alt
www.heartmountain.org
307-754-2689
Open all day

In 1942, almost 120,000 Japanese Americans were forced from their homes in California, Oregon, Washington and Arizona in the largest forced relocation in U.S. history. Many spent the remainder of the war in one of ten "relocation centers" across the country run by the War Relocation Authority, or facilities administered by the Department of Justice or U.S. Army. By the time the last internees were released in 1946, Japanese Americans had lost homes and businesses estimated to be worth, in 2000 value, four to five billion dollars. Located at the foot of Heart Mountain near Powell in northern Wyoming, this quiet site once held more than 11,000 Japanese detainees from the Los Angeles area and is now on the National Register of Historic Places. The camp, constructed on property that was part of a federally funded farmland project called The Heart Mountain Irrigation Division, was in operation between September 1942 and November 1945. Commemorative plaques have replaced many of the original buildings. The area is easily toured by car and includes a small, roadside park on U.S. 14 Alt. A learning center on the premises is being planned.

8. National Atomic Museum

1905 Mountain Rd. NW
Albuquerque, New Mexico
505-245-2136 or 505-284-3243
www.atomicmuseum.com
Daily, 9 a.m.-5 p.m.
Closed Thanksgiving, Christmas,
New Year's Day and Easter
$4

The story of the New Mexico-based Manhattan Project, from inception and testing to the bombing of Hiroshima and Nagasaki, is chronicled in this informative atomic energy archive located in Old Town Albuquerque. Exhibits include replicas of "Little Boy" and "Fat Man" as well as an hour-long documentary, *Ten Seconds That Shook the World*.

9. Luna Mimbres Museum

301 S. Silver St.
Deming, New Mexico
505-546-2382
www.cityofdeming.org/museum.html
Monday-Saturday, 9 a.m.-4 p.m.,
Sunday, 1:30 p.m.-4 p.m.
Closed Thanksgiving, Christmas,
New Year's Day and Easter
Donations requested

Among the many hats worn by Deming's small museum—art gallery, antique auto show, cowboy exhibit—is a military history section that pays a personalized tribute to victims of the Bataan Death March. Close to 2,000 New Mexico National Guard recruits were dealt this fate, half of whom died during forty months of brutal captivity. Displays on some of the prisoners and their struggles have added poignancy in this very local red brick facility.

10. The National Museum of the Pacific War

340 E. Main St.
Fredericksburg, Texas
830-997-4379
www.nimitz-museum.org
Daily, 10 a.m.-5 p.m.
Closed Christmas
$5

The only museum in the continental United States dedicated exclusively to the Pacific War, this seven-acre estate in Texas Hill Country includes the Admiral Nimitz Museum, George Bush Gallery, Veterans' Walk of Honor, Pacific War Combat Zone and Japanese Garden of Peace. The recently opened Bush Gallery alone boasts 23,000 square feet of innovative exhibit space, including a B-25 bomber with spinning propeller "preparing for take off" and an interactive Henderson Field, Guadalcanal set complete with wartime voice-overs. Walk-through dioramas help "visitors become quickly engaged in the very stories of all kinds of Americans from all branches of the military involved in the long struggle to fight aggression in the Pacific." The Japanese Garden of Peace is a replica of Admiral Marquis Heihachiro Togo's traditional garden in Japan. Togo's meditation study was duplicated in Japan, disassembled and shipped to Fredericksburg, then reassembled (without nails) by the same craftsmen who built it in Japan. The Chester Nimitz story is spotlighted next door in the historic Nimitz Hotel where the famed admiral grew up. A large collection of Allied and Japanese planes, tanks and artillery are spread throughout the grounds. There's much more to see.

11. U.S.S. *Lexington* Museum on the Bay

914 North Shoreline Blvd.
Corpus Christi, Texas
361-888-4873
www.usslexington.com
Daily, 9 a.m.-5 p.m.
Closed Christmas
$10

One of America's most illustrious aircraft carriers, the U.S.S. *Lexington*, was the flagship of Fast Carrier Task Force 58— pushing its way from Tarawa to Tokyo before following up with nearly fifty more years in service. The retired vessel now sits on the Corpus Christi waterfront, where it's one of Texas's top attractions. Visitors on the 33,000-ton "Lady Lex" can tour hangar and flight decks, engine room, captain's quarters and virtually everywhere else
of interest. Several vintage aircraft are exhibited on board. A large-format theater offers screenings and presentations at an extra cost.

12. The National D-Day Museum

945 Magazine St. (Entrance on Andrew Higgins Drive)
New Orleans
504-527-6012
www.ddaymuseum.org
Daily, 9 a.m.-5 p.m.
Closed Thanksgiving, Christmas, New Years Day and Mardi Gras
$10 (Adult), $6 (Senior, Military, Student), Free (Child under five, military in uniform)

"D-Day" has become synonymous with the June 6, 1944, Allied landings in –Normandy, but the term originally applied to the beginning of any military offensive. This museum—founded by Stephen Ambrose and opened in 2000— is a spectacular facility that dedicates a 5,000-square-foot gallery to the more than 125 amphibious assaults carried out in the Pacific. Exhibits include a fragment from the U.S.S. *Arizona*, bomber jacket worn by one of the

Doolittle raiders, weaponry, animated maps, theaters with films on Midway and the Philippines, oral histories from American and Japanese war participants and examinations of race, propaganda, brutality, Tokyo firebombing and atomic bombs. A separate gallery dedicated to ship builder Andrew Higgins—his factory was located in New Orleans—includes a full-size reproduction of a Higgins LCVP landing craft. All of World War II is depicted here in stunning fashion. It's one of the more worthwhile museums on the list.

13. U.S.S. *Alabama* Battleship Memorial Park

2703 Battleship Parkway
Mobile, Alabama
251-433-2703
www.ussalabama.com
Daily, 8 a.m.-6 p.m. (April-September);
8 a.m.-4 p.m. (October-March)
Closed Christmas Day
$10 (Adult); $5 (Child);
Free (Child under six)

Visitors can tour the 680-foot-long battleship U.S.S. *Alabama*, which earned nine World War II battle stars after action at such key locations as the Marshall Islands, New Guinea, Mariana Islands, Leyte Gulf and Okinawa before steaming with the American Fleet into Tokyo Bay for Japan's September 1945 surrender. Nearby is the 311-foot-long submarine U.S.S. *Drum* (thirteen Pacific War patrols, fifteen Japanese ships sunk) and a collection of twenty-three combat aircraft that includes a P-51D Mustang, B-25J Mitchell and SBD-3 Dauntless.

14. National Museum of Naval Aviation

Naval Air Station
1750 Radford Blvd., Suite C
Pensacola, Florida
850-452-3604 or 800-327-5002
www.naval-air.org
Daily, 9 a.m.-5 p.m.

Hailed as Florida's "most visited museum," it traces the history of naval aviation from the early twentieth century to Operation Desert Storm. More than 140 Navy, Marine and Coast Guard aircraft are spread throughout this 300,000-square-foot, world-class facility, which includes climb-in cockpits, a fifteen-passenger, full-motion flight simulator and an IMAX theater. Most of the building's West Wing is devoted to World War II carrier aviation. The centerpiece is a full-size replica of the flight deck of the aircraft carrier U.S.S. *Cabot*. It's surrounded by Corsairs, Hellcats, Avengers and other legends of their time. One of the country's better Pacific War exhibits.

15. Flying Tigers Warbird Air Museum

231 Hoagland Blvd.
Kissimmee, Florida
407-933-1942
www.warbirdmuseum.com
Monday-Saturday, 9 a.m.-6 p.m.,
Sunday, 9 a.m.-5 p.m.
Closed Christmas
$9

Half museum, half body shop, this unique air museum on the west side of Kissimmee Airport specializes in the restoration and display of World War II aircraft and parts. Guests are welcome to watch B-25s and Corsairs being revived. Return visitors are often rewarded with new additions to the old fleet.

16. Kalamazoo Air Museum/Guadalcanal Memorial Museum

3101 E. Milham Rd.
Kalamazoo, Michigan
616-382-6555
www.airzoo.org
Monday-Saturday, 9 a.m.-5 p.m.,
Sunday, Noon-5 p.m.
Closed Thanksgiving, Christmas Eve,
Christmas Day, New Year's Eve,
New Year's Day, Easter
$10

This pair of museums under one roof at Kalamazoo Airport features an excellent display of World War II classics in the larger Air Museum—including four

Grumman Cats (the Wildcat, Hellcat, Tigercat and Bearcat). Visitors are welcome to watch new acquisitions being worked back into shape at the on-site restoration facility. The Guadalcanal Memorial Museum occupies a large room filled with artifacts commemorating the first Allied offensive in the Pacific.

17. U.S. Air Force Museum

Wright-Patterson Air Force Base
1100 Spaatz St.
Dayton, Ohio
937-255-3286
www.wpafb.af.mil/museum
Daily, 9 a.m.-5 p.m.
Closed Thanksgiving, Christmas
and New Year's Day

Not strictly a World War II museum, but with more than 300 aircraft and missiles on display, it's one of the best military flight museums in the world. The Air Power Gallery concentrates on the World War II years, with sixty original aircraft and missiles on display. Beautifully restored aircraft include a B-25B Mitchell bomber (used for the 1942 Doolittle Raid on Tokyo), B-29 Superfortress, P-51 Mustang, P-39Q Airacobra and many others. History displays cover the entire Pacific Theater of Operations. Video features include a film on the Doolittle Raid. A must-visit site for those with even a slight interest in WWII aircraft.

18. Canadian War Museum

General Motors Court
330 Sussex Dr.
Ottawa, Ontario
819-776-8600 or 800-555-5621
www.civilization.ca/societe/annrpt95/rp2
mcge.html
Friday-Wednesday, 9:30 a.m.-5 p.m.,
Thursday, 9:30 a.m.-8 p.m.
Closed Mondays from mid-October
to March 31
$4 (Canadian)
Free Thursday nights,
half-price on Sunday
Closed some holidays (call in advance).

Because the vast majority of Canadian troops in World War II were engaged in the fight against Nazi Germany, Canadian forces were committed to just two Pacific ground actions—Hong Kong and Kiska, in the Aleutian Islands—where they served with distinction. In addition, about 100 officers were attached to American units fighting throughout the Pacific (three were wounded in action). Following the defeat of Germany, about 30,000 Canadian troops were being prepared for the invasion of the Japanese main island of Honshu (Operation Coronet) when the atomic bombs dropped on Hiroshima and Nagasaki ended the war. This museum chronicles the history of all Canadian armed forces, but the second floor, devoted to World War II, includes a large exhibit on the 1941 battle for Hong Kong, where Canadian troops fought valiantly, after which many suffered enormously in Japanese prison camps. A POW-camp is re-created behind barbed wire with a mannequin of a soldier who endured the entire war in a prison camp. A number of sketches and paintings deal with the Aleutian Islands campaign. Monthly movie and speaker series occasionally deal with World War II topics. The —museum's Vimy House (221 Champagne Ave., North Ottawa) is an auxiliary location twelve minutes by car from the main museum. It houses tanks, artillery and other large military equipment. It's open Saturdays only, 10 a.m.-4 p.m.

19. Museum of World War II

46 Eliot St.
Natick, Massachusetts
508-651-7695
www.museumofworldwarii.com
By appointment only

"If a visitor is overwhelmed with the enormity and the complexity of the war," notes Kenneth W. Rendell, director of this private, Boston-area museum, "I have achieved my goal." Few galleries, public or private, house such an impressive array of World War II artifacts and collector's items. Most of the exhibits in the facility's eighteen sections are, refreshingly, not encased in glass. The list—Patton's battle helmet, Hitler's SA shirt, Montgomery's beret—is exhaustive. Honorable mentions in the Pacific Theater include MacArthur's draft of the Japanese surrender terms and an intact LCVP landing craft.

20. Battleship Cove

Fall River, Massachusetts
508-678-1100
www.battleshipcove.org
Daily, 9 a.m.-5 p.m.
Closed Thanksgiving, Christmas,
New Year's Day
$10

The remarkable display of World War II naval vessels in this anchorage begins with the U.S.S. *Massachusetts*—a Pacific war horse (aka "Big Mamie") that pounded through three-and-a-half years of service from the Solomon Islands to Iwo Jima, Okinawa and Japan. The submarine *Lionfish*, the destroyer *Joseph P. Kennedy, Jr.* and a Japanese suicide boat are other highlights. Further attractions at the Cove include the Marine Museum and an eight-acre park.

21. Intrepid Sea-Air-Space Museum

Pier 86
12th Avenue and 46th Street
New York, New York
212-245-0072
www.intrepidmuseum.org
April 1-September 30:
Monday-Friday, 10 a.m.-5 p.m.
Saturday, Sunday, holidays,
10 a.m.-7 p.m.
October 1-March 31:
Tuesday-Sunday and holidays,
10 a.m.-5 p.m.
Closed Mondays, Thanksgiving
and Christmas Day
Last admission one hour before closing
$13 (Adult); $9 (Veteran, Student); $6 (Child 6-11); $2 (Child 2-5); Free (Active military, Children under 2)

Launched in 1943, the U.S.S. *Intrepid* served thirty-one years as one of America's most effective aircraft carriers. The ship took part in history's largest naval engagement, the Battle of Leyte Gulf, and during the course of the Pacific War withstood seven bomb attacks, five kamikaze strikes and one torpedo hit. An uncanny ability to continually return to action earned her a reputation as "the ghost ship." Now berthed on the Hudson River in Manhattan, the colossal and inspiring ship is the focal point of a superb museum that includes the Vietnam-era destroyer U.S.S. *Edson*, guided-missile submarine U.S.S. *Growler* and more than twenty-five aircraft.

22. Smithsonian National Air and Space Museum

7th Street and Independence Avenue, SW
Washington, D.C.
202-357-2700
www.nasm.si.edu
Daily, 10 a.m.-5:30 p.m.
Closed Christmas

Factoring in the Smithsonian National Museum of American History (14th Street and Constitution Avenue, 202-357-2700), more than one visit to this monolith may be required. Each of the museum's twenty halls—with a rotating display of more than 300 aircraft—comes with its own aviation theme. The second floor has World War II aircraft and displays. Top exhibits include recovered Japanese bombing balloons, an intact Mitsubishi A6M5 Zero and an interactive display that simulates an aircraft carrier hangar deck. Considering the entire collection, this is one of the world's top museums of any kind.

23. The Navy Museum

Washington Navy Yard
805 Kidder Breese St. SE, Building 76
Washington, D.C.
202-433-4882
www.history.navy.mil/branches/nhcorg8.htm
Monday-Friday, 9 a.m.-4 p.m.
Closed weekends, Thanksgiving,

Christmas Eve, Christmas Day
and New Year's Day

Washington, D.C.'s second largest
museum (after the Smithsonian) commemorates U.S. Navy battles, heroes
and artifacts from the eighteenth century
to the present. Comprehensive coverage
of World War II is permanently displayed
in a three-section exhibit (Pacific, Atlantic,
Home Front) titled, "In Harm's Way: The
Navy and World War II." The Pacific
Theater's impressive collection of planes,
artillery, submarine chambers and equipment are joined by popular exhibits that
include a radio broadcast of President
Franklin Roosevelt's declaration of war,
Japanese aerial photos of Pearl Harbor,
a kamikaze plane retrieved from the
American carrier *Enterprise* and replicas
of the atomic bombs dropped on
Hiroshima and Nagasaki.

24. U.S. Marine Corps Air-Ground Museum

U.S. Marine Corps Base, Quantico
Quantico, Virginia
703-784-2606
Tuesday-Saturday, 10 a.m.-5 p.m.
Open Sunday, Noon-5 p.m., from
April 1-November 26
Closed Monday, Thanksgiving and Easter

A fine collection of military aircraft and
ground equipment is set in beautifully
restored 1920s-era hangars at the Marine
Corps Base, Quantico. Marine achievements in two major wars and several
other campaigns are the focal point.
Standout World War II specimens include
a Mitsubishi Zero and "Baka" suicide aircraft. Plans for a larger national museum
on these grounds are in development and
scheduled to be completed by late 2005.

25. Hampton Roads Naval Museum

Nauticus: The National Maritime Center
One Waterside Dr., Suite 248
Norfolk, Virginia
757-322-2987
www.hrnm.navy.mil
Tuesday-Saturday, 10 a.m.-5 p.m.,
Sunday, 12 p.m.-5 p.m.
Open until 6 p.m. from Memorial Day
through Labor Day
Closed Monday

The U.S.S. *Wisconsin*, one of the largest
and last battleships built by the U.S.
Navy, is parked in semi-retirement at
downtown Norfolk's massive Hampton
Roads naval shipyards where it's now
an equally large public attraction. Four
of the ship's decks are open for self-
guided audio tours, the latest runaway
exhibit of its neighboring Naval Museum.
The *Wisconsin* steals the show, but the
museum's naval displays are also worthwhile. Artifacts and interactive exhibits
include the role of Hampton Roads in
the Battle of the Atlantic.

Auxiliary Sites

AUXILIARY SITES

R ed tape, development and politics have limited access to a number of significant Pacific War battlefields. Travel to these destinations can be pricier, less satisfying or more problematic than travel to locations covered more extensively in this book. In most cases, however, none are impossible to visit.

BURMA (MYANMAR)

Officially part of the China-Burma-India theater, the 1942-1945 Burma campaign produced figures and achievements—"Vinegar" Joe Stilwell, William Slim, Orde Wingate, the Chindits, Merrill's Marauders, Burma and Ledo Roads—that stand among the war's greatest legends. Unfortunately, the places where the Burma campaign unfolded were for many years nearly impossible to visit. But Myanmar's repressive military regime has loosened its gates over the last few years, and tourism is now trickling into one of the most hermetic (and beautiful) countries in Asia. Though rewarding, travel here can still be relatively involved, costly and unpredictable—especially outside the main drop zones of Yangon (Rangoon), Pagan and Mandalay. Next door, in Thailand, there are more River Kwai tours than there are readily accessible World War II sites in Burma. One of the country's most worthwhile sites is the beautiful Allied cemetery in Thanbyuzayat, several hours by train down the coast from Rangoon (permission required). In the north, parts of the famous Burma Road are open (most of the time), and outfitter Mountain Travel Sobek (888-687-6235) now offers a Burma Road to Yunnan tour. Chiang Mai, Thailand-based Gem Travel (66-0-53-818754) operates a World War II & Battlefields tour through Burma. Tackling many of these areas independently is tricky, but not impossible. For updated information and travel visas contact the Myanmar Embassy in Washington, D.C. (202-332-9044) or visit www.visatogoabroad.com, then click on "Myanmar."

DARWIN, AUSTRALIA

Australia's Asian gateway and port town of Darwin was pummeled for nearly two years by more than sixty Japanese air raids. Today, it's a sedate, cosmopolitan mini-city with a vast, impressive backyard (Australia's "Outback") and a prohibitively slim supply of Pacific War attractions. For most travelers, Darwin's East Point Military Museum (089-81-9702), Aviation Heritage Centre (089-47-2145) and sparsely scattered plane and shipwrecks won't justify coming all the way out. Factoring in a trip to Kakadu National Park, Katherine Gorge or Bali for that matter might change that.

ENIWETAK

Getting to this thirty-island atoll on the western periphery of the Marshall Islands is impractical, expensive and, for most, undesirable. Three swift American amphibious assaults left their modest share of relics here, but Eniwetak is perhaps better known for its fifteen-year status after the war as a U.S. atomic bomb testing ground. The atoll's main island, two-mile-long Eniwetak, has regained a clean bill of health (others here still have not). Air Marshall Islands (692-625-3731) flies to Eniwetak just once a week on a puddle-jumping commute with three stopovers. The island isn't set up for visitors, who may or may not—depending upon whom one talks to—have to arrange official permission before coming here, presumably for the week. (Marshall Islands Embassy in Washington, D.C., 202-234-5414; Eniwetak Atoll Government in Majuro, Marshall Islands, 692-625-3296)

HONG KONG

Surprisingly, Hong Kong's sixty years of runaway development hasn't entirely paved over its dramatic World War II past—the former British colony was attacked on the same day as Pearl Harbor—but preservation hasn't been a priority, either. The Hong Kong Museum of History (852-2724-9042) has a permanent "Japanese Occupation" exhibit in a dark air-raid-shelter-designed room. The Museum of Coastal Defence (852-2569-1500) devotes two of its dozen small galleries to the war. There are a smattering of pillboxes, barracks, batteries, memorials and cemeteries on the island's quieter pockets such as Stanley and Sai Wan. And a bronze lion flanking the entrance of the Shanghai Bank Building has some nicks on it, apparently caused by a Japanese shell. Local tour operator Jason's Walks (852-2476-5057) offers World War II walking tours through Hong Kong. Whether or not this all merits a special trip is debatable. But visiting these sites can add an interesting day to a trip to Hong Kong.

INDONESIA

Known before the war as the Dutch East Indies, the enormous battleground of Indonesia has been left off the main list of sites due to a paucity of relics and travel difficulties created by continuing political turmoil. For those willing to embrace a limited risk, Indonesia remains an exotic and fascinating country in which to travel. The best war remains are found around Irian Jaya, the western half of the island of New Guinea. At Jayapura, near the border of Papua New Guinea, is a hillside monument to General Douglas MacArthur near the site of his Hollandia wartime headquarters. Tanjung Ria Beach there was known as Base G by the Allies. At Hamadi Beach, a monument commemorates Allied landings of April 1944. Far west of Jayapura outside the town of Manokwari is a Japanese monument at Table Mountain. Diving wrecks around Irian Jaya (www.iriandiving.com/Wreck-Diving.html) are some of the best in the Pacific—among others at Dore Bay are an intact P-40 aircraft and the *Shinwa Maru,* a Japanese cargo ship still loaded with mine-sweeping equipment, ammunition, sake bottles and other relics. At Tulamben on the northeast side of the touristy island of Bali is the wreck of the *U.S. Liberty,* an enormous cargo ship sunk during World War II and now surrounded by coral, sponges and a wide array of marine life. There are also a number of relics and wreck dives around the island of Borneo. In Malaysian Borneo, the Kinabalu National Park was established to honor 2,400 Allied prisoners of war, many of whom died on what is known as the "death march" to the foothills of 13,451-foot Mount Kinabalu during World War II.

IWO JIMA

The entire eight-square-mile island of Iwo Jima remains one of the world's most hallowed and preserved war mausoleums. More than 100,000 soldiers once crammed onto this sulfurous, volcanic speck, catacombed with Japan's most impregnable underground defense fortress—where mummified Japanese soldiers were unearthed as recently as 1984. The island's dominant Mt. Suribachi—atop which was taken the famous photograph of Marines raising the American flag—was the focal point of one of the war's most important and terrible battles. Iwo Jima is now a tightly secured Japanese military installation with no tourist infrastructure and only one U.S. operator on its highly restricted guest list. Virginia-based Military Historical Tours (800-722-9501) includes a single day on Iwo Jima during its annual weeklong Guam-based trip in March. Spots fill up several months in advance. Otherwise special permission must be obtained, which for the casual traveler is no small task (Japanese Embassy in Washington, D.C., 202-238-6700).

MIDWAY

Closed to the public for fifty years, this decisive 1942 battle site, former U.S. Navy base and famous gooney bird (Laysan albatross) colony opened its doors in 1996—becoming a Galapagos-esque National Wildlife Refuge overnight. For six years, Midway was managed by the Midway Phoenix Corporation (MPC) in conjunction with the U.S. Fish and Wildlife Service (USFWS). Financial and regulatory disputes have since dissolved this partnership and shut down the tiny three-island atoll once again. MPC has boarded up its 100-guest ecotourist resort on Sand Island, where a smattering of preserved pillboxes, bunkers and shrapneled hangars remain. Aloha Airlines charter flights to the atoll have ceased, and the USFWS is shopping for a new on-site operator. As of this writing, they haven't found one, and Midway remains (temporarily, most likely) closed—save for emergency landings and visitors with special permission. For updates contact the USFWS in Hawaii (808-541-1201).

WAKE ISLAND

In Japanese hands for most of the war, Wake Island has been almost as off-limits to travelers ever since. No tourist facilities are set up on this three coral-island atoll 2,000 miles west of Hawaii, which operated for years as a restricted U.S. military base and missile-launch support facility. More recently, it has served as a "temporary" storage bin for U.S. toxic waste shipped from Japan, and continues (along with Midway) to have ETOP (Extended-range Twin OPeration) status as an emergency flight landing field. Visiting restrictions on Wake Island have eased somewhat, but the real challenge is finding a ride. There's no indigenous population, and the number of residents on Wake Island, an unincorporated U.S. territory, amounts to about 100 contract workers.

BIBLIOGRAPHY

In addition to specific works cited in each chapter, the following books were consulted frequently during the preparation of this text.

Allen, Thomas B. and Norman Polmar. *Codename Downfall: The Secret Plan to Invade Japan.* London: Headline Book Publishing, 1995.

Arnold-Forster, Mark. *The World at War.* London: Thames Mandarin, 1973.

Bradley, John H. *The Second World War: Asia and the Pacific.* The West Point Military History Series. Wayne, N.J.: Avery Publishing Group, 1984.

Cressman, Robert J. *Official Chronology of the U.S. Navy in World War II.* Annapolis: Naval Institute Press, 2000.

Dower, John W. *War Without Mercy: Race & Power in the Pacific War.* New York: Pantheon Books, 1986.

Dudden, Arthur Power. *The American Pacific: From the Old China Trade to the Present.* New York: Oxford University Press, 1992.

Dull, Paul. *Battle History of the Imperial Japanese Navy, 1941-1945.* Annapolis: Naval Institute Press, 1978.

Dunnigan, James F. and Albert A. Nofi. *The Pacific War Encyclopedia.* New York: Checkmark Books, 1998.

Gailey, Harry A. *The War in the Pacific: From Pearl Harbor to Tokyo Bay.* Novato, Calif.: Presidio, 1995.

Ienaga, Saburo. *The Pacific War: 1931-1945.* Tokyo: Iwanami Shoten, 1968. English translation published in New York by Pantheon Books, 1978.

Inoguchi, Captain Rikihei and Commander Tadashi Nakajima with Roger Pineau. *The Divine Wind: Japan's Kamikaze Force in World War II.* Annapolis: Naval Institute Press, 1958.

Keegan, John. *The Second World War.* New York: Viking, 1989.

Keegan, John, ed. *Who Was Who in World War II.* London: Arms and Armour Press, 1978.

Leckie, Robert. *Delivered From Evil: The Saga of World War II.* New York: Harper & Row, 1987.

Lundstrom, John. *The First Team: Pacific Naval Air Combat from Pearl Harbor to Midway.* Annapolis: Naval Institute Press, 1984.

Morison, Samuel Eliot. *History of United States Naval Operations in World War II.* Vols 1-15. Boston: Little, Brown, 1947-62.

Nunnely, John and Kazuo, Tamayama. *Tales by Japanese Soldiers.* London: Casell & Co., 2000

Parker, Robert Alexander Clarke. *Struggle for Survival: The History of the Second World War.* New York: Oxford University Press, 1989.

Smurthwaite, David. *The Pacific War Atlas: 1941-1945.* London: Mirabel Books, 1995.

Snyder, Louis L. *The War: A Concise History 1939-1945.* New York: Julian Messner, 1960.

Spector, Ronald H. *Eagle Against the Sun: The American War With Japan.* New York: Free Press, 1984.

Sulzberger, C.L. *The American Heritage Picture History of World War II.* New York: American Heritage/Bonanza Books, 1966.

Thompson, Robert Smith. *Empires on the Pacific: World War II and the Struggle for the Mastery of Asia.* New York: Basic Books, 2001.

INDEX

Chuck Thompson is a writer, editor and photographer
whose work has appeared in *The Atlantic Monthly*,
Maxim, *National Geographic Adventure*, *Playboy*, *Spy*,
Reader's Digest, *Fitness*, *Islands*, *Publishers Weekly*,
American Way, *Southwest Spirit* and many other
magazines, newspapers and television including MTV.
He's the former executive editor of *Travelocity* magazine
and a former contributing editor for *Escape* magazine.
Originally from Juneau, Alaska, he received history and
journalism degrees from the University of Oregon and has
lived and traveled extensively in Asia and the Pacific.